The Hungarian Quarterly • Vol. XLVI • No. 180 • Winter 2005

Cover illustration: Tourists on Gellért Hill. *Photograph by Hungarian Film Bureau, 1930s. Courtesy Historical Archives of the Hungarian National Museum.*
Back cover: Budapest at night in 1938. *The Chain Bridge was first floodlit in the previous year. Courtesy Historical Archives of the Hungarian National Museum*

György Spiró

Captivity

Excerpts from the novel

From BOOK ONE
From Rome to Jerusalem

"You will leave for Jerusalem the day after tomorrow."

Uri woke up with a start.

His father was standing over him.

Uri pulled himself up from his ragged bedclothes, picked up the scroll that had slipped from his hand, and while still in a sitting position, looked up apologetically. An embarrassed half-smile appeared on his lips, as always when he was caught, and he was always caught, even when he hadn't done anything wrong.

His father tarried a little longer in the dim alcove. From the courtyard, the grey February afternoon illumined his serious, bearded face, his prominent cheekbones and deep-set eyes; the small square cut into the wall glimmered right above Uri's tousled, greasy hair. His father stood there looking grave, not casting another glance at him, just staring out the window. Then he turned on his heels, and with his shoulder pushed aside the rug hung over the doorway with a force that bespoke deep dissatisfaction with his son, his own lot, and Creation in general.

Uri wasn't himself yet; he hadn't resurfaced; all he felt was shame that his father had caught him. He'd fallen asleep while reading. He often fell asleep in the

---

György Spiró

is a novelist, playwright, essayist, poet, translator and Slavic scholar. As a child he spent some years with his family in Belgrade and studied Russian and Serbo-Croat—in addition to Hungarian—at Eötvös University in Budapest. His books include five novels, collections of plays, short stories and essays, a volume of poems, a book on Miroslav Krleža and a book on role-doublings in Shakespeare's plays. His translations include plays by G.B. Shaw, Wyspiański and Gombrowicz. A collection of his short stories has appeared in French translation, a novel in French and Czech. His plays have been staged successfully both in Hungary and abroad. The excerpts here printed are from his latest novel Fogság *(Captivity), Budapest, Magvető, 2005, 770 pp.*

A review of the novel and an interview with the author also appear in this issue.

afternoon. And though he had nothing to do and could withdraw into his corner anytime and even sleep, he had a guilty conscience about it. It was as if reading was a self-imposed punishment, a painful obligation to make amends for some primal sin he hadn't committed. Actually, he liked to read; it was the only thing he liked to do.

Clutching the scroll, he stood up and stretched from the waist up, feeling his aching back, turning his head this way and that, bending his body, trying to get the stiffness out. Then he stared out the window.

A cold and clammy early February in Rome. Uri gave a shudder. The fragments of a dream still wavered in his soul, sinking deeper and deeper, like fish melting into the mud of the Tiber, only to dissolve in the dull halo of light that was seeping in from the courtyard. It could not have been an unpleasant dream; an agreeable feeling lurked in him still, an image of hope perhaps, but he couldn't retrieve it anymore. It was as if in his dream he was truly alive. People were loitering about in the courtyard, but they were too far for him to recognise; all he could see were their multiplying silhouettes. They must have been women, because men at this time were still going about their business.

Uri had poor eyesight.

His feet also gave him trouble; his ankles hurt when he walked. He had back pains, too, ever since he was little; his right hip turned out to be somewhat bigger than the left. But it was his eyes above all that were cursed. He saw things clearly only from up close. It wasn't always like this; until the age of eleven or twelve he was able to do everything boys his age were, but then he began to stay away from their games, move more precariously than they, and when he read, he had to lean his head closer and closer to the scrolls. At first, this didn't bother him, as it happened gradually; but he also had frequent headaches.

The teacher, Eusebius, who gave lessons to Uri and ten to fifteen other boys in the prayer hall, and whose salary was therefore paid by the congregation, had told Joseph that he thought Uri didn't see well. Joseph protested; no one in his family had bad eyesight, so his son couldn't, either. The teacher shook his head. Only Joseph's first-born was a boy, and after the birth of his younger daughter, his wife couldn't conceive again. The teacher appreciated the difficult situation Joseph found himself in.

That evening his father confronted him.

"Is it true that you don't see well?" he asked sharply.

He went to the far corner of the big room and asked how many fingers he was holding up. The big room wasn't all that spacious, but the hand was still far away; it was getting dark, the oil lamp barely flickered, it just smoked, as always, and that, too, interfered. Uri sighed and took a guess: "Two." From the silence he knew that he had guessed wrong.

That's when things turned bad between him and his father.

Until then he was the only son, the only complete person Joseph had been able to father. He was the favourite up to that point. His father was happy to know that his son learned to write and count before others his age did; he bragged about it, and shared with him his business plans as though he were a grown man.

Six months later his father repeated the experiment. This time Uri told him honestly that he didn't see how many fingers he was holding up.

"Because you don't want to see it," he cried angrily.

Uri would forever be haunted by this admonition.

After that last incident, his father began avoiding him. He didn't want to see that his son couldn't see. According to doctors, the dried resin of the balsam tree had a curative effect on cataract and myopia; and since Joseph at one time had dealt in balsam and dates, too, and even now received shipments of these products from Judea, he told Uri to prepare a compress of powdered resin and apply it to his eyes. Uri did as he was told and applied the compress diligently. The resinous odour made him nauseous, but his vision did not improve. After another half a year passed and Uri again could not see how many fingers his father was holding up, Joseph told him to stop the treatment; balsam was much too expensive.

Uri was relieved and also desperate.

He could read all right, and if he squinted hard, he could see pretty far; and if he cupped his fingers and put them to his eyes and looked through them, he could see even farther—in small segments, but still far. He tried to look out the window this way often; more and more, he withdrew into his little nook and didn't go out much; inside his alcove, everything was near so he saw everything. He could take in the courtyard through the cracks between his fingers and make out the remotest corners.

The courtyard was big; you couldn't even tell where it ended. The truth is it didn't begin or end anywhere.

The houses beyond the Tiber—the area was called Transtiberim in Latin, while the Jews of Rome called it simply "Yonder", as if they, too, were looking at themselves from somewhere else, the real Rome, with the condescending pity and even disdain of outsiders—became one with their courtyards. Indeed, over time, old Yonder turned into a continuous, chaotically winding and flaring labyrinth of houses and courtyards; and because its residents built their houses the way their ancestors had long, long ago, in Palestine, all that could be seen from outside was one unbroken wall, with windows and doors giving onto the many courtyards; so what emerged before long was one endless, impenetrable, zigzagging network of fort-like one-story structures, haphazard alleys and reinforced gates—quite mysterious and exotic to those unfamiliar with this part of Transtiberim. That Jews lived in miserable poverty, most outsiders knew. In the area around Porta Capena, where the Via Appia began, there were Jewish mendicant lepers for all to see; many Roman residents came this way, because—aside from the nearby Via Ostiensis—this was the only gateway to trade from the south; and since produce was cheaper than in the neighbourhoods around the Forum, many from the inner city came here to do their marketing. People could also see stooped, haggard men carrying jugs—bearded men in worn-out sandals and frayed togas. They were here to get drinking water, for the water arriving in conduits in the Yonder district was said to be polluted and at best suitable for watering only. The inhabitants of the district had been petitioning the authorities for generations to no avail, because they still hadn't received better water from the City and were thus forced to buy it from districts blessed with good water, which residents of those better quarters enjoyed for free. Water from the Tiber was supposed to be potable, but Jews considered it unclean, because from time to time there were too many corpses in the river; consequently, they didn't drink its water and didn't even use it for washing—they preferred water from cisterns. There were stubborn ones, stricter followers of their ancestors' laws than most, who considered water from other districts unclean, too, and forbade their families to use it. They may have been right: water flowing through lead pipes caused a gray coating to form on children's skin, and these children turned out to be slower and duller than the others.

Lepers were treated decently by their own; they were not cast out of the community, but sent to large holding pens designated for this purpose where their minimal needs were met. They received the *cupa,* which even the poorest of the poor, and also travellers, could count on in Jewish communities the world over. But because lepers, too, were considered unclean, not even members of their own families could have any contact with them; they could communicate with one another only by shouting from a distance. The very sick were obligated to break their clay pots after a single use and bury them in the ground three feet deep, to the delight of crockery merchants. The lepers were otherwise free to wander about and allowed, like other sick people, to go begging even beyond the walls of the Jewish quarter. A priest, however, not only could not touch them, he couldn't even cast eyes on them, lest he become unclean himself. Thus, lepers were restricted to a partitioned-off rear section of the prayer house; they had to arrive well before the priest and leave only after he was gone. The ritual cleanliness of the priest was safeguarded by the most ancient and strictest of regulations, if only because there were not too many of them. It was they, descendants of Aaron, who were sent to Rome for the more important holidays so they could give their blessing; but afterward, they quickly returned to Jerusalem. Over the years, some Levites were also sent over from Judea, though they could never be priests, only their assistants. Levites blew the shofar on certain holidays, they sang and played instruments and collected taxes. The ritual slaughterers and butchers were also selected from their ranks; Levites were far more numerous in Rome than priests.

Apart from their prescribed religious duties, the priestly and Levite families could not interfere in the life of the Jewish community, which was not the case in the East. In Rome the wealthy and prestigious families would not cede the right to make important decisions to anyone. Seeing this, many of the Levites asked to be sent back to Jerusalem—and the Roman magistrate was only too happy to let them go. Others from Jerusalem took their place, as visitors: members of the lower clergy and poorer Levites. It seemed that not even in the Holy City did every priest and Levite do all that well. After some bureaucratic wrangling, they were usually allowed to enter Rome, especially if wealthy Roman families assumed responsibility for their support. In such cases, the magistrate's assistants were relieved: they didn't have to provide free grain to the newcomers and their families, for the entrants naturally brought their dependents along; in fact, this was the real reason behind their leaving the Holy City and coming to stay with the unclean Diaspora. But after a few weeks or a month at most, they had had enough of Rome's climate and returned to Jerusalem, after which they were either replaced or they weren't. Later, a few Levite families did settle in Rome and became wealthy, mostly from dealing in ritually pure oil and wine which they imported from Judea and Galilee.

In truth, the non-Jewish inhabitants of Rome were not that much interested in how Jews lived on the right bank of the Tiber.

There were many small ethnic islands in Rome, and outsiders had no way of seeing into their lives, either. What is more, the Jewish enclave was not even among the larger, more significant outposts; at the time, their number, in a city of one million people, could not have been more than thirty or forty thousand—the majority of them the descendants of slaves, brought over at slender intervals, who over the years were gradually given their freedom. They had their prayer halls, twelve in number, one of them on the Via Appia, where they also had a catacomb, or underground cemetery; believing in their future resurrection, they didn't burn their dead, like the foolish Latins. Seven of their prayer houses were located along the road to Ostia, the land route used to transport goods arriving by sea.

The first prayer house, later named after Marcus Agrippa, a rich Roman protector of Jews, and built close to one hundred years earlier, was still in use. And though Uri's family did not pray there, Joseph pointed out the edifice to his young son and told him that the members of the first batch of Jewish prisoners had refused to work until the Roman slaveholders conceded that these prisoners rested on Saturday, observed their laws in all circumstances and had to have their own house of worship. A few of them were killed during the initial confrontations, but the rest still wouldn't submit. On hearing this, Uri was so happy, he started clapping and decided that if necessary, he was going to be just as brave.

He was also happy when his father told him that slave masters would have their male and female slaves marry each other in order to increase the number of slaves at no expense to the masters, but that Jewish slaves would consent only if the non-Jewish women chosen for them for purposes of procreation first converted and became Jews themselves. Later, to make things simpler, women were brought over from the Jewish Kingdom. Herod the Great, a friend of Marcus Agrippa, was on good terms with the Emperor Augustus and got him to agree that women of marriageable age be sent to Rome. There were prostitutes, thieves, even some plagued with the white flow among them, but they were Jewish women, and the slave owners did not have to bother with conversions.

Their transportation, however, cost money, his father told him, and no one in power likes this sort of expenditure. Both Herod the Great and Augustus conceded as much, and the supply of women from Judea soon declined.

According to Roman law, the descendants of slaves had to assume their masters' religion; but with such a law in force, Jews were not willing to produce heirs, so an exception had to be made in their case. Non-Jewish slaves—since they couldn't claim that their religion, too, required them to marry within their faith—did not merit such an exemption, and therefore hated the Jews, which was nothing new: ever since Alexander the Great conquered the East, the people of those lands were furious at Jews demanding special treatment and citing wherever they went the rights extracted during Persian rule. It was one thing when both Jews and Greeks were under the same foreign—that is, Persian—rule and quite another when Jews came under Greek domination. But for centuries Jews refused to accept the difference. And ever since both Greeks and Jews had been under Roman rule, the latter looked upon Rome as the new Babylon, and in daily practice paid homage to it more eagerly than the Greeks. Female slaves were in any case ready to become Jewish; they knew that Jews, unlike Greeks and Latins, would not abandon their children. There were male slaves, too, who converted to Judaism; in their case, the decision was prompted by the knowledge that Jewish congregations contributed to the price of slave redemption; some religious groups were known to have bought the slaves' freedom outright. What gave would-be converts pause was circumcision, a painful procedure in adulthood, and not without danger. Women were not threatened with female circumcision—that is, excision of the clitoris. That the Jews of Rome did not require. Thus, large numbers of Syrian, Greek, Arab, Abyssinian, Egyptian, Germanic, Gallic, Hispanic, Thracian, Illyrian and other female slaves became Jewish in Rome, to the greater glory of the One God, and gave birth to children in the maze-like slum called Yonder. But the teeming district also known as Transtiberim—which at this time wasn't yet walled, though the municipal authorities already considered it part of the city, albeit not officially—was the home not only of Jews, but of many other conquered people as well. Converted Jewish girls who were no longer needed in their own homes often had to move only a few houses down and could easily visit their parents if they wanted to. Most of them didn't want to; every non-Jewish parent was happy to be rid of his or her daughter, and they let her know it in no uncertain terms. Besides, a woman who moved in with her husband's family had to remain there for good; nothing tied her anymore to her own family—in this, Latin and Jewish law was in agreement. These girls could be grateful to the One God, to whose bosom they now returned, for having had parents who at least did not cast them out, thereby turning them into the prey of wolves and men, and who also didn't strangle them right after birth.

And that is how it came about that there was a Jewish Diaspora in the Empire's capital.

Joseph considered it unfair that they had to live in a strange land, for strictly speaking, everyone who did not live in the Holy Land was unclean, and no amount of water could wash that away. But he also said that this was not a new development in Jewish history and reminded Uri that the Jews of Rome were very useful to the people back home, who knew this themselves. They in Rome functioned as a kind of large, overstaffed, permanent embassy; and if they conducted their affairs cleverly and strengthened the ties between Rome and the Jews, which they were bound to do anyway, then they did what the Creator had, by all indications, bidden them to do.

The huge, unpredictably winding and twisting inner courtyards of the Jewish quarter were a single, labyrinthine network, a spontaneously expanding fortress from the beginning, although the wealthiest residents had high walls built to separate their courtyards from the common areas and even had guards protecting their properties, as happens invariably where Mammon rules, may it be cursed to the very end of time. If anything, the tendency was on the rise of late; there was a growing number of rich Roman Jews and an even greater number of poor Jews. There may even be a connection between the two phenomena.

The original Yonder stood in the middle of the Jewish quarter. Newer houses were built around it, but more recently, rich entrepreneurs began building multi-story lodging houses. Joseph was afraid that one day his ramshackle hovel would be razed along with the other smaller houses in the neighborhood, and four- or five-story apartment buildings erected in their place. This was what happened in the neighbouring, non-Jewish section of Yonder, where Egyptians, Syrians and Greeks from Asia Minor lived under the same miserable conditions as the majority of the Jews, moving as familiarly in the Jewish section as they did in their own neighbourhoods.

One reason why the courtyards occupied contiguous but whimsically odd-shaped spaces was that on holidays a Jew is not permitted to walk more than two thousand cubits, or elbows, or ells from his dwelling. One ancient cubit is about eighteen inches, but depending on the length of one's forearm, it can be shorter or longer, because a cubit is the length of the arm from the elbow to the end of the middle finger. So Jews couldn't walk farther than about a half mile from their homes, or roughly four antique stadia, one stadium being 605 feet in length.

They had many holidays: there were the four major holidays of the year, all of them multi-day affairs, and there was the Sabbath, from sundown Friday to sundown Saturday; and on these days, too, people wanted to be able to walk more than 2,000 cubits, the equivalent of only about one hundred steps. They loved to visit neighbours and chat and gossip, which is not forbidden on a holiday, except if it involves work, but chatting isn't work; the Creator Himself knows this, and must surely chitchat sometimes with His archangels, since His six-day labour had long been done. At any rate, people built those interconnected courtyards, which made it possible for them to walk not 2,000, but 10,000 cubits, even on a holiday; for they were staying in their own backyard—or at least they could explain as much to their strict Creator, who had to appreciate the soundness of their reasoning. This, then, was the way the Jews of Rome circumvented the Law, like their brethren, the approximately five million Jews living around the world at the time. Or rather, this was the way they observed the Law, observed, that is, the letter of it.

To further justify this bit of trickery, a special rule was conceived, the blending rule, which eventually included handy sub-rules. One of these, still in effect in Rome, was that old Yonder could be considered one vast courtyard, so on the Sabbath and the holidays, whatever was permitted inside one's house could be done outside as well. There were fierce debates over the question of whether this rule applied to Jewish homes built outside the walls of old Yonder. There were those who argued that the entire city of Jerusalem was considered a single "blended" (i.e., interconnected) courtyard, where on the Sabbath it was permitted to move even heavy objects. Others disagreed, saying that Rome was not a Jewish city, and neither was Transtiberim (already then, people pronounced it Trasteberin, dropping the nasal "n" before the "s" and slurring the last syllable, so the word became simply Trastevere, which is how this part of Rome is called even two thousand years later). Rome was unclean and so was Yonder, argued those who intended to return to the fundamentals of their religion, but who themselves were unclean, since in the Diaspora every Jew was. In any case, the residents of old Yonder continued to enjoy the benefits of the blending rule.

In Yonder's labyrinthine courtyards, there was no need for the act of pious fraud committed by just about everyone in Judea, where, before the start of a holiday, people set out food two thousand cubits from their home, indicating that their household extended to that point, so during the holiday they could walk another two thousand cubits from where the food had been placed. They, too, observed the Law in ways that suited them. This ploy wouldn't have worked in Rome, if only because the food set out would be stolen immediately. The outside world corrupted a way of life; the polytheists, the godless Romans, undermined the closeness of the Jewish community—one could have a good grumble over such things. It said something about the Latins' obtuseness that even their first emperor believed that the Jews ate nothing on Saturday, as if the Sabbath were a fast day! Roman Jews chuckled about this for decades. They did pray in their prayer houses on Saturday, and read from the Torah and from the writings of the Prophets, but no less important were the communal meals, whose ex-penses were covered by congregational taxes. And the holiday fare could not be paltry: both wine and meat had to be served, as well as vegetables and fruits, to say nothing of unleavened bread. The poorer families may have had little to eat during the week, but on the Sabbath, they could fill up for free.

The unique mode of construction favoured by Roman Jews was rooted, then, primarily in religious—that is, starvation-fighting—considerations. The fortress-like character of the sprawling neighbourhoods was also no accident.

When sixteen years earlier Emperor Tiberius decided to banish followers of the Jewish religion from Rome, as well as devotees of Isis; the Roman mob, getting wind of the news, tried to storm this mysterious network of walls, but they couldn't penetrate it because they couldn't really size it up, they couldn't brake a breach in it—the Jews defended themselves, shooting arrows and throwing spears from their low roofs.

In the end, however, they all had to leave their homes; Joseph, too, fled Rome with his wife and three-year-old son.

They took shelter in the small village of Ariccia twenty miles from Rome, in a stable with holes in its roof. Joseph hauled out the manure, ploughed the land; his wife cleaned the horses' stalls, and Uri chased after the chickens all day long. Then, a half year later—thanks to the kindness of a Roman patrician, his patron, whose client he also became with the help of his own freed father, Joseph was able to return with his family to his plundered and ravaged home.

With the exception of four thousand unmarried young Jewish men, who were pressed into military service and taken to Sardinia, supposedly to fight bandits, sooner or later, almost all Jews and their families returned to Rome; only a few hundred were killed by murderous highwaymen. The Emperor did not resort to banishment again.

The houses were repaired; little by little they replaced the stolen furniture. There wasn't much to replace. The Jews of Rome were by and large poor.

Uri hardly remembered anything of the move to the country or the return to Rome, only the smell of chicken shit stayed with him, and the image of his father putting him on his shoulder and carrying him around—it felt so good that even now, at the age of nineteen, he would dream about it. In his dream he'd think how wonderful it would be if his father stood in front of him when he woke up and said: "Come, I'll carry you on my shoulders again."

What remained of their temporary banishment was his mother Sarah's cry of pain whenever she remembered a particularly pretty dish of hers that was missing. They were not returned by those non-Jewish freedmen, their patron's other clients, who agreed to hide their valuables. She would whine at length about this every time. The truth was, though, that a few of these people did honestly return the objects deposited with them, they still used those very dishes, as his father often pointed out. But this didn't stop Sarah from whimpering about her loss.

His father no longer looked up when she did this; he would glumly continue eating his food, and even if he did look up at his wife, at her plain, kerchief-covered head, what burned in his eyes was deep resentment. He hated her, not the thieves. But he remained silent. For Roman Jews, getting a divorce was hard; there weren't enough men to go around. In Judea, it was much easier—and this wasn't mere hearsay; the law itself made it easy. If a married man found a prettier woman, it was considered reason enough to get a divorce. He also had the right to drive away his wife if all she did was walk around naked, even though this, under certain circumstances, was not prohibited between two people who were married to each other. But then, Judea was not the backwaters of Judaism, but the heart and soul of the nation; many things were allowed there. In Rome, a Jew, unlike a Latin, could marry his own cousin, because Jews were fewer in number, and thus the older principle applied. In Judea and Galilee, such marriages were considered incestuous and therefore forbidden, for there were more people to choose from. On the other hand, a Roman widow was not obliged to marry the brother of her deceased husband, while in Palestine this was still the law.

His father never talked about their six-month ordeal. It was said that the banishment was caused by four depraved and evil Jews who somehow persuaded the wife of Satirninus, a woman by the name of Fulvia, to donate money for some expensive rugs for the Temple in Jerusalem, after which the miscreants promptly absconded with the money. Fulvia was so indignant, she told the story to the Emperor, who was supposed to have flown into a rage.

But on the bases of other speculation he had heard, Uri suspected that this was a mere pretext and that their banishment from Rome had more to do with Germanicus.

From BOOK TWO
Judea

He had a pounding headache, but the cold was even worse. He shivered, huddled up, and felt that he was lying on a thin layer of straw over stone. He opened his eyes.

It was still dark in the room, which had a tall, vaulted ceiling. Two hefty-looking men sat on the stone floor with their knees drawn up. They rested their backs against the wall and kept staring at him.

"What's all this?" Uri asked in Greek

"Prison," answered one of the men in Aramaic.

Uri raised himself with difficulty, and when he managed to get on all fours, he tried moving his limbs, then turned his head this way and that. Nothing was broken. He felt a strong but dull pain in the nape of his neck

The builders had left small, palm-sized spaces between the blocks of stone all the way on top, and some light filtered through these chinks. To the left, in the wall facing the room's shuttered window, Uri noticed a door with iron bars. Clearly, it could be opened only from outside. Uri got up and took a closer look at the window; it was cut into the wall under the vaulting, in the middle. As was his custom at home, he kept touching the wall, and even smelled it. The section under the window had pieces of rough-hewn stone smaller than those used in the other walls, and it reached only as far as the vaulting. The spaces between the stones were filled up generously with a cement-like material, which had trickled down and hardened. They must have thrown this part up later.

He walked around and felt the other walls, too. Near the lower end of the wall opposite the window, there was a long ledge-like protrusion on which one could sit. Here more or less square-shaped stones of equal height were placed next to one another. The spaces between them were filled with earth and pebbles.

What on earth could this have been before they turned it into a jail?

He sat down and tried to size up the two characters. They were young lads with coarse features. Although they were sitting, he could tell they were strong. Both wore tunics and coats. That's why they could lean against the cold wall. Where was his coat? It was in his sack. His father's coat. He really missed it now.

"How long have I been here?" he asked in Aramaic.

"They brought you in last night."

Uri looked up. Rays of sunlight frolicked high above the door, only there, grazing the wall at a slant and leaving the rest in the shade.

"It's morning now?"

"It will be noon soon."

The window then must have a northern or rather northeastern exposure.

Uri kept pressing the area around his stomach with his finger.

"Do they feed you here?"

"You slept through breakfast. There'll be supper."

"Wonderful."

He was testing one eye and then the other. That blow on the back of his neck didn't make them better. But they didn't seem any worse either.

He felt relieved. He thought of Matthew—who denounced him and got him in jail—with gratitude. Now I am where I belong, and he laughed happily.

The two men looked at each other.

Everything became clear to Uri.

There would still have been time in Rome to put his name in the passport, as Plotius said. He joined the delegation even later, and his name they did enter; only Uri's name was not in it. Matthew didn't even mention him to the magistrate the day before they left—that was the only time he could have gone and told him that he'd be travelling with six people, not five. Plotius did get on the list, though it was decided even later that he, too, would be coming. At the request of Agrippa, he, Uri, had been put on the list of the elders two days earlier. Still, Matthew didn't report him as an additional passenger. He could have done it when he made sure they knew about Plotius, but he didn't.

Matthew had decided already then that once they got to Jerusalem, he was going to turn in the man he thought was Agrippa's spy.

Actually, he said as much in Cæsarea the evening when he, Matthew and Plotius were having a few cups of wine. He couldn't be too explicit, but Plotius had to know what he was talking about. Plotius also knew what was going to happen, but he didn't say a word—he agreed with Matthew.

It didn't hurt Uri that the two men he preferred over all the others in the group were the ones that betrayed him.

I am not cut out to be a member of such a delegation. Even prison is better. At least it's a straightforward situation.

Uri had the feeling now that he wasn't afraid of anything. He'd make it out of here for sure, he wasn't in any kind of real danger. There were adventures waiting for him, the kind he would never have dreamed of. What Roman Jew could say that he was imprisoned, and in Jerusalem!

Uri laughed out loud.

He no longer had to cower among people of dubious intentions and slovenly appearance, who were also secretive and stuck in the world of petty political and business calculations.

I will never again be a member of any kind of delegation, he decided. No power on earth can force me to join one.

He noted gladly that his instincts had not abandoned him. He sensed all along that there was trouble ahead. He would have liked to believe that he was simply imagining things, but he wasn't. On the contrary, he always sensed what he was supposed to.

I am safe and sound!

He took deep breaths. The back of his neck still hurt, but he felt strong. He will tell his father that overnight he became an adult. This is just what happened to him, and it happened now.

"What's the custom here? Do they question the prisoners at all, or do they just let them rot in jail?"

After a moment's silence, the one sitting under the window said:

"Where are you from?"

"Rome."

"You don't say... Listen then. They must pass a sentence, so they have to hear you out. First, you say it was like this and like that, but you didn't do anything, in fact just the reverse; then somebody steps up announces the charges, and if there are witnesses, they'll hear them out, too. And then, one by one, the members of the court have their say. In a village three judges will do, in town there can be as many as twenty-three; and for a decision to be valid, there has to be at least a two-vote majority. They begin to recite the judgment at the two ends of the row of judges— first, the younger ones and then the older judges who are seated in the middle of the row. While all this is going on, you stand there facing them, remorse had made your hair grow long, as if you were in mourning, so you stand there with your head bowed, looking repentant even if you had pleaded innocent. If someone spoke in your favour, he can speak once more before the vote, but the ones against you can't speak again. Then the vote is taken. If you are acquitted, you can go straight home; but if they find you guilty, they won't announce the sentence until the following day, and if that day happens to be a holiday or the Sabbath, then only afterward."

"I don't understand," Uri said. "If three judges are enough, how can there be a two-vote majority?"

"In that case, there isn't," the other said. "Either the judgment is unanimous, or they call in two more judges, and from that point on there must be a two-vote majority."

"Twenty-three judges?" Uri asked. "Even in a small town?"

"The towns aren't that small. Where there are five hundred adult males, you have a town. That amounts to at least fifteen hundred or two thousand people, in all probability a lot more. Our towns aren't so small."

"A booster for the home front," Uri thought cheerfully.

"There are that many judges in one town?" he asked. Or there are also attorneys among them? Who are sometimes prosecutors and sometimes defense attorneys? Is that what you mean?"

They didn't understand what he was asking. Uri tried to describe what a prosecutor was, what a defence lawyer does, and what a judge is supposed to do. Eventually they got it.

"We don't have such people here," the one sitting under the window said. "There are men, there are tailors, blacksmiths, carpenters, tentmakers, robbers, thieves—you know, people like that." He laughed at his own joke and then continued: "If they have to judge a case, the master sends for them. Then they go to the prayer house and sit in judgment. And if there isn't a two-vote majority, they keep summoning more judges, until there is one. Twenty-three is the most they can have, and if they can't come to a decision even then, the case goes to the Sanhedrin, who meet right here above us... But even they don't meet as a body right away, they also begin with just three people... and keep adding more, up to seventy-one. But that rarely happens; sooner or later the two-vote majority is reached locally.

"I never heard of a case that couldn't be decided where it took place," said the one sitting closer.

"And that master... how does he have the right to invite outsiders to judge. Is he the *archisynagogos*?"

They didn't understand the word. Uri explained that he was referring to the leader of a congregation. They shook their heads.

"But that would be the master; it's that simple."

"And that is how he makes his living?"

"Of course not," said the one sitting under the window. "He is not allowed to accept money for teaching or for giving counsel or adjudicating a case. He has an occupation: he is a tiller of land, or burns lime or makes furniture—that's why he is a master."

"Or he steals or robs," said the other one.

They all laughed.

This was a different world, all right.

"Did you two have your trial already?"

"Not me," said the one sitting under the window.

"Me neither."

"When will it be?"

The one sitting under the window looked up toward the light.

"Either today, very soon, or after Passover."

"If it's not today," said the other one, "then it will be more than a week from now."

The earliest date was a week from the following Monday. In eleven days, in other words. The court was in session Mondays and Thursdays. On other days there were no trials.

In short, the court met in Jerusalem the same day it did in the countryside: on Sunday. If they didn't come by sundown today, Thursday, then, because of Passover, they couldn't have it next Monday or Thursday either—those days were only half-holidays, but they couldn't hold trials. There were many things one could do on half-holidays that were forbidden on full-fledged holidays, for instance, hold a burial or heal the sick, but a court of law could not meet.

He wouldn't like sitting around for eleven days. Let them come today and clear up this whole thing, after which he'd go back to Rome. He didn't yet know how. Of course, if they fed him, he could bear to stay for eleven more days.

"What did you do?" asked the one sitting under the window.

"Nothing," Uri said and laughed again. "You won't believe it, but nothing."

"You're right. We don't believe you."

"Doesn't matter," Uri said. "My name is Gaius Theodorus."

The other two didn't say anything. Uri shrugged his shoulder.

"Why are *you* here?"

"We're also innocent," said the one sitting under the window sarcastically.

"But we're being accused of committing robbery."

"So I am locked up with robbers; that's funny. And they can't even rob me; I have nothing."

"That's a serious accusation."

"Serious, my foot," the other said. "At most we'll be sentenced to four or five years of slavery, and after our time is up, we'll be free without having to buy our freedom. We're not lousy little thieves; we're robbers."

"Rather, they say we are," added the one sitting under the window sarcastically. "But first they have to prove it."

Uri thought he didn't hear them right, or maybe they used words differently here; so he asked what they thought was the difference between a thief and a robber.

The two of them looked at each other in amazement. But then the one sitting under the window proceeded to explain, shouting helpfully and stressing each syllable so that Uri would understand that a thief steals and a robber takes away by force.

Uri did hear it right.

"A robber gets a milder sentence than a thief?" he asked with great surprise.

They again looked at each other.

"Are you sure you're a Jew?"

"Of course I am."

"Then you are an idiot," said the one sitting closer and, taking a deep breath, explained, "The thief not only steals but offends the Everlasting God, because he hides from His visage and commits evil in stealth; he seeks to hide his deed from the Almighty. But the robber attacks courageously, openly, and therefore does not offend the Everlasting, because he doesn't hide anything from Him. The thief's sin is therefore much more serious."

A fine, clean, religious explanation, Uri thought. They've got different laws here.

In Rome's Jewish community, a robber was punished by death, while a thief was usually sentenced to slavery for several years or permanently. There were two further classes: as a slave, he could stay in the Yonder district; or he was sold in the Italian provinces—in Puteoli, for instance—which had a well-known slave market. Shipments of humans arrived in its harbour from every corner of the empire.

If the guilty Jew happened to be a citizen of Rome, then, in theory at least, the Jewish court's verdict had to be approved by a Roman tribunal, but in practice the Curia gave every Jewish verdict its nod; it was plenty busy with other things. The death sentences were also usually approved by the Latins, and if once in a while there was a retrial, neither the defendant nor the witnesses were invited; the verdict was formal, and approval almost automatic. However redundant this process may have seemed, the Curia reserved the right to retry a case, because it could happen that for political reasons they wanted to save a Jew who'd been condemned to death—he may be the favourite of an influential senator or of the emperor himself: a much favoured actor, a lover or some such person. Then the Curia dug in its heels, until of course a large bribe was offered.

"What kind of sentence does a thief receive in your courts?" Uri asked.

"A death sentence."

Must be a new law.

He learned back in Rome that in the past a thief had to repay four times the value of the stolen goods, and when he did, they let him go. But then Herod the Great's decree stipulated that a thief had to be sold into slavery; that's how a whole lot of Jewish slaves, the "new ones", ended up in Rome. After the death of Herod the Great, the Roman prefects put an end to this practice.

"Once," said the one sitting closer, "I saw a thief's execution. Not a pretty sight."

"Did they stone him?" asked the one sitting under the window.

"He was burned to death."

The one sitting closer recounted the incident with much relish. Everyone from the village was there, women and children included, so they could all witness the event. Actually, they were told to be there, so they would learn from it. The blacksmith, over a great fire, heated up a piece of iron in a dish, and when the iron was already dripping, the tied-up thief was made to stand. After wrapping a scarf around his neck, two people began to pull on the scarf on both sides. The thief was strong and could stand it for a long time without breathing, but finally he did open his mouth and gasped for air. And then the blacksmith's assistant poured the hot iron down his throat; he had him drink it, and sure enough, the thief's insides burned up; the red-hot metal came oozing out of his burst-open chest. He was still alive but couldn't scream, because he didn't have a throat anymore, he was just writhing and burning from inside out, and couldn't fall down either, so he was propped up by the two who'd been pulling on the scarf. He turned into a live, dripping metal statue.

Uri gave a shiver.

"And what if he doesn't open his mouth?" he asked.

"Then he suffocates," said the one sitting closer, "but since the verdict was burning and not choking, the corpse's mouth is forced open and the liquid iron poured down, for that was the verdict."

"I wouldn't like to burn to death," mused the one sitting under the window. "I'd prefer choking."

"That's not good either," opined the other. "If they don't do it right, it can take a long time."

"Stoning also takes a long time," said the one sitting under the window. "They keep throwing and throwing, and you're still alive. I'd rather have them choke me to death."

"The best," said the one sitting closer, "is to have your head chopped off with one clean swipe."

"That's a foreign way of doing it," said the one sitting under the window with contempt. "I want no part of an Edomite execution. Come the resurrection, the angels would have to look for my head, which may have rolled away somewhere, or match my body with another head, maybe a whore's. No, thank you; I'd rather have them choke me to death."

Judea... what a strange place. Jerusalem must be strange too. Uri smiled: he is inside the city, yet he hasn't seen any of it.

"Where exactly is our prison located?" he asked.

"The high priests live right above us," said the one sitting under the window, motioning with his head toward the vaulted ceiling. "A nice big building this one. They don't have it much better up there; we live in the same house now." He laughed haltingly as he said this.

"Where is this palace, in the Temple Square?"

"No. This is the upper city. But the Temple is close by, northeast of here. You count to five hundred while you walk, and you're there."

Uri gazed up at the tiny slit of a window and saw a small, blurry patch of blue; the sun no longer shone through the crevice. These amiable rogues also knew which way was northeast; and when it was be time to say the evening prayers, they'd be bowing in that direction. From now on, he wouldn't have to bow toward Jerusalem while praying; for, he was inside the city, in the very centre of it. He'd have to bend his knees toward the Temple, which was a mere five hundred paces from here.

"There used to be shops where we are now," said the one sitting closer, who got up cumbersomely to take a little walk. He was tall and muscular, and could easily have been hired by the Jewish police force; and if he weren't a Jew, he could be one of the carriers of Pilate's litter. "The shopkeepers paid a high rent to the priests. But then these merchants moved to the marketplace in front of Herod's palace; they make more money there, and so do the priests; business is brisker. Something had to be done with those shops, so they put up a wall and turned them into a prison."

"It's more convenient for them this way," the one sitting under the window put in, and he, too, got up. He wasn't short either, but looked kind of chubby. "Lately the Sanhedrin have been holding their meetings upstairs. The accused don't have far to travel. It's better to have us right in the same building. They don't need a whole squadron, like in the old days, to march us all the way to the Xystos. Cheeky devils that we are, we might slip away."

Uri's stomach rumbled—he hadn't eaten anything for a full day. He also had to relieve himself, so he looked around.

"Over there," said the chubby one, pointing to the corner on the other side of the room.

A wide-lipped crock stood there, covered with a square-shaped sheet of marble. This lid was off centre, suggesting that the crock wasn't empty. Uri kept turning and fumbling; while holding his pulled-up tunic in one hand and his untied loin-cloth in the other, he tried to squat down on the crock in such a way that the pile of the previous user would not get smeared all over his skin. He crouched with his back to the other two, who were having a hearty chuckle. It wouldn't be a bad thing if they started questioning me already tonight, he thought.

Hours passed. It was getting dark outside.

"Well, boys," said the chubby one as he sat down again under the window, "for the next eleven days we'll be shitting in each other's shit."

The door opened. Two guards entered, one of them, holding a torch, remained at the door, while the other put two bowls on the floor. One contained some food, the other was filled with water. The taller jailbird made for the crock, wanting to give it to the guard, but he waved him away: Not now. Then the guards left and locked the door behind them.

It was almost completely dark outside, but Uri could still see the two cellmates dip their hands in the water bowl and then turning in the direction of the crock and bowing repeatedly, recite the evening Shema. Uri, too, splashed water on his hands and joined the other two in prayer. Toward the crock was northeast.

The cellmates knelt down beside the food bowl and smelled it like two dogs. Each made a face and shook his head. Then they sat on their heels and stuffed a solid piece of food in their mouths. Uri didn't move. The two jailbirds finished eating and crawled away from the bowl. It was Uri now who crawled over to the bowl; he too, smelled it and even poked it with his finger. It was some kind of cake; he licked his finger. Maybe there was even a drop of honey in it, he never had this before. He didn't eat much, mainly because they didn't leave him a whole lot.

With his hand, he scooped up some water from the bowl.

By right he should start eating around this time.

It was the first night of Passover. They should have gotten lamb, it's what Jews eat at the Seder everywhere.

Maybe there were a few bites of meat in that cake, but the jailbirds must have gobbled it up.

He saw nothing around him. This is what blindness must be like. He got scared.

"You can't see anything, either?" he asked.

"How the hell should we see, you nitwit, when it's dark," said the one sitting under the window.

Uri calmed down.

Later he woke up to loud knocking. The door opened, and between two guards with torches, another two led in an older, heavier man, holding him by the arm. The torches blazed in the draft; shadows danced on the prisoner's face and tunic. One of the guards cut the rope on the heavy man's wrists, which were tied behind his back, and then they both left. Uri quickly looked around, his cellmates remained in their places. The new prisoner just stood there, he didn't look anywhere. He was balding, and his greying, unkempt beard gave him a scruffy look; he stood there barefoot. The door was closed now, so it was even darker than before. They were all silent. The hay strewn on the stone floor crunched softly under the new prisoner's feet. Then he sat down to the left of Uri and heaved a deep sigh.

"A man can't even sleep here," said the one sitting under the window.

It was quiet again. The new prisoner's breathing seemed laboured.

"Did they beat you?" asked the one sitting under the window.

"No," the new prisoner said. He had a deep, pleasant voice, and though he spoke softly, it sounded loud enough. Judging by his accent, he could have been from Galilee.

"Let's sleep," the other said, who sat to the right of Uri.

It was quiet, but all four were up.

"What did you do?" asked the one sitting under the window.

"I caused a disturbance," said the new prisoner.

They were all silent.

"Not enough of a disturbance unfortunately," he later added.

"Why aren't we asleep?" the other asked rather angrily.

"You go to sleep, we'll talk," said the one sitting under the window. "What was the disturbance?"

"We went up to the Temple Square, to the women's courtyard, last Tuesday, to buy the doves, and I saw they were cheating. I told them to stop cheating, but they went on doing it. Then I turned a few tables on them.

They were quiet again

"And where did they keep you since Tuesday?"

"Nowhere, we were allowed to leave. We are staying outside the city."

"I don't get it. They didn't arrest you then, on Tuesday?"

"No. We went back on Wednesday, and I told them again not to cheat, because they were still cheating. The guards came over, we argued, and then we went home. They came over tonight, to the place where we are staying. I told the others to run, but they didn't give them chase; I was the only one they caught.

"I still don't get it," said the other, to the right of Uri. "They looked for you afterwards, so they could arrest you? Why didn't they arrest you right away?"

"I don't know," the new prisoner said.

"It couldn't have been much of a disturbance," said the one sitting under the window. "Our police are quick to arrest you even for something minor, especially on the Temple Square. One wrong word and they move in. They get a reward for it, especially on a holiday; extra money for each arrest, I know.

"What do you mean by cheating?" inquired Uri.

"What he means is," said the one sitting under the window, answering for the new prisoner, "that the money changers charge more for the exchanges than the kalubon."

"What is that?" asked Uri.

"The exchange fee: one silver meah," said the one sitting by the window, "that is, one sixth of a zuz. You know how much a zuz is?"

"I don't."

The two began to stir, getting rather excited

"One zuz is half a shekel, or to put it another way, a zuz is one dinar or a like amount of Attic drachma, or four sistertia... And one silver meah is worth two pondions. So how many sestertia is the *kalubon,* big boy?"

Uri tried to figure it out, but he got all mixed up.

"Give it to him in perutah, that's the smallest copper coin. The little dimwit must have handled that... Thirty-two perutah: that's how much the *kalubon* fee is."

"The perutah is also called lepton," Uri said proudly. "This much I know."

"No other coin was ever in your hand, down-and-outer that you are," said the one sitting closer contemptuously.

"So, how much is it in sistertia?" asked the one sitting under the window.

"I don't know."

The robbers laughed; they couldn't get over somebody not being able to do the arithmetic.

"Two-thirds of a sistertius," said the new prisoner.

There was a short silence.

"That's correct," the one sitting under the window said glumly, disappointed that somebody had put an end to his little game.

They were silent now.

"How much more do they charge over there?"

"As much as seven or eight pondions," said the one sitting under the window. "I even saw them asking for seven or eight tresiths. And those morons don't even notice it. They come from villages and haven't the foggiest idea."

"Try to understand, birdbrain: one meah equals only two pondions and one and one-third tresith. Instead of one-sixth of a zuz, they rake in two-thirds. Four times as much. These country bumpkins come into town, and they're clueless as to how much things cost, like you there; it's the only time the peasants have money in their hands, so of course they get clipped."

"Half the profit goes to the high priests," said the other one; judging from his noisy movements, he must have sat up. "Of course, they cheat. And it's mostly the high priests, the rotten foreigners."

"And they cheat with the doves, too," said the new prisoner. "They charge twice as much for the doves, since it's supposed to replace the paschal lamb. But they are not allowed to do that. I told them to charge the regular price, but it was no use." He sounded tired and resigned. "They are a shameless bunch, feeding off people's faith. And the miserable poor give them all they have, since they need the two doves for the offering..."

"The third-dove tax," the other said sarcastically, "that's what people call it. And it ends up in the priests' pockets... They're the biggest thieves, the high priests. That's why they live here, above the prison... They know where they belong... Right here, next to us. They're bigger scoundrels than we are, that's why their rooms are so much bigger than ours."

They were quiet again. Uri was sorry that he hadn't yet handled Palestinian money and he didn't pay attention in Cæsarea when his companions were arguing about the value of the local currency. Now, at least, he knew that one meah is two-thirds of a sestertius. First chance he gets, he'll tell them.

He smiled. He will probably never see them again, thank the Lord, blessed be His name.

"Did you come from Galilee?" asked the one sitting under the window.

"Yes," the new prisoner said, somewhat startled.

"You pay taxes there, right?"

"Yes."

"Wait a minute. Then you changed money on your own, for the sacrificial doves, in which case they weren't supposed to ask for kalubon. You were entitled to change money without a fee. For free! Did you know that?"

"No, I didn't," the new prisoner said, sounding very tired.

"What cheek," cried the one sitting under the window. "Rotten bastards! Scum of the earth! But they'll never end up here. Because they make sure the high priests get their cut. Oh, the dirtbags!"

When the morning light appeared, Uri awoke with a start. The new prisoner was praying quietly, on his knees, bowing in the direction of the crock. The other two were still asleep, with their coats pulled over their heads, facing the wall. Uri couldn't stop shivering; he didn't have a coat. His side hurt, and his back, and his shoulder. The new prisoner didn't have a coat either, only a linen tunic, but he didn't appear to be cold. Perhaps praying kept him warm. While praying, he looked at Uri. There he was, this older man, one step away, Uri saw his face clearly in the early morning light. His mussed up hair was turning gray, and he had beautiful, clear, light-coloured eyes, gray perhaps, set deep in his swollen face. At one time he may have been a handsome man. He's probably as old as my father, Uri thought and gave him a smile. The new prisoner nodded toward him and continued praying.

Then the door flew open, the torchbearers came in, pulled the cover off the two men who were sleeping, held the torch to each one's face, and finally came to a stop in front of the new prisoner. He rose. The guards grasped him by the arm on both sides, and led him away. Once more they bolted the door from outside.

"Let's get some more sleep," said the one lying to the right of Uri and turned back toward the wall.

From BOOK FOUR
Rome

The great fire broke out on July 17, the very same day that the Senon people many years earlier had set fire to a still miniscule Rome.

Uri crouched in his little hut and blessed the Everlasting God that he'd also bought the goats and chickens from the farmer, who didn't want to bother with them. Now Uri drove them into the pantry, and with the strongest lock he had, locked them up—there was bound to be a food shortage. He had his own private well; he blessed the Everlasting for that, too. On the third day Hagar returned from Yonder where she had run as soon as the fire broke out. In Yonder nothing burned down, the fire did not spread across the Tiber—no one thought of starting a fire there.

"But the city, the city!" wailed Hagar, as though she had lived in that part of Rome all her life, and proceeded to sprinkle ash on her head.

Soon after Hagar, Marcellus arrived, too.

"He will come again, the second time," he cried. "It is all true! The prophets, His prophets, are preaching the truth! He sent Satan ahead, as it is written. Nero cleared the way for Him. This fire is His fire. He is coming; He will soon be here, any minute. It has begun, it has begun! So pray!"

"You're crazy," screamed Uri. "Don't do this, it's so very dangerous."

"Here's the proof," Marcellus shouted back. "The unbelievers can see it for themselves; the pagans can see it! This is His Work!"

"You want them to accuse the Jews of setting the fires themselves?"

"The unbelievers will go to hell," howled Marcellus. "You'll be the first to go. You deserve it, too."

He asked his mother to join him and his friends, because they'd be praying in Yonder. Many had already congregated there, waiting eagerly for the Anointed, who had sent word with the fire, and will appear with a sword. The faith of His followers makes Him walk on clouds; the smoke is His smoke; the fire is His fire. But Hagar was too tired to walk back to Yonder.

"You'll go to hell, too," he growled at his mother and ran off.

Uri groaned painfully.

We're in for big trouble.

The ruins were still smoldering when Nero from the undamaged Rostra announced majestically that he would rebuild Rome; it would be more beautiful than ever. He said the conflagration was a blessing; he could now build a larger palace, full of gorgeous gardens, to the greater glory of Rome. He promised to build a canal leading from Lake Avernus to the mouth of the Tiber, so there would be enough water to put out future fires. Rome will become a well-ordered city at last, and not a filthy maze of dark and narrow alleys; it would be better laid out than Alexandria. He ordered that the rubble be loaded onto boats, shipped down the Tiber and used to fill the swamps around Ostia. He also decreed that houses below the second story could no longer be built of wood—blocks of the hardest stone from Alba must be used. Houses may no longer have common outside walls; each one must be surrounded by a separate wall. He asked his people to pray to Vulcanus, Ceres and Proserpina, and asked women to appease Juno in the Capitol, which was untouched by the fire. He said he had heard the rumour that he himself had set his own city on fire—he, the Emperor. What an unprecedented, unheard of accusation, what base calumny! He commanded that those insidious, dark-souled, mad and evil Jews who call this terrible fire the revenge of their God should be arrested forthwith. For these miscreants have cursed Rome, cast an evil spell on the city, and confounded, becharmed and bewitched the Roman people's soul—they dared to do this, who had caused this fire themselves, and were behind Rome's misery, and were guilty of the death of hundreds of innocent citizens, as was seen, and would be attested to by many.

The citizens hissed and booed and cursed the Jews, and ran off to exact revenge.

They rounded up all the Nazarenes, or whoever was said to be one, and proceeded to torture them. The Nazarenes readily confessed to arson and named their accomplices. Hitherto unharmed Jews, in their turn, preemptively denounced the innocent Jews; it was an easy way to get rid of rivals and enemies. The Augustinians picked up innocent passers-by, stripped them and stabbed to death anyone whose foreskin was missing; those who had it, they beat to death in their helpless rage. During those days it was not advisable to walk the still passable streets of Rome. Superstitious beliefs from Alexandria began to spread in the capital, too: Jews drank the blood of non-Jews on Saturday; they slaughtered Greek children and roasted them, and that is why they didn't eat pork. Not only Jews escaped from Alexandria, Greeks fled too, in large numbers, and brought these tales with them. The most perfect accusation against the Jews was that they cast spells. They were able, just by muttering some curse, to set things ablaze; they needed no live coals or tinder. Most of those who were tortured declared, just as the wheel was about to crush their skull, that yes, the accusation was well-founded. Political commentators reminded people how eminently credible the accusation was. At the time of Germanicus's death, Piso had also been accused first and foremost of casting spells, and he in effect had pleaded guilty to the charge, for he committed suicide, though his trial was still in progress. He, too, had been bewitched by the Jews.

The first people to be executed were sewn into the skin of beasts, pressed against monkeys, rats and dogs, like those guilty of matricide—the official charge against them was, in fact, that they betrayed their mother city—and then thrown into the Tiber. But they ran out of monkeys. So the wretches sewn into animal skins were simply thrown to the dogs. Soon there was a shortage of skin, and the dog owners also protested; many of them had trained their dogs to run in races, and once they gorged themselves on human flesh, they would never obey orders. Thus, Nero had an amphitheatre erected in the Field of Mars and there the Nazarenes were thrown to the wild beasts. Dressed as a charioteer, Nero stood close to the arena and watched the proceedings from there. After a time the animals had their fill, and there weren't enough of them, either. The Emperor decided to crucify the remaining victims in his burned down gardens and made entry to the spectacle free for everyone.

When Uri heard what was happening, he hurried over to the gardens. He had fathered Marcellus; he should at least be with him at his death, though he could easily have been devoured already by dogs or tigers. Uri wasn't afraid of being recognised and dragged to a cross; he felt he had lived long enough.

Many hundreds of people were hanging on crosses, some of them upside down. Quite a few of them were still alive; many were dead. Mounted guards kept order; desperate relatives wandered about with pitchers of water in their hands or on their heads; no one bothered them. Mourners were bowing toward Jerusalem, with their clothes rent and with clods of earth on their heads. Large groups of onlookers simply enjoyed the spectacle; it surpassed by far the best circus entertainment. Ever since the rebellion of Spartacus was put down, they hadn't crucified this many people—and that uprising happened a long time ago.

Uri slowly and carefully made his way through the gardens; he had to go up to each cross and look at every person hanging on it. The walk tired him out, people kept pushing and poking him. Those still alive moaned and begged for water, and twitched and gasped as faeces trickled down their legs; blood dripped from the mouths and noses of those who were strung up by their feet. The youths and the stronger ones who were crucified upside down could still tense their muscles and raise their upper torso until it was almost level, but then they fell back again.

Uri recognised many acquaintances from Yonder, of whom he would never have imagined that they, too, had joined this insane, fanatic sect; or perhaps they didn't even join, only their denouncers had their eyes on their fortunes. He was shocked to discover the dead body of old Honoratus. One of his legs was missing; it must have been cut off before he was nailed to the cross. He surely did not become a Nazarene. A revolution was taking place in Yonder; young people were replacing the old leaders who did not know how to handle the Nazarenes. Many faces made him think they might be Judeans who came as missionaries. He spent a long time looking at an old man hanging by his feet. He was dead, his long white beard fluttered in the wind, and even this way, with his head upside down, he appeared to be smiling. What terrible sins he must have paid for with his death, happily.

Uri roamed about the garden all day long, because they kept bringing more people to the crosses, but he didn't find Marcellus. Did he come to his senses in time? Was he killed before all this started?

When the sun went down, Nero gave orders to set fire to the crucified—let them light up the sky, and let the populace see it. They put straw under each cross and sprinkled oil on it, so that the fire would emit plenty of smoke. The dead crackled silently as they burned; those still alive squalled.

Rome caught up with Alexandria. Until now the Romans simply looked down on the Jews and laughed at them; the Nazarene zealots succeeded in inspiring hatred for them.

Marcellus turned up late at night, emerging from the goats' hideaway when Uri finally made it home.

"I didn't see you among the crucified, my dear boy," Uri greeted him matter-of-factly.

Marcellus wiped goat shit off his foot.

"Did you betray them then, son?" inquired Uri with a smile "You ran and sold them down the river? To save your own skin?"

Marcellus said nothing. Hagar, as expected, wrung her hands.

"I don't believe I would have done that," Uri mused. "They were your family, your brothers and sisters..."

"They lied," Marcellus hissed darkly.

"And you realised that only now? When they are massacring them? What kind of faith is yours?"

"He will come," Marcellus whispered. "He will come at night, in stealth, like a thief... And by morning there will be a new world. And He will forgive the sinners first."

Uri fell silent.

"I still have a lot to learn," he thought and began to laugh. And kept giggling to himself for a long time; he couldn't stop.

Hagar looked at him in horror; Marcellus, with hatred in his eyes. Then Hagar plucked a chicken, cooked it, and after saying the prayer for the dead, they feasted on it in silence. ❧

Translated by Ivan Sanders

András Imreh

Poems

Translated by David Hill

Birds

Madarak

All morning they persecuted me
As if I were a cat, creeping through creeping
shrubs, to make my breakfast from their chicks,

that was the fluttering racket they gave me.
At least it's better than the dive-bomb treatment.
"What's going on?" I pondered, lobbing stones their way.

And then I almost trod on one. Beak open,
head back, like one of its own hungry young,
it sat, and couldn't budge.

Perhaps it had a sunstroke. Or, from laying eggs,
it had lost all of its vital elements. "Don't be
afraid, little bird," I said. But then,

what can a sick bird understand of human talk?
I padded out the lid of a shoe-box
with straw. I brought it water, too.

András Imreh

trained as a lawyer but is now a free-lancing poet and translator. He has published one volume of poems (1998) and is working on a second. A selection has been published in Spanish translation.

It just looked at me. But the others did leave off
their screeching. Probably coincidence.
Nearby, another thrush rummaged through fallen leaves,

a member of another clan. It sang once.
Mine vomited—the colour of bird faeces.
It seemed to get some strength from that.

Away it flew, past my neighbour's garage,
and then one more garage farther along.
And then I no longer cared where it went.

I'm going to get a beer from my garage.
And to be honest, yes, I think
they'll persecute me again.

Phobia

Fóbia

At eight-fifteen is when it likes to get
the whole thing started. Promptly. I suppose
it's eating through the wall. Inhuman, yet
not even animal, it blindly goes

its course. A functional, unfeeling sound.
I picture it as some strange bug, the hue
of rotting flesh, the size of one stretched hand,
obscure in darkness as it clambers through

a crack it's cut out with its jaw-like things.
And now in this small room where I sit lonely,
it creeps in crazy automatic rings,
and closes in. On me? Or am I only

a living landmark that's of merely passing
concern? Something digestible, that may
be useful later on? A dull amassing
of various smells? Some kind of pulp or whey?

Perhaps I'll be the object of a fairly
disinterested killing operation;
a snail-fleshed prey that registers just barely
above the threshold of its stimulation,

whose chemicals it will assimilate?
And now within my brain—though I don't will it—
a sense of preparation's taking shape,
pulsating, pounding: telling me to kill it.

Afternoon

Délután

They give the dog a bath. Face twisted to a frown,
they pull their sleeves above their elbows with their teeth.
They play a bit of soccer, until the sun goes down.
They let go of the wheel as the road descends beneath.

They shower, then they iron, in just their underwear.
They open up the window. The hinges give a screech.
They give the lawn a mowing. The radio starts to blare.
They reckon that tomorrow they'll go check out the beach.

They have a few soft drinks before the evening news.
They oil the rowboat's hooks, in which the paddles go.
They bet a crate of beer that the German team will lose.
They occupy the roof to watch the firework show.

They phone their granny up, and give their nails a trimming.
As scissors dance through fingers, a long long chat is had.
The tablecloth gets shaken. A little spoon goes skimming.
The joy of early evening, auto-destructive, mad.

Set to Go

Indulás

We're set to go. We've turned the heat off,
we've ditched the compost, locked the gate.
We've polished all we had to eat off,
pre-set the light to shine at eight.

We're set to go. Garage is locked.
Small keg beneath the water-course.
I've brought the deck-chairs in, but not
the chopping block, the sawing horse.

We're set to go. Got pad and pencil.
Got laptop next to driver's seat.
Filled all the bags. Packed each utensil.
Put out the trash can on the street.

We're set to go. But hey, look fresher!
Our time is good. Let's keep it so.
What say we quickly check the pressure?
We're set to go. We're set to go.

Sonnet

Szonett

I'm not old. But I like to be alone,
to lounge around the house, procrastinate;
grow fond of aging undershirts, and hate
to throw them out, however soiled they've grown;

advice, delivered in a friendly tone,
by caring friends, can make me quite irate;
some items of my furniture, whose state
could be improved, I want left in their known

condition; and I never lift my voice
at times when someone has to make a choice;
some sentences of mine, which start out good,

I break off, and they're never understood.

Géza Buzinkay

Antal Szerb, the Inquisitive Martian and Budapest in the 1930s

We, the present readers of Szerb's *Budapest Guide,* are the Martian, the creature from far away. The city today is different, its landmarks are found elsewhere, associations (if any) different than those of Antal Szerb seventy years ago will come to mind when roaming the streets. It is best to read the *Guide* as if it were the gentle recollections of a distant, sunken world by a Romantic author of the early nineteenth century. Yet Szerb actually intended it as a "persiflage of a tourist guide", as one critic put it at the time of its publication in 1935.

Antal Szerb (1901–1945) is best known in his native country as a literary historian and critic, the author of a *History of Hungarian Literature* (1934) and a three-volume *History of World Literature* (1941), two ground-breaking and immensely popular works which challenge the sweep of any novel. Szerb was an essayist of the first rank, who produced translations from four languages and whose knowledge and erudition were legendary. His two novels, *The Pendragon Legend,* an ingenious and enthralling ghost story (1934), and *Journey by Moonlight* (1937) have been everybody's secret favourites. The novels, as well as his brilliant evocation of the notorious affair of Marie Antoinette's necklace in the *The Queen's Necklace* (1943), were regarded as side products, as it were, of his many talents and interests. Still, Szerb regarded himself first and foremost as a writer. It is a belated compensation for his early and tragic death that the two novels have recently been published to resounding success in Germany and Italy. Their recent success in England can also be attributed to the congenial translation of Len Rix, translator of *A Martian's Guide to Budapest* for this journal.

Antal Szerb's short life, a life spent very much among his beloved books, can be summed up in a line or two. He studied Hungarian, German and English

---

Géza Buzinkay
is Professor of History at Esterházy College, Eger. He has written eleven books on the history of journalism, cultural history and museology.

literature at universities in Graz and Budapest, lived for five years in France, Italy and London, took a teaching position at a secondary school on his return to Budapest and was killed in the Holocaust for being Jewish.

A Martian's Guide to Budapest, his "whimsical and gently ironical love-letter to the city", as Nicholas T. Parsons puts it in an essay in this issue, first appeared in *Nyugat*, Hungary's leading literary review of the first half of the twentieth century, and was subsequently published in a limited edition with a handful of illustrations and ornamental capitals in 1935. The publishing house Officina, known for its serious and handsomely produced small books, was the undertaking of a Budapest printer and stationer, Dávid Löbl. The translation published here is accompanied by drawings and initials, some by Sándor Kolozsváry for the 1935 edition and others by József Pintér.

A Martian's Guide to Budapest is a wealth of observations infused with fine irony. The reader will find a special delight and a challenge in the pyrotechnics of literary and other references provided by this exceptionally widely read and original writer. How forceful, and yet enigmatic, the image is of the "Habsburg radish" topping the belfries of St Anne's Church in the Watertown District—it takes some looking to discover the similarity in shape between the spire and the root. Sometimes it is an adjective, sometimes a paragraph, devoted to a building, area or city district that makes readers forget whatever image of it they might have had before seeing it through Szerb's eyes.

The Martian was a favourite symbol of Szerb's. In his *History of World Literature,* Szerb epitomised Goethe's singular significance by saying that "if we die out, the Martians will have to study the greatness and weaknesses of our species through his legacy." The naive Martian, without previous knowledge or preconceptions, was the appropriate figure Szerb could show his beloved city to—and in the substance and manner he perceived to be his own. Familiar tourist sights do not appear in his *Guide* because he did not relate to them; but he had no difficulty presenting radish-belfries—why not, when onion domes are famous elsewhere? A Martian can be told something other than the clichés proffered in the usual travel guide and can have quoted to him rhymesters of old with the same

Alajos Fuchstaller: Panoramic view of Pest, *1846, engraving. Budapest Historical Museum, Kiscell.*

gravity as our finest bards. Szerb must surely have known that "the otherwise unknown Emil Vidor" (there could hardly have been an aspect of Hungarian literature he would not have known) was none other than Frigyes Kerényi, the classically trained poet popular in the eighteen-forties who had staged a "poetic contest" with the great Sándor Petőfi. But why should a Martian have been interested in that?

Szerb cites the poets of the eighteenth century with their charmingly artless descriptive passages: Pál Ányos, the poet monk and doctor of philosophy, who died at the age of 28; Major General Count József Gvadányi, who created one of the enduring figures in Hungarian poetry in the person of the village notary from Peleske, a country squire who came up to the capital; and the priest and poet Benedek Virág, who lived in the Tabán and scraped along as a one-man literary centre there. Having struggled through their clumsy stanzas, Szerb finally arrives at the lines from that genius who meant most to him, Mihály Vörösmarty (1800–1855), "that wonderful liberator of the Hungarian language".

Even a hundred years after his time, Vörösmarty was important enough for Szerb to practically sacrifice his life for him. With the anti-Jewish laws coming into force and under the shadow of spreading Nazism and its modus operandi, Szerb was invited to lecture at Columbia University in New York. He agonised over the offer. In the end, he declined, arguing that it would be bizarre to be teaching students who were not able to read Vörösmarty.

What is it a Martian could have seen in the Budapest of 1935? Primarily Pest, or more precisely, more of Pest than of Buda, since Szerb was a Pester—there he felt at home, there he lived. He crossed over to Buda only for a specific purpose, as had been natural already for the "urban" writers and journalists of the eighteen-sixties. Pest bustled with trade and the lively exchange of ideas this brought; Buda was a sleepy place, permeating tradition and nostalgia. A real intellectual could only be a man of Pest. The Pest intellectuals had always agreed on that—even when they were strolling over to Buda to end up in one of the small inns or cafés in the fairytale world of the soon-to-be demolished Tabán to chat about old love affairs and old poets.

Greek Street in the Tabán, around 1900. Photograph by Albert Petrik

Still, Szerb's Budapest tour is mainly on Buda. It begins with the Chain Bridge, and rightly so, since across this beautiful piece of engineering, the first permanent bridge, "old Hungary marched into new Hungary", as Gyula Krúdy recalled. Facing the bridge on the Pest side, next to the Gresham building, still stood a famous relic from Biedermeier times, the Hotel Európa, though at that time it housed the police headquarters and not travellers. After the Second World War, the building (with its splendid ballroom undamaged) fell prey to the wrecker's ball to make room for a much-disputed monstrosity.

The book devotes a paragraph to the core of the old Inner City of Pest—without whose gracious Baroque mansions "the city is now a bit gap-toothed"—in which a group of edifices long since gone was described. They were callously pulled down when the Elizabeth Bridge was built and the dream of Budapest as a metropolis was conceived. The disappearance of this part of the city took with it the vestiges of two famous people Szerb considered worthy of mention. One was József Ürményi, the author of the sweeping education reform during Maria Theresa's reign (*Ratio educationis,* 1777). The other was Ferenc Kazinczy, poet, writer and literary organiser, who launched the Hungarian language reform. What had been left standing has also lost its original function. The Greek Church in Petőfi Square lost one of its steeples during the Second World War and Greek, Hungarian and Russian are now used in worship.

Across the river, Gellért Hill roused not just Szerb's imagination but that of the old residents also. Its steep, romantic cliffs have always evoked the presence of witches and gave it the name "Blocksberg", in reference to its German counterpart. Below stretched the Tabán, the quarter favoured by writers, artists and all bohemians, razed, allegedly in line with urban development plans and against stiff resistance, during the time Szerb wrote his *Guide*. Nothing remained of the centuries-old tavern on whose wall Imre Vahot had once written his initials (Vahot was a playwright and "literary factotum", a fellow editor to the great poet and freedom-fighter Sándor Petőfi. Nor was anything left of all the places frequented by Gyula Krúdy, the celebrated novelist of the first third of the twentieth century, lover of evanescence and of the Tabán.

On Castle Hill, over the Tabán, rose the Royal Palace, in its gardens the enormous Turul bird, the totemic animal of the medieval House of Árpád and regal sym-

The Karátsonyi House in Krisztina Town around 1900.

bol of Hungarian rulers. In Szerb's eyes, the Turul was a harmless beast sporting the ceremonial dress public figures donned, leaning forward slightly, like the fiery orators in Parliament. As he recalled the apocalyptic days of the Hungarian Soviet Republic of 1919, he saw a vision of the coming of the Prophet—images like the grande finale to a Fellini film.

On the Bastion Promenade he imagined spying the professor of philosophy at the university of Pest, Ákos Pauler, among the strolling crowd, then jumped unexpectedly to the image of budding lovers sketched against the background of the sauntering philosophers and generals. The Fishermen's Bastion brought to his mind its southern steps, the eerie Jesuit-stairway named for the Jesuit house that once stood there, and, in recounting his vanished Jewish jeweller ancestor's fate, he evoked the mystery that cannot fail to accompany a site of this sort. Not far from the top of the stairs, in Tárnok Street, stood a Palace of the Esterházys. In view of Szerb's account, one can only be sorry to see the school which stands in its stead today. Further on, at the northwestern corner of the Castle quarter, the Garrison Church fared no better than that stately mansion; nowadays only the Mary Magdalene Tower remains.

Down in Krisztina Town, next to Vérmező Park, Buda's jewel, the Romantic-style Karátsonyi Palace was razed at this time. When the counts died out, the palace had been sold and pulled down: the new owner, the German Reich, planned to build a school on the site. As a fitting illustration of the twists of history in this part of Europe, instead of a Nazi German building a Socialist-Realist-style ministry in the Soviet mould was erected here in 1951.

Now Szerb directed his steps into the Buda hills, to the new villas and apartment blocks in outer Pasarét, to the look-alike boxes designed by the Hungarian followers of the Bauhaus. Here stands also what was then a new church, one of the prides of modernist Hungarian architecture.

In a jump over the hills one reaches Óbuda, parts of which still retain their rural atmosphere. Its traditional residents—Jewish money-changers, merchants and artisans—after banishment from the free royal boroughs of Pest and Buda, had long since left to settle near the town-wall of Pest, in the massive Orczy House with its many courtyards on the Király Street corner. Of Óbuda, Szerb noted only a single name, that of Gábor Halász, a wonderful essayist and his great friend. It proved to be a premonition, since less than a decade after the *Guide*'s publication, both would fall victim to Nazism in Balf, a notoriously cruel labour camp.

Between Buda and Pest lies Margaret Island (Margitsziget), which for a man-of-letters cannot but recall János Arany and the cycle of poems he composed there as an old man. With fine irony Szerb notes that the man regarded as the greatest of all Budapest poets in actual fact didn't like Pest very much. Arany is present on the island also in the form of a statue by Alajos Stróbl. On either side of it stood two vases (destroyed in the war) derived from originally smaller drinking vessels with rams heads and alluding to Arany's proclivity for Hungarian prehistory. The actual originals belonged to the Nagyszentmiklós gold treasure hoard which had made its way into the Imperial and Royal collection and is on permanent display in Vienna's Kunsthistorisches Museum.

Szerb concluded his walk on the Pest shore facing Margaret Island, in Újpest, a factory district whose workshops and working men and women he found utterly romantic. Here he could formulate a Pest citizen's real worldview: "Buda may be on the far side of the water, but the real far shore is Újpest"—as if he sensed the end of his own comfortable city and the coming of the proletarian city of the masses.

"If ever I had to turn my back on the city forever, on that day I would become as old as the Monk of Heisterbach," he wrote tongue-in-cheek, as he cannot have been certain that his readers would understand his reference to the Cistercian of a medieval legend of the Rhine. But he had to turn his back on Budapest: he became an inmate of a forced labour camp. "We learned about the turn of events on 19 March 1944 from Antal Szerb, who telephoned in the afternoon whether he could come and sleep over," recalled his friend Pál Granasztói, the architect and writer on Budapest, of the day the Germans occupied Hungary.

> He came, and from him we learned for the first time... about the upheaval in our entire social circle, their trying to seek sanctuary back and forth. He finally went home and stayed there. Shortly they sent him into retirement from the Vas Street school. We heard he was at home all day and reading all the time. We visited him—it must have been the end of spring—my wife got there first. She stepped in quietly and found him in his study, lying on the couch among heaps of books. He looked up at the ceiling and did nothing. My wife, hiding her concern, greeted him with feigned cheerfulness and asked him how he was.
>
> "I am just thinking," he replied with a sweeping motion at his books, "I have read everything that is worth reading and may just as well die."
>
> Not much later he was called up for forced labour service, and he complied obediently. Just like he had once gone to camp as a scout, to play, now he went into the looming horror. But first he asked to let him bring over his books. We cleared out the small room, and the two of us carried perhaps two thousand selected and properly packaged books up into the flat in the attic. It was warm, we both sweated and panted. ... He seemed tired, but not broken or dejected. Maybe determined. I knew he did not want to hide and made no attempt to talk him into it. ... His concern was his books, not himself. We said goodbye, I escorted him to the stairs, hugged him. I had a strong sense of his vulnerability, that I would not see him again, and so it was. The room at our place where we had put the books was shelled during the siege, the only damage to the house. Nothing more happened than a hole in the wall and a few books got scorched. Even here Fate aimed a swipe at him. ❧

ANTAL SZERB

A Martian's Guide to Budapest

TRANSLATED BY LEN RIX

One fine day a Martian turned up in Budapest, took a room in the Bristol Hotel, brushed the stardust from his suit and telephoned to inquire if I might show him round the town.

First and foremost, honoured visitor, I must urge you to ignore the newspapers and other egregious pundits who will tell you that the citizens of Budapest are like this or like that. The people they are talking about are no different from any other commercially-oriented folk in need of cash. How should such creatures be of interest to a Martian? Indeed, how important are the inhabitants of any town? In Paris, it is only the people who are dull and unattractive. I shall acquaint you with a city where, in my opinion, the beings that really matter are the houses. Or rather, not the houses but the erotic way they beckon to one another, with their displays of manly strength or feminine grace; the fevered traffic; the charged atmosphere around the statues in the squares... even the bus-numbers are imbued with obscure literary references—or some such thing. But you know what I mean.

THE CHAIN BRIDGE. Perhaps we might begin here? Budapest is the city of great bridges. The Chain Bridge was begun in the early years of the last century, taking several decades to complete. It was the subject of genuine popular enthusiasm and was celebrated by the otherwise unknown poet Emil Vidor, writing in *The Athenaeum* in 1842:

Out there, beneath the flood, they have buried a seed
From which—to the headstrong current's blushing shame!—
An arch, Intelligence's brandished blade,
Will soar in triumph to everlasting fame!
The ancient river, so mighty and so proud,
Shall bend its neck in stooping subjugation
As patriot-poets hymn their praises loud,
And all men bow before the Mind's creation.

The construction work apparently went on through all four seasons of the year, which makes it the bridge of winter in particular—of winter and the night, with its characteristic colouring of black, or the dark chocolate-brown of asphalt in the rain. It is also the winter bridge in the sense that its predecessor was not.

Before it, Buda and Pest were connected by a pontoon crossing, along which the saintly old Benedek Virág would stroll with his devotees. But in those days the Danube regularly froze over, and you could skate across to the other side. If the ice failed to freeze, but simply broke up and drifted, they say that you had to go all the way round via Vienna to dine in Krisztina Square. Well, possibly.

The Chain Bridge as we see it now is in the Empire style, as are the entrance to the Buda tunnel on the right bank and the Police Headquarters on the left. Essentially there are two historical layers in Pest: the Baroque—in the spirit of the old German (and Catholic) Burghers, and the Empire, preserving the memory of a great Magyar impulse that has since dwindled to nothing. But here, between the Tunnel and the Police Headquarters, something of it lingers. If, a hundred years ago, the Palatine were to gaze down from his apartments, this is the scene that would have met his eye. And he would have thought, with a sigh, of Széchenyi (whom he only ever addressed as "Count Stefi") and turned back to his desk, stubbornly devoted, like all his Habsburg forebears, to his work.

The Chain Bridge is infernally long. But you must try it once, Sir, and you won't regret it. Stroll, with a woman on your arm, across to Buda, and then stroll back again—possibly with the same woman. You will find it conducive to romance simply because it is so long. Budapest is truly, and profoundly, the City of Love. Believe me, Sir, those who really know this town can only speak of it with tears in their eyes.

But as you cross you must look neither right nor left. Keep your eyes focused on the Police Headquarters, that noble, finely-proportioned, silent presence. Don't even glance at the Academy, with its fiercely independent dignity so suited to a Hall of Learning. It is best addressed as "Your Excellency". "Your Honour" might be more appropriate, but when it comes to titles one should always err on the side of caution. And don't stare at the Gresham Palace either. The poor thing was new and daring, once. This is how we live, poor souls of Budapest, caught, like the Police Headquarters, between stern formality on the one hand and the flashily ornamental world of commerce on the other. So, don't look to either right or left.

HE RIVER BANKS. Like a great many rivers, the Danube has two banks. Here, as in Paris—and many other cities, I believe—each bank is an entirely different world. As the chestnut trees close down for the night on the Buda side, the coffee-houses open up in Pest, alive with music.

I suggest you avoid the Pest bank in daylight. I'm not sure what your standards of taste are, but I'm fairly confident you would not like what is generally to be seen at that time. This bank is at its loveliest on winter evenings, when the only people strolling about (in pairs) are teachers from the Piarist Gymnasium. Dressed in their flowing cassocks, they set out from the priory in the direction of Parliament. The point of these mysterious missions is the dinner they will enjoy on their return. On name days, the porter trundles a barrel of beer into the refectory. It is drunk amidst a steady flow of gentle monastic jokes and the discussion of scholarly and pedagogic questions. I'm sorry I can't show you the old Friary, the Grassalkovich Palace with its gracious balconies, or the drab (but truly ancient) tenement blocks attached to it. Since they went, the city is now a little gap-toothed between the Greek Orthodox and the Inner City Parish churches. This was once the most distinctively eighteenth-century quarter of Budapest. In those days you could still half-expect the Serbian tugboats to smash up against the tramway railings as they came in to moor, just as they did decades earlier, when Councillor József Ürményi bathed his aching old feet in the water and chatted away with the smooth-tongued Ferenc Kazinczy.

N INNER CITY STREET (part thereof). But Galamb Street (Dove Street) is still there, and beside it, the Kriszt House and the Greek Courtyard. The former is several feet below street level: in this town, the lower the level the older the building. It seems Madách was right: the dust flies up, a few centuries level the pyramids, jackals howl on the esplanade and cars roar past where the present third floor stands.

Lying in the very heart of the city, between two major thoroughfares, Galamb Street has been unaccountably forgotten. It remains just as it was in the days of Maria Theresa. No sunlight has entered these rooms for two hundred years. Little old people totter down the street—I can't tell whether they actually inhabit those shuttered apartments or simply remember them. I do know that some of them live in the Greek Courtyard. There you see bearded priests and small children everywhere, and these Greeks, they say, are the real thing. Even today they hurl abuse at one another in parish meetings in the old Hellenic tongue.

ELLÉRT HILL. Recommended for a Sunday afternoon in spring. The hill is topped by a ruined building, the Citadella. Along the wall you can make out narrow slits, like military embrasures, out of which horses occasionally poke their heads. Behind the Citadella lies a plain. Every Sunday there would be a pilgrimage up here by the local people and soldiers—all of them quite indistinguishable from the people and soldiers you see at St Cloud, and no doubt on the outskirts of every other large and not-so-large city at the same time of the week and the year. In fact these people are the same everywhere. Only at the highest levels can one make distinctions. A soldier is a soldier wherever you look: Hölderlin and Vörösmarty are very different.

But this isn't what I want to talk about. Rather, Sir, consider the scene. At the top of the Hill the people, and the soldiers, take part in a rather unusual game whose origins go back into the densest mists of folklore, when witches still posed in groups for their copper engravings. No one knows who introduced this game and who keeps it going: it simply happens every Sunday in spring. People stand in a circle, in pairs—a man and a woman, as I understand. One of the couples inside the ring walks around, stopping from time to time before another couple standing on the perimeter. The man inside the circle asks the man on the perimeter, "Are you fond of your partner?" If he says yes, he is, they move on. If the answer is no, the women are exchanged. This goes on all day. When darkness falls—to put it rather grandly—every Tristan has found his Isolde. What happens next, I never managed to find out.

HE TABÁN. I'm not sure whether it breaches tourist office rules to show you something which isn't actually there. For, in truth, all you will see next is a row of muddy fields where they meet, rather boringly, at the foot of Gellért Hill. In their centre, like the left-over detritus of some gloomy flood, stands the higher elementary school in White Eagle Square. Once, Sir, there were houses here—but what houses! And little streets wandering about between them—but what streets! The houses were all single-storey. In their midst, beside a mulberry tree, stood a washing trough, its watery suds trickling their way down the middle of the street, where they had cut a deep channel between the irregularly-shaped cobblestones.

Every second house used to be a famous old restaurant resounding with the old Viennese *Schrammelmusik*. Here, if you please, stood the Basement, and Uncle Poldi's, with its five-hundred-year-old vaulted cellar, where the Turkish lords once maintained a bordello at public expense. There was a painted quail on the wall, next to Imre Vahot's initials, and everywhere the sacred, if somewhat inebriated, memory of Gyula Krúdy. The Tabán could be visited at any time of year, in winter or summer, by day and by night. It was always wonderful, always unique. You made your way down its sloping streets, trundling the prospect of some newly-dawning love, one of the sort that occur to you in the early hours of the morning, when it is still dark and you are lying in bed with no prospect of a bath and a shave to wash the sweetly soporific resin that is love from your soul. Yes, here, Sir, there once were real streets, and the spirit of youth.

But I'm not suggesting this youthful spirit is confined to one area of Budapest. There isn't a single district which doesn't embody it for me. If ever I had to turn my back on the city forever, on that day I would become as old as The Monk of Heisterbach.

THE BUDA PROMENADE. Best to stroll along on an afternoon in late spring, for the chestnut trees. This part of the river bank draws back rather timidly at the foot of the two hills: indeed it is hardly there at all. Dogs wander about, and once

I came across an elderly married couple, the man in a grey jacket and grey bowler hat. If you like walking, it's better to take the lower embankment from the Franz Joseph Bridge to the Margit Bridge. This part of the city has a distinct nautical flavour, and there is evidence everywhere of this way of life. I once, for example, sat there, just like a sailor, on an upturned rowing boat; and sometimes you can get down the little stairway to sit directly over the water, as if you were in Venice, and count the streaks of light cast by the embankment lights onto the river. You cannot imagine, Sir, how rich the city is in possibilities.

HE DANUBE, POETS AND TRANSIENCE. The poets of old did not concern themselves with detail, were not interested in the particular: they saw the wood and not the individual trees. So in both Pest and Buda they celebrated nothing beyond Gellért Hill and the ancestral field of Rákos over in Pest. The melancholy Pál Ányos wrote once to a certain Imre Kreskay (who is otherwise unknown to me):

Let's sit awhile on Gellért's rocky peak
And send a dirge to distant Rákos mead.

Such was the travelling-power of the poet's voice in those days.

But most importantly, and quite correctly, they identified the river as the life-giving centre of the Budapest landscape. Gvadányi, the most congenial general in our history, was more jubilant when he observed:

Danube! Oh you precious embryonic Neptune!
Your beauty enhances all the rivers of Europe.
How many sturgeons does your mighty torrent shelter?
Every grain of your golden sand is dear.

(Perhaps he might have spared us the sturgeons.)

The Danube is a truly ancient river, and will no doubt continue to flow long into the future, whereas the life of a poet is a relatively short thread in the hands of the Fates, and perhaps for this reason it arouses a feeling of transience. Benedek Virág, the holy old man of the Tabán mentioned earlier, frequently sang the river's praises. Once, in the heat of one of his odes, he charged it with flowing backwards, but he came close to greatness as a poet when he observed:

I often go down to watch as the Danube
carries away the old and enfeebled year
on its back. Ah, take it and bury it
in the tumultuous depths of the sea!

Virág's sentiments seem to have hovered over the river unchanged until the arrival of Vörösmarty. Then, in a few short lines as weighty as Gellért Hill itself, that wonderful liberator of the Hungarian language invested it, and the whole landscape of Pest, with a sombre dignity that can never be taken from it:

Infant streams set out with a leisurely babble:
The country-long Danube roars as it gathers them in
Transforming their diffident ooze to a fearsome flood.
The heavens gaze down with a hundred glittering eyes
As it flows ever onwards, bearing them down to the sea,
And with them, borne on its transient waves,
Time itself, lest it ever turn back.

ALACE GARDENS. We could go up in the cable car, but there's no need, as we can travel there in the mind. No need to be alarmed by the Turul: he's never harmed anyone. He's a serious old bird, in full Hungarian regalia, leaning forward slightly, like the fiery orators in our Parliament. He watches over the Palace Gardens. When I was little, you could go in on Sunday afternoons. I found this very moving, because I imagined that the King himself had invited us, as his own children. But then, during two appalling and apocalyptic months in the life of the country, a notice was put up: "Everything belongs to us." Meaning: "Nothing belongs to anyone now." The city had gone to the dogs. But now all that's in the past. The one good thing was that you could now get into the Palace Gardens at any time of the day. And in we went, and stayed there the whole day. Here at least production had not been collectivised. The trees delivered their delectable scents on a strictly individualist basis, in memory of the Palatine.

It was here that I waited for the coming of the Prophet. (As I say, those were apocalyptic times, and for many reasons I am not sorry to have lived through them.) I imagined us all suddenly setting off downhill, hand in hand like children, singing the *lánc-lánc-eszterlánc* song—the song that was to resolve everything. Women standing on balconies would roll out their newly-beaten rugs and weep, the lions of the Chain Bridge would bound up to us like enormous shepherd dogs, the whole Pest embankment would become one great orchestra, the ships and the Parliament building would suddenly sprout little flags, and herds of cattle, their udders bulging with milk, would stream in from the ring roads with banners between their horns proclaiming: Peace to Mankind.

CASTLE HILL, BASTION PROMENADE. A miracle, and still standing. But they would have knocked this down, too, as they did the Tabán, because it too is beautiful. The whole of Castle Hill is a delight. Generals can be seen strolling along the Bastion Promenade, as once did Ákos Pauler, the great schoolmaster of our youth, wearing his characteristic wide hat and busily analysing fundamental principles. Nowadays he instructs little angels: "Take this star, for example..." And when he utters his favourite phrase "not so?", the ranks of the heavenly host nod in agreement. Of course we have forgotten the fundamental principles, but the generals are still there, as is the view towards the vibrant amphitheatre of the Buda hills.

This, Sir, was where we began our little romances. Why here, as opposed to anywhere else, no one can be sure. Perhaps the promenading generals inspired some unconscious recognition that the country needs soldiers. So: you sit on a bench with a girl, then it gets cold, except that your heart is overheating. Sometimes a well-manicured little dog will jump up onto the bench between the two of you, curious to know how far things have progressed. He notes with satisfaction that the first kiss is about to break. But this is a worrying time, since you are a little apprehensive about the consequences, both short-term (perhaps a slap on the cheek) and long-term (perhaps marriage), but the need to get deeper into this first kiss is too urgent if you wish to move on to the second. This road leads to so many endings, Sir...and, all the while, the worldly-wise bell of the Krisztina Church rings out knowingly somewhere down below.

ISHERMAN'S BASTION. Kitsch, but wonderful. From its rampart, Sir, you can receive the acclamation of the people, and then make your way, very slowly, down its wide stairway with a lady—the queen, it should be stated—her train held up by thirty young pages in line. I suggest you bestow this honour only on the sort of woman who likes this sort of thing. But pause awhile on the Jesuit steps. An ancestor of mine, a jeweller, once set off for the Castle to deliver some diamonds to a count and never returned. I am convinced he was murdered on this particular stairway.

ASTLE HILL, TÁRNOK STREET. Here stands the wide-fronted and tranquil Esterházy Palace. It is only a single storey high, but it occupies the space of six houses. Inside it: memories of schooldays. Halls and long rooms without number, the furniture mostly under covers. Where it is not, there will be some simple Empire piece so lovely as to make you weep. The little prince's room is smaller than mine, with photographs of the Palace in Eisenstadt and his favourite bits of fishing tackle. The whole building is pale-gold, wise and melancholy. The Esterházys of the last century plunged into every kind of revelry, shot their most prized racehorses, and, exiled in far-off England, acquired mythical status for their spending. The present head of the family can now only wonder at them with a silent shake of the head. All around, the setting sun bathes the streets in a timeless pale-golden gloom. So if you please, Sir, tread a little more softly in your walking shoes. Behind these windows, old retainers still recall Franz Joseph's shooting parties.

MATTHIAS CHURCH. Once there was a tall, pointed tower here, but it now looks so much better as a ruin covered in scaffolding—so much more stylish. If, Sir, you study pictures of any medieval city, you will see that the cathedral is always just being built. There is something dreadfully modern and parvenu about a finished tower.

ARRISON CHURCH, KAPISZTRÁN SQUARE. There is nothing ornamental about this infernally big building: nothing to raise a smile, no hint of a lighter touch anywhere. It just sits here, like the centuries. Westminster Abbey is bigger than it, yet beside it you don't feel the same sense of sheer insignificance. You just stand in the bleak, empty square and pull your neck down into your collar, as if some grim Puritan God were raining curses down on you from the top of the tower. All round you are the hideous, silent barracks, "in memory of so much spilt blood".

On the nearby Rondella, dead cannons and other contraptions of warfare and siege bristle pointedly out towards the peaceful hills. Make the sign of the cross and clear out fast.

VÉRMEZŐ (BLOOD FIELD). Budapest's one great luxury: a piece of land this size left unused in the middle of the city. Behind it stands the Karátsonyi Palace, finely sardonic in its melancholy—the sort of aristocratic statement you expect to find only in London. But that doesn't mean it is particularly old. In my youth there was a plaque on the corner with the following inscription: "It is strictly forbidden to deface the banklet." What has become of the beloved banklet of my youth?

ASARÉT. Nothing to do with the Pasha. Some giant with modernising tendencies unpacked a series of enormous little boxes next to the tram line, gathered together a few affluent Lilliputians and announced, "Here you will live." And here they live. They toddle off every morning in their little cars to the little banks where they work. People who live in little boxes pay each other little social visits and compliment each other on their little gardens in the spring. Just like real people.

ÓBUDA. Once the Twelfth Tribe of Israel lived here, the bony sons of Zabulon, the anaemic, ivory-skinned offspring of Naftali and all the rest. They cooled their heels in the ante-rooms here because the Germans would not allow them into Pest and

Buda. Some time later they did get to Pest, to the Orczy House and elsewhere, and in recent years, following their wandering instinct, they transferred from Pest to Buda. In Óbuda it is now only the sloping earth of the wild and wonderful Pálvölgy cemetery that preserves their memory. No Jews live there now. The only person left is the reclusive essayist Gábor Halász.

T ANNE'S, BATTHYÁNY SQUARE. The charming secret of the chosen few. Let us stroll past it with a conspiratorial smile, for we know that this is the loveliest building in the whole city. On its tower is the Habsburg radish. This same architectural idiom praises the Lord, the God of pious kings in Spain, Burgundy, Austria and Hungary. A few years from now everyone will be in on the secret and we will have to find some other building to admire—perhaps the box church in Pasarét. By then it will have become every bit as *passé* as St Anne's is now.

ÓZSEFVÁROS. This entire quarter is out to rent. Its tenants are the future of Budapest—medical students from their clinics, fine-minded philosophers, the staff of the City Library. Every evening in The Good Ship Adria, where the hubbub is loudest and liveliest, the fug thickest and the love you can buy sweeter than in Montparnasse, they set fire to their brains with a sprinkling of wine to help prepare for examinations. One day they will all be famous.

But exactly who their landlords—and landladies—are, no one can determine. Where are the men who left all these widows and orphans? The landlord answers to your ringing. There is a sort of fishnet round his head, rather like the moustache-nets worn in my father's day. He complains bitterly about his current lodger, who hasn't yet got out of bed. In time, this man's entire body will take on the shape of an enormous ear. He no longer has a life of his own; it has been totally absorbed into the business of spying on his lodger. In his single room, above the paper flowers and beneath the stuffed golden eagle, hang pictures of his ancestors. But he seems to have no further use for them.

Indeed, Sir, you might begin to suspect some mystery as, at the approach of Christmas, you wend your solitary way in the shadow of the neighbourhood houses, unable to free yourself from the thought that somewhere among those jars of preserved fruit is a recipe, the secret to absolute order in life, that might flower (only, of course, in places such as Józsefváros) in the form of golden-haired maidens (here and everywhere).

BEHIND THE GREAT MARKET HALL. Now please don't spread this around. No one but myself knows about this quarter. As twilight descends, it suddenly becomes Paris—the small, dirty coffeehouses, the shops with their exhilarating flood of fruit, vegetables and meat, the people looking like characters from a novel, the neglected riverbank behind them (like the Seine) and the Citadella lit up above them (like the Eiffel Tower). If you walk at night through the square behind the market, chickens suddenly stir—a hundred, a thousand of them—and start to racket. "You can't park here," a late policeman tells a solitary delivery truck. "The engine's stalled," replies the rough-looking driver, evasively. "Cobblers, Sir," says the policeman. And they argue for long hours through the night—just like Parisians.

This was once the abode of a way of love long since gone. You might look for it in vain in the sheer canyon of Lónyai Street, or the deep-sea loneliness of Köztelek Street. Kálvin Square has grown so large it seems that, just as in the old days, you could wait there for hours for someone to come, and she never does.

ÚJ-LIPÓTVÁROS. When I was young, the houses in this part of the town stood behind fences. Dogs would squeeze half way through the gap underneath and bark furiously, making you slip on the icy road, then stand up feeling thoroughly embarrassed. But this was all part of the charm, and you could continue on your way towards Újpest, which I knew only from legends and my own fears. Nowadays it's full of modern mansions in the flat-roofed Bauhaus style. Inside them, youthful psychoanalysts spread out one another's souls to dry on their couches, strapping amazons of the bridge table dream in the depth of their snow-white bathrooms, and amazingly clever clerks tune in to Radio Moscow. On Sundays in winter the entire neighbourhood sets out, walking stick in hand, and goes on pilgrimage to Svábhegy, leaving only the poor abandoned barber behind. Everything here is modern and simple, objective and uniform. It is an area of two-room-plus-lobby apartments. With the defiant insistence of the young, their inhabitants conceal the only genuine secret of their wan little lives—that they have no money, none of them.

ARGIT ISLAND. In the narrow park, where you catch occasional glimpses of the Danube, the river of transience, glinting to right and left between the too-lovely flowers, you often see children between the upper and lower restaurants. Here we were brought when young, and here we return in our declining years. The greatest of all Budapest poets, János Arany, was one of those who grew old here. In actual fact, he didn't like Pest very much. He yearned constantly for his village, as a great Indian chief might, and he felt bitter:

My birthplace Szalonta
Was more than any salon;
And every day I long
For a cottage in the far beyond.

But the townspeople love him all the more for this, even today. They recognise in him the pattern of their own lives. Like his neighbours, Arany was sober and hard-working, was fond of money, and just wanted to be left in peace. I must repeat, Sir, what I said about not believing the newspapers. The citizens of Budapest are solid, dependable folk, and János Arany, their poet, was the most dependable of all Hungarian poets.

These are his oak trees. Here he would sit, a leather-bound book with a lockable clasp in his hand, composing his *Little Flowers of Autumn.* Monuments seldom manage to convey the essence of their subjects, but these two ram's horn motifs on the vases on either side of his statue do evoke something of the ancient, inner voice of the forest celebrated in his epics. The rams' horns, I believe, Sir, are from the Hunnish hoard found at Nagyszentmiklós, so this is not mere retrospective mythologizing. It is as genuine, Sir, as the buffalo in the city zoo.

And now I would ask you to listen to some lines Arany wrote about the island of the Blessed Margit, and also about himself and the transience flowing past on either side.

These orphaned shoots of willow may perchance
Survive protected by her royal presence
Who interweaves past years with those to come,
That this lovely isle might ever flow through time—
But leaves the nightingale of the wood
To pour his heart out in a dying ode
Then wait, in silence, for his hour of dread:
Better to follow Toldi's epic thread.

Poor old nightingale!

JPEST. From the romantic point of view, we now leave the ruined castle for the boiler house. Oh, the huge machines, those biddable monsters! How they reach out with their thousand glittering tentacles! How they howl and stamp their feet in rage! How contentedly they purr at other times! How they spew out smoke, and goods, and oil! How does life begin, Sir? Is not a mighty machine a thousand times more alive than an old woman? Their technical experts look on them as serious, demanding creatures. They are their tamers. If they didn't keep them under constant surveillance, the machines would run out onto the streets and gobble up their puny owners.

At midday the sirens blare. The square in front of the factory becomes colourful and gay, a little village. Working girls in tennis shoes stroll arm in arm before the men, who flash glances at them over their slices of bacon. How many of the girls are truly beautiful, and how mysterious they are! Their simplicity conceals a terrible secret: their minds are the atom I can never split with words of love. I am afraid of them. In my nights of yearning I think of their large, unlovely hands. The far shore? Buda may be on the far side of the water, but the real far shore is Újpest.

And now farewell, my dear companion. I see that you are already glancing at your watch, and need to get home. It's a clear winter's night, and our mutual friends the stars are flashing whitely above Budapest. Don't forget to turn a little to the right, once you reach the Lyre, and give my greetings to the Little Bear. I hope you have a good journey through space. May God go with you. ❧

INTERVIEW

The Classics Are Patiently Waiting

János György Szilágyi
in Conversation with Ferenc László

Ferenc László: *In your essays, you repeatedly refer to Nietzsche who said that each age must enter into a new relationship with antiquity and measure itself against that. Can the study of antiquity help us gain our bearings and find solutions to the problems of the present?*

János György Szilágyi: Yes, it can. The study of antiquity, the examples antiquity offers, can at least assist us to see things clearly and to come to proper judgements. Let us take the topic that I find the most exciting and the most important at the moment, which is the problem of fictions regarding early history and what is closely related to them, the issue of modern nationalisms. One of the mainstays of every form of nationalism, as we have all experienced, is fictive protohistory, a nation's creation myth. Well, in point of fact, all prehistory is fictional, because there is no such thing as a genuine protohistory. This has been widely known since antiquity, given that there was a huge production of these mythical stories among the Greeks and Romans. In the end, it was Livy, one of the greatest of Roman historians, who squarely faced the problem in the Early Imperial Age: speaking about the foundation of Rome in the Introduction of his *History of Rome,* he declared that as far as the traditions of what happened prior to the foundation of Rome are concerned, he had no intention of establishing either their truth or their falsehood. He then went on to say, "Now, if any nation ought to be allowed to claim a sacred origin and point back to a divine paternity that nation is Rome. For such is her renown in war that [...] the nations of the world accept the statement with the same equanimity with which they accept her dominion." Straight from the shoulder. He finally added dryly that these were comparatively trivial matters and he, for one, set little store by them. To put it

---

Ferenc László
teaches in the Department of Ancient History of Eötvös Loránd University, Budapest. He is also on the staff of the weekly Magyar Narancs.

J. Gy. Szilágyi (1918–) is a disciple of the Classical scholar Karl Kerényi. Between 1951–92, he was Head of the Department of Classical Antiquities at the Museum of Fine Arts in Budapest, an institution he has worked in since 1941. This interview took place in the Museum, the scene of his legendary university lectures and tutorials. As the wide spectrum of his publications testify, Szilágyi is acutely aware of the relevance of antiquity to the present. He wrote notable essays on the historical aspects of forgery and on how ancient cultures are seen differently with every new approach. His main work, however, concerns Etruscan pottery, on which he is a widely recognised authority. One of his major publications is the catalogue of the Museum's holdings of Greek and Etruscan vases (Corpus Vasorum Antiquorum. Hongrie *I. Budapest–Bonn, 1981), which made this important collection accessible to the international scholarly community. It was followed, in 1992 and 1998, by his magnum opus,* Ceramica etrusco-corinzia figurata, *Vols. 1–2, Florence, Leo O. Olschki, the definitive work on Etrusco-Corinthian vase painting.*

another way, Livy's example demonstrates that we must use our mind when we set about relating to prehistory and legends of this kind.

Reflection is not generally a strong point with nationalists, yet they dabble all the more in early history.

All those concerned must be aware that in Hungary, and elsewhere, a fictive protohistory is one of the foundations of right-extremist ideologies, and even for not so extreme right-wingers; indeed, such protohistories are almost always rooted in antiquity. In a small country like ours, which suffers from a permanent inferiority complex—and let us not go into whether that is justified or not—that's something one has to be careful with. How can anyone believe—and what is more, ascribe tremendous social significance to—stuff like it was the Hungarians who invented writing? That's nothing new, of course. In 1825, it was started by István Horváth, an otherwise serious scholar, when he recorded that Hungarian was mankind's most ancient language, the tongue of the biblical Adam and the Scythians—and that the Pelasgians, the Parthians and the Philistines were in reality all Hungarians. Such notions have been ineradicable ever since. A hundred years ago, for example, one has the sculptor János Fadrusz claiming that the language of the Etruscans was actually Hungarian; he had a fixation that the Etruscan script and Hungarian runic characters were the same. It was still fairly innocent back in those days, but to go on about that sort of thing nowadays is downright harmful stupidity. In a present that is falsely interpreted from the past, the view of the past is also false.

Stupid nationalism also has a connection with the other subject that greatly interests me these days, and that is acculturation, a term used by American anthropologists in the 1930s to refer to the interaction between two different cultures in such a situation when these two cultures come up against one another. It is a crucial issue—essentially the problem that globalisation presents. One may say that this can be studied admirably in Classical cultures. These days a great deal is said, usually with a political undertone, about losing our identity, our national character, under foreign influences. In my opinion, if there is such a thing as European culture as a whole—that is, the culture that rests on Greco-Roman and Judaeo-Christian traditions—then its most conspicuous distinguishing mark is openness. This is a legacy of the Greeks in the first place; Europe inherited its openness from them. They genuinely accepted foreign influences. To give just two examples, a significant portion of their mythology is traceable to the Near East, yet they still went on to fashion all that into a peculiarly Greek mythology. Their sculpture, the very acme of their art, was similarly evolved from elements taken from various cultures. We can say precisely, to the centimetre, what was adopted from where: the manner of representing the male figure from Egypt, and the female figure from Mesopotamia. All the same, in under half a lifetime those foreign models had become totally Greek, but in such a way that they retained their original Egyptian or Mesopotamian characteristics as well. True, the great Mediterranean cultures were surrounded by a clutch of peoples that chose isolation—the Egyptians or, let's say, the inhabitants of Arabia Felix, the territory of modern-day Yemen. It was not them but the Greeks who—in effect and by good fortune—were to exert an influence on Europe's future mentality, because the Greeks proceeded to hand their culture on to the most diverse peoples: the Scythians, Thracians, Iberians, Celts—even, as it happens, the Etruscans. It was the Greeks who transmitted to the Etruscans the defining forms, means and subjects; it was through these that Etruscan art came into being. Thus, the end-result everywhere was that these peoples were awakened to the possibility of giving form to their own culture and their own art. This is the true meaning of acculturation, and it can be examined in an unadulterated state in these instances from antiquity. I feel that this is also the answer to irrational present-day fears that spring from ignorance.

Is that why you look on Classical scholarship as the philology of European consciousness?

Yes, because that openness, the readiness to receive, survived. If I jump ahead two thousand years, then I see the same curiosity, the same receptivity. When Chinese culture made its appearance in Europe in the eighteenth century, it immediately enjoyed a massive resonance, with a great many elements being adopted right away. When Japanese woodcuts became known around the year 1900, European art speedily integrated them, and the same happened with African sculpture. Our art did not become any less European as a result; it did not break away from the tradition of which it was the inheritor and continuer. But let's take some examples that are Hungarian and at one and the same time Classical. Is our literature the poorer—or for that matter, less Hungarian—because Mihály Vörösmarty wrote his epic *The Flight of Zalán* in hexameters, or because Dániel Berzsenyi used a Horatian ode form, rather than rhymed strophes, in his poem *To the Hungarians*? It is an extremist, embittered, and most of all, ignorant myth, a pseudo-myth, that Hungarian culture is under threat from contact with either surrounding or more distant cultures. Quite the contrary! One of my favourites, Mihály Fazekas's comic epic back in the Age of the Enlightenment, *Mattie the Gooseboy,* which is about a peasant lad who exacts a threefold revenge for the wrongs done to him by his despotic landlord, was found on a Mesopotamian cuneiform tablet—the story just as we are familiar with it, the entire plot. Nevertheless, that did not stop Mihály Fazekas's work from becoming a characteristically Hungarian story and a part of our national identity.

In your approach, Classical studies are very much a living discipline with things to say to the present. But many others complain that they have had a dramatic loss of prestige.

There were indeed huge changes in attitudes to antiquity in the twentieth century, and not just within European culture overall, but also locally. The way in which Germany switched from Greece to Rome following Hitler's rise to power—that was a massive turnabout. Neither beforehand nor afterwards were the Romans particularly esteemed by German Classical scholars, but under Hitler their exchange rate rose sharply all at once. Then there's the way that Classical studies, under the influence of the experience of the world wars, started to devote growing attention to antiquity's dark, volcanic-demonic aspect. These were considerable changes. Despite that, during the last thirty or forty years there is no doubt that a certain defeatism has been discernible even within the world of Classical studies.

There is too much talk to the effect that Classical culture and the branch of learning that rests on it have lost the status they had enjoyed earlier, or that they are not in a position to claim a leading place among the social sciences. Yet, it has been a long time since anything to the contrary was the case. It was never more than a nineteenth-century German, and in part English, illusion which was responsible for bringing the institutionalised forms of Classical humanist grammar-school education into being. In reality, that education was never all that effective, usually making do with testing all the Latin and ancient Greek conjugations and declensions—in Germany and England just as much as here in Hungary. Not that even that sort of training was always totally useless, because an eminent scholar who has spent a lot of time studying the role of antiquity in British culture has shown that a training in Classical scholarship developed precisely the qualities and skills that a good official needed in the colonies. For what did it take for someone to become a good Classical scholar—to be able to translate from ancient Greek into English, and from English back into ancient Greek? Diligence, creativity, obedience to teachers and superiors—those are the paramount virtues of a good official. And indeed, a great many Oxford and Cambridge Classics graduates served exemplarily in the Colonial Office. Even Arnold

Toynbee, one of the greatest historians of the last century, spent 25 years working in Britain's colonies and was only able to turn to writing history in the evenings. I do not wish to suggest that I see the importance of Classical scholarship as residing here, but the training certainly had this ancillary market value, if one may put it that way. Indeed, it still has it, because banks and big companies are increasingly willing to employ Classics graduates for their ability to solve intellectual problems more readily. Their brains are simply more polished by virtue of their university training.

Another common complaint is that the young are no longer interested in antiquity and that the Classics are no longer being read.

I think fears of that kind underestimate the Classics. There is no reason for anxiety; the Classics are patiently waiting their turn and will come to the fore again. Whether we are aware or not of how and to what extend our common past is rooted in the Classical heritage, its influence is alive. It is the classicist's job to study the undercurrents and the byways—problems which are not necessarily important for other people. Still, the influence infiltrates into the present, provided people do not take deliberate steps to screen themselves from it.

How antiquity is viewed is constantly being redefined from one era to the next. This ever-shifting image is the topic of the series of essays Legbölcsebb az idő *(Time is the Wisest of Things), your own now classic study of forgeries.*

In that, I attempted to show, through examples from four eras, how the subjects and types of fashionable forgeries—in fact, of what we happen to see or would like to see in antiquity—are functions of the current concept of antiquity in the era in question. In the concluding section, to which I gave the title "Meditation", I ruminated on what exactly constitutes a forgery in this sense, because a forgery is more a category we tend to think of in commerce and criminal law than in the arts. There you are! That, too, is a trendy topic: the high value placed on originality, the near-hysterical fear of forgeries. The explanation for that lies primarily in a lack of aesthetic education, as a result of which people are driven to external props. That same insecurity was also the reason why visitors to the Museum of Fine Arts, which is where I have had my quarters for more than sixty years, often look at the captions of the labels first and only then at the pictures and objects themselves. The captions decide for them whether or not they are going to like an artefact. One of the former directors, Andor Pigler, made it even easier for visitors by having an exclamation mark placed next to any outstandingly beautiful paintings in the Old Gallery to signal that one should take particular pleasure in it.

I ended up concluding "Meditation" by asking why one should not regard a forgery as an original, thereby signifying that we live in a forged world. The example I used here was the well-known "Pseudo" series by Gyula Pauer. There is a couplet by Frigyes Karinthy which I might aptly quote, *"An age that yesterday dealt you false measure / Tomorrow will enjoy the self-same pleasure."*

Over the last sixty years, your name has become inseparable from the Department of Classical Antiquities in the Museum of Fine Arts. When did collecting begin there?

The idea of an Antiquities Collection considerably predated the establishment of the Museum of Fine Arts, being suggested by Ferenc Pulszky when he was the director of the Hungarian National Museum. He was thinking primarily in terms of a collection of plaster casts that would convey to visitors an impression of the leading works of ancient art. That remained the basic consideration during the setting up and planning of the Museum of Fine Arts, from 1896 until its opening in 1906; and accordingly, the ground floor of the new building was designed so that some of the rooms should offer space to casts that are copies of the main sculptural styles of antiquity (and later ages). Collecting original works began in 1908, when 135 antique marbles were purchased, and a few years later, a set of 650 small terracotta pieces. The Museum Act of 1934 designated the Museum of Fine Arts as the country's primary repository for antique artefacts that had come from countries outside Hungary, which led to a substantial number of acquisitions. Over the years, five times the space that had been given over to plaster casts was soon taken up by original objects. With material of the most varied genres (bronzes, glassware, painted vases, etc.), an inventory was made that aimed to provide as complete a display as possible of Greek, Early Italian and Roman art in historical order. Though there are some partial changes in concept, the exhibition that opened in 1951 is essentially in the form which can still be seen today, along with the Egyptian Gallery, which became a separate department in 1957.

The year 1989 was a turning-point, the point at which the Antiquities Collection was able to add to its material by making regular purchases abroad. These systematic acquisitions were directed first at correcting the painful lacunae concerning certain centres of production and genres in the permanent collection, but a few years later we made a start on implementing an old plan of ours, which was to acquire representative pieces of the peripheral cultures in antiquity in order to broaden the one-sided Greco-Roman-centred perspective. This has given us a chance to obtain, when the opportunity arose, representative pieces of Palmyran, Phoenician, Southern Arabic, Iberian, Parthian and Sassanid art. We then display these every quarter within the framework of the series "Work of the Month", accompanied by an explanatory booklet in Hungarian and English. If the opportunity presents itself, the Collection also mounts temporary exhibits of material from foreign museums, such as those on Thracian art, the gold treasures of Scythia, or most recently, post-Pharaonic Egyptian art.

Nowadays there is much talk everywhere about the changing role of museums. How do you assess the nature of these changes?

Museums never did have a uniform role. Sometimes the object was to promote the prestige of a ruler or lord; at other times it might be to preserve values or to give an introduction to the world at large… As I see it, in some countries there is a growing emphasis on the aspect of instilling or reinforcing a national identity (or indeed, a local identity, whether that be in Foggia or Nyíregyháza)—though without this becoming a matter of international rivalry. I see the generation of revenue streams (with coffee bars, bookshops, gift shops, etc.) as a new and ever more important trend, which is linked with efforts to boost visitor numbers—or to put it another way, catering to, rather than guiding, tastes and cultivation. Another new phenomenon is what one might call museomania, with new museums for everything springing up everywhere. I don't know where these various tendencies are going to lead. I personally see a museum's cardinal task as being the conservation of values, traditions and documents; and consequently, the perfection of the techniques of restoration. After that, each era, community and museum administration does what it sees fit with the material that it has preserved and used its ingenuity to augment. I, for one, would see it as essential to carry out a thorough sociological survey of museum visitors as to what they look at and why, what background and expectations they bring, and what they take away with them from their visit. And then what remains of that, say, five years on.

What then remains of the value placed on individual scholarship? Even such a brilliant scholar as Karl Kerényi, the man you acknowledge as your master, is no exception. The relevance of his oeuvre is also diminished as the images of antiquity change with time.

I often cite a German saying: having a branch of learning as your occupation means making yourself obsolescent. That's a basic fact of life that everyone who takes up a scholarly discipline has to come to terms with. Over time, scholarly hypotheses go out of date. New papers are published; new finds are excavated; and not least, new ideas are advanced. Kerényi, for instance, showed not the slightest aptitude for the social and sociological aspects of antiquity. What interested him was mythology, which in point of fact—as his favourite disciple, Angelo Brelich, was to point out—was actually the brainchild of eighteenth-century thinking. The scholarly disposition that characterised Kerényi, on the other hand, did not go out of fashion, nor the example that he set for his pupils, myself included. His view was that scholarship was a way of life, and he devoted his life to his chosen tasks and truths. Kerényi taught us that we should not pursue a branch of learning because we want to be professors or academicians, or we are seeking to impress someone or other. We should take up a branch of learning simply because we cannot do anything else. We should be cultivating a branch of learning for pleasure and out of a sense of duty. That was a project that appealed to me, that suited me down to the ground. ❧

A Grand, Elaborate Story

Interview with György Spiró on the novel *Captivity*
by Magda Ferch

The place is the Roman Empire; the time, the first century A.D. We follow the unusual life story of the novel's ungainly, bookish hero from around Christ's crucifixion to the end of the Jewish war—his journey from Rome to Jerusalem and other parts of Judea, and back to Rome via Alexandria. In some of your previous works you also dealt with the complex subject of the rise of Christianity. Not being a religious man, why are you drawn to this subject?

My interest in religious thinking goes back to the nineteen-sixties; it was then that I realised that even atheists think in religious ways. I came to the conclusion that in all human thought there are irrational leaps. We try to weigh things rationally, but that doesn't always work. I guess it has something to do with our instinct for self-preservation. The more individualistic a society, the less inclined we are to face the fact that we shall die, and there will be no resurrection and no hereafter. I thought that if somebody creates and develops characters and wants to say something about how the human psyche functions, he cannot ignore this phenomenon; it must become part of his representation of human reality. But I was also afraid to broach the subject, because I had absolutely no background in theology. For a previous novel, *A jövevény* (The Newcomer) I had to immerse myself in Jewish and Christian mysticism because my main characters thought in terms of those beliefs. It occurred to me at the time that I should take a close look at the original story. First, I thought I could get away with just sticking to the Old and New Testaments. Well, that's not how it turned out.

Originally the story was to take place only in Jerusalem. But it wound up having four, or rather four and a half, focal points.

First, the idea was that the action would get underway sometime after stories of Christ's resurrection began to take hold, and it would centre around the

---

Magda Ferch,
a critic, is on the staff of the literary supplement of the daily Magyar Nemzet.
A volume of her interviews appeared in 2005.

Nazarene sect. I realised that this story cannot be told in isolation, though I still believed that it would be enough if Jerusalem and Galilee served as background. But then I saw that merely describing Pontius Pilate and his circle would not do, especially if I wanted to situate this very provincial city in a global context. I began to study all the relevant sources I could get my hands on and learned that Pilate was an insignificant historical figure and, as Roman governors went, by no means the bloodiest. It became clear that Rome could not be left out; after all, it was the leading power in the world in which the crucial events of Jesus' life occurred; what is more, none of these events could be divorced from Roman power politics. My research material kept growing, and at this point I still didn't know whether it was going to turn into a play or a novel. I continued to believe that it would be enough to ground the story in two cities, Rome and Jerusalem. But then I had to realise that the centre of world trade, as well as of world Jewry at the time, was Alexandria. I also came to the conclusion that the pogrom which occured in Alexandria in 38 A.D., a detailed and faithful description of which can be found in two works of the philosopher Philo of Alexandria, contributed greatly to the spread of Christianity. I couldn't leave out Alexandria because I was very much interested in this breeding ground without which Christianity would not have spread as it did. That's how the story became "tripolar". That it ended up consisting of four and a half parts is due to the nature of the material—to aesthetic considerations, in other words. If one is intent on telling a grand, elaborate story, one has to choose one of the familiar aesthetic forms of one's culture. Tripartition has deep roots in the European tradition; it manifests itself in many things from the concept of the Trinity through dialectical thinking to the three-part division of the sonata. My tripartite division would have been Rome–Jerusalem–Rome, but then Alexandria got in the way, so I finally chose a four-part division, which is also deeply ingrained in the European tradition: it is the mystical form of eternal recurrence. Swedenborg described it most clearly, but in the nineteenth and twentieth centuries it appears in the works of Chekhov and Wyspiański, as well as in the Russian formalists' writings. The four-part division precludes the notion of progress; in this form everything always begins anew. But the material I was working with did not fit this pattern, so I tacked a long coda onto the final Roman chapter—this way the structure points to an odd number. There is no real difference between three- and five-part divisions. Tragedies were written in either three or five acts. The odd number always connotes some kind of progression, a developing story; the two- and four-part division, on the other hand, implies eternal recurrence. The latter form doesn't necessarily reject progress within each of the four parts, but with regard to the whole, it does. It is for this reason that the book came to have this unusual structure.

One of the reviews pointed out that the story takes place outside of historical time, in a kind of "no time" zone, and that the traditional, conventional features of the novel are at odds with the anachronistic elements you employ.

That reviewer focused mostly on language, I think, and he is right in the sense that I did not opt for archaic language; I couldn't, since Hungarian as we know it did not exist two thousand years ago. I don't agree, however, that I resort to anachronisms. It is true that "commandos" sail from Rome to Alexandria to capture the local governor. The word refers to modern conditions, but it so happens that French and English works treating this period use that very term. The term is the same because the function is the same. In this sense there are no anachronisms in the novel. For me it was natural to use a contemporary idiom in writing *Captivity;* I am convinced, you see, that our ancestors were the same sort of people we are. They felt the same things, had the same kinds of desires, and were just as shrewd and smart and stupid as we are. So in principle, there is no difference between their world and ours.

Why was it so important to you that the story should have historical credibility down to the last detail?

If I am after the specific reality of everyday life, the smallest factual detail can become very important, although I can't say in advance precisely what that will be. For another writer something else may become extremely important. I am fully aware that my sensitivity to things has its limits. I also realise that twenty years ago I would have responded to different details, and if I live another twenty or thirty years, I will again respond to different ones. A historical novel is always about the author's own time as well—after all, his very thought processes are determined by the world in which he lives. In this sense every historical novel takes place in a kind of strange in-between time and space—neither at the time it was supposed to happen, nor in the author's own time, but rather in some imaginary dimension. How many of these authentic minor details does a writer try to track down? The more, the better. I have always considered narrative credibility very important and tried to understand the spirit of a given age even when I did not set out to write a realist work. For example, in my play *A békecsászár* (The Emperor of Peace), which takes place in a totally fictitious Rome, I gleaned the various beliefs and superstitions then current from Strabo's *Geography* in an attempt to feel at home in that period. For some reason this was important to me. Perhaps it's because realist art is closest to my heart, even if the work in question is not written in a realist style. And this affinity acted now as a command to check out and get right even the smallest detail. Facts always come in handy; they gave me wonderful ideas that I couldn't possibly invent myself. For example, I never gave any thought to how high priests cheated, or how people were defrauded when exchanging the currencies of different Roman provinces. The small acts of fraud and corruption are necessary—they add to the accumulated anger and despair that eventually bring about a new religion. I discovered many things in Flavius Josephus's *The Jewish War,* and I was helped by my archeologist friends, who gave me very good books on Alexandria. Of course I picked and chose from the available material; there are many things I did not use, they would have pushed out the limits of the novel. This story is still a piece of fiction, though it does try to take people's daily lives seriously.

Your piece of fiction takes place two thousand year ago; nevertheless, the world that emerges from it bears an uncanny resemblance to our own, and the characters, too, remind us of people living among us.

I could never have written this novel if I hadn't realised that our own world, structurally, in terms of power, does resemble the early imperial period of Rome. I myself was surprised by the similarities, but this is what emerged from the historical material I examined, so I had to take it seriously. The similarity has become striking ever since there is only one superpower left: America. If our world again becomes bi- or tripolar, other patterns will seem inescapable. Then a writer will react differently to the same historical material. I consciously tried to make Uri one of us. I came to realise that the German literary theorists and George Lukács were seriously mistaken when they thought that the novel was the product of bourgeois culture and that before the seventeenth and eighteenth centuries the genre didn't even exist. The truth is it did exist, but few examples have survived, and even those are fragmentary. However, novelistic techniques made their way into historiography. For example, Philo's historical-political works abound in novelistic elements, which he remembered from Greek novels he had read, but those were lost. I had to give a lot of thought to how misleading it is to believe that in ancient societies there were no social classes comparable to the bourgeoisie or the intelligentsia. The fact is there were. Friedrich Engels asserted that in the ancient world, love in our sense of the word did not exist. Of course it did. These are inanities, which could be traced back to the idealist concept that there was once a golden age which was lost, but which we shall one day restore.

You mentioned in interviews that you consciously set out to write a book that would be a good read, otherwise people would loose interest. Aren't you underestimating your readers?

No, I am not, or else I wouldn't have written such a long book. The fact remains, though, that people's reading habits and skills have deteriorated in the past twenty years. This is true even of people who have been taught how to read books, and all the more of those who have never been taught how to read. It's not their fault; I see it at the university where I teach: the majority of students cannot read. I had to keep in mind while producing this book that those on the receiving end are tired and easily distracted, and because I chose a subject that flies off in different directions, I had to use the simplest possible form. The story has one central hero, and I pursue him through myriad adventures; along the way the world in which he moves opens up. I've long been convinced that you must try to express complex things simply rather than talk about simple things in a complicated way, which is what is usually done around here. The way I see it, aesthetics, literary history and criticism—or at least, certain fashionable schools within these disciplines—do not accomplish what they are supposed to, which is to bring works closer to the reader. Instead they stand between a work and its potential reader. This is primarily a question of power, but the explicators use such convoluted language that at first blush it's impossible to tell which aesthetic argument is the damning blow of which artistic powerhouse.

A number of critics have said about your new novel, quite admiringly, that it opened a new path in contemporary Hungarian prose, and it may well signal the end of the dominance of postmodernism here, if by the postmodern condition we mean a waning interest in traditional grand narratives.

I am no trailblazer and never intended to be one. That is a collectivist notion of literature, which I am dead set against and always will be. The assumption is that there aren't individual works, there are trends and currents, and works that don't fit into the mainstream are not worth talking about. My favourite period in prose is turn-of-the-twentieth-century Russian literature. That's when Chekhov and Gorky wrote their masterpieces, and alongside them you had the first, and to this day greatest, flowering of avant-garde literature, with the extraordinary formal innovations of Leonid Andreev, Andrey Biely and, later, Mikhail Bulgakov. Did this diminish Chekhov's and Gorky's art? Of course not. Did it invalidate their style, or make them outdated? No. Varlam Shalamov was a realist, though he wrote his books long after the heyday of the Russian avant-garde. Officially the entire avant-garde movement was banned, without much success of course, for what is good in it is still good and can be taken further. Everyone should be able to write as they see fit. Some have tried to pit me against the postmodernists, but I was never willing to play along. Not that I am that much interested in postmodern art, I consider it an essentially romantic phenomenon. All my life I defined myself in opposition to romanticism, but why shouldn't somebody write romantic ravings even today? When I felt that I could make use of them, I didn't hesitate to employ romantic or postmodern devices. And if at times I was forced to break new ground, I did it because the forms I needed for a given work were not available, so I had to come up with something different. I did this with great reluctance, for I am a conservative in this, and have an abiding respect for the rules pertaining to literary forms. I believe they still work, they will always work. I couldn't disagree more with the notion that there are trends and currents and not individual works. I consider this a Bolshevik cultural view. It's as if a singular masterpiece cannot be included in the canon unless it is followed by dozens of derivative works. Mihály Vörösmarty's *Csongor and Tünde* was not followed by a similar masterpiece, and after *The Tragedy of Man* there was only one, Ferenc Csepreghy's *Flood,* which no one knows anything about nowadays. Should we therefore throw out the *Tragedy* and *Csongor*? Nonsense. It's a long time since we lived under a Bolshevik system, yet those who feel they are in a position to tell writers how to write still think in terms of dominant tendencies and mainstreams. These people should not tell me how to write. Writing is not their strong suit. It is mine. ❧

CITYSCAPES

Victor Határ

Leeds Town Hall

At the end of 1950, all the engineers and architects who were doing time in Hungarian gaols were concentrated in the notorious Kisfogház, or 'Little Prison',[1] of the Central Prison in Budapest's Kőbánya district. There, on the first floor, they installed a secret technical bureau that was their pride and joy—not out of any misplaced 'humanity' but simply so that all that expert knowledge should not go to waste and the regime should get its cut of that, too. We drew up plans for fortifications for the Yugoslav frontier as well as standard designs for barrack blocks. In the 'drawing-office', formed by knocking three cells together, we were able to enjoy the latitude of the carefully dosed 'freedom' of being able to traverse a whole fifteen metres; the opulence of having a drawing-board, a typewriter, tall racks of foreign journals and comfortable genuine chairs (an unheard-of luxury); two cigarettes a day (heavenly manna for a smoker); as well as our own 'liaison officer'—a reliable party-activist colleague who fetched and carried the blueprints and maintained contact with our mysterious 'Control'.

We were slick, there's no denying it. We were delighted that we did not have to pass on messages from cell to cell by the prison Morse code of tapping on the pipes, but were able to sit down next to one another and chat; delighted that we could push a T-square and slide-rule about and pass the time by devising ground plans on a pile of tracing paper (for a born architect a form of tinkering that renders him oblivious to the world around); and delighted not to feel 'ready to eat a horse', because First Floor inmates were in line for double the usual rations of a mess-tin of beans.

Except that after the first three 'inspections' the comrade liaison colleague made himself increasingly scarce; in the end, the 'visits' ceased for good.

General consternation. We held a war council. We busied ourselves with feverish sham activity—anything as long as the screws noticed nothing unto-

1 ■ The death row cells were on the ground floor. Hangings took place on Fridays. On these occasions we were ordered to the back of the cell, along the bearing wall, and made to lie on the ground so that we would not be able to spy out of the window; yet even so we could hear the unfortunate 'faction-mongers' who were dragged there still hymning the praises of Comrade Stalin and the Party, and we were only allowed to get up when the all-clear was sounded, at which point we resumed our 'business' as if nothing had happened.

Victor Határ, *born in 1914 in what he calls an "obscure little backwater in eastern Hungary", has been living in England for almost fifty years. He studied architecture (as well as musical composition) and began writing novels while working as an architect. In 1943 he was court-martialed as a member of a subversive organisation, barely escaping the death penalty. After the war he worked for UNRA, and was imprisoned again in 1950, this time for attempting to leave the country illegally. Freed in 1952, he made his living as a translator, with versions of Russian, French and German classics to his credit, not to mention Sterne's* Tristram Shandy *and* A Sentimental Journey. *Unable to publish, he left the country in 1957 and settled in England. He worked for the Hungarian Section of the BBC until retiring in 1976, when he started working for Radio Free Europe and for the Foreign Office, tutoring diplomats in the language and culture of Hungary. His vast oeuvre consists of novels, plays, poetry, essays and philosophical works, as well as a three-volume autobiography. This text is part of an essay devoted to Budapest's architecture but also discussing Leeds Town Hall and Cuthbert Brodrick, its architect.*

---

ward. We designed heaps of whatever came to our minds—in my own case some four dozen family homes (we kept these in bound 'albums' which we dreamed of publishing after we were released). After that came a National Theatre Colosseum. (This was a complex incorporating an Opera House, National Theatre, Experimental Theatre, Theatre School, Institute and Museum of Theatre History, Drama Library and restaurants, below which was a two-level car park, and so on, apparently seeking to outdo Jean-Louis-Charles Garnier's glittering structure for the Paris Opéra. It was somewhat neo-Art Nouveau in appearance, almost postmodern, its planned scale far bigger than a small nation would have need of.) A full set of plans for this existed, along with all the associated ground plans, cross-sections, longitudinal sections, interior and exterior perspective views.[2]

It was good fun, and a noble occupation; we were obviously 'keeping up our profession'. Witnessing our diligence, the screws could self-contentedly puff on their gaspers without suspecting anything.

It sometimes happened that 'work' would be set aside and I would pitch into the tall rack of professional journals from abroad. One after the other, I would pick up *Domus* from Switzerland, *Architecture d'aujourd'hui* from France, and *Architecture* from the UK, drinking in the illustrations and articles until lights out. It was on one such occasion that it happened. As I was taking the volumes of English *Architecture* down from the tall rack, I spotted on the cover of one issue a colour picture of a building complex that knocked me back on my chair and left me unable to take my eyes off it. This depicted a palatial, colonnaded building,

2 ■ This set was destroyed in early 1952, in the course of an onslaught on and trashing of the planning office by the state security police. István Fehérváry, a fellow prisoner at the time, witnessed this and recalls it in his autobiography.

obviously monumental. But what purpose was served by this splendid monstrosity, dazzling out from the townscape around as it did, and where could it be, who could know? Of a caption or clue, whether on the cover or inside—there was no sign. For weeks on end, that issue of the journal became my 'mandala'—an object of meditation. Of a morning, on awakening on my palliasse, that perspective apotheosis of my dream palace would be waiting there, laid out beside my seat.

Set on a one-storey basement in order to enhance its importance, the broad flight of a grand staircase swept up to a Corinthian order portico, on the seemingly endless colonnade of which the entablature was crowned by an 'attic' of baroque balustrades. Inset in the middle, over wall embellishments on a divided plinth, was a topping, a sort of square 'drum' around which ran a likewise square 'peristyle' of slender columns; and on that, set in an ornamental entablature, four large clocks, one on each of the four sides. A strange dome, soaring from that square base, was closed off by a graceful scrolled cupola. The tall, slender-looking tower could no doubt be seen from miles around.

I was instantly alive to the fact that this magic mansion was a blend of professional know-how and inventive genius: a brazen, emotion-grabbing confection in the worst possible taste, and at the same time, such a supreme expression of classicising monumentality that I was in thrall to its spell, unable to break away. There were times when that captivating stone tower would float by in my dreams: nothing could be more shamelessly kitschy yet equally an enthralling blast of a Berliozian fanfare transfixed in stone (not for nothing did Schlegel call architecture 'frozen music'). It was that kick in the pit of the stomach, the infatuation of a Vitruvius, a falling head over heals in love. Placed ready on the seat beside my palliasse, that was where my look would be cast on upon awakening. My eyes would fill with tears.

I was ashamed of being overcome by my emotions, but I vowed with tears in my eyes: one day, when all this was over and done with. Even if I had to wear my legs down to the knees and walk to the ends of the earth. But would I recognise it?—oh, and how! With an indelible image of that tower and colonnade inscribed in my memory as long as I lived. I would search until I came across it somewhere on the face of the earth. But where?

Oneiromancy is what that was. Divination by dream.

Let us skip the ten years that I had to wait.

It must have been around 1963. I was working as a BBC correspondent and the Home Service dispatched me on a six-week tour with a senior colleague, who took me round the British Isles in his scarlet sports car. Every place has its particular *lares* and *penates,* its own household gods: customs, cooking pots, tools, superstitions, words of abuse, body language. In Hungary, a carpenter smoothes wood by pushing the plane away from his body; a Chinese chippy, on the other hand, pulls it toward him, and the instrument itself is differently constructed.

Well, I was supposed to be paying attention to dyed-in-the-wool English peculiarities like that, and whenever anything struck me to dictate the distinction out loud and at length, in my choicest (thick) English accent, into a microphone, 'marvelling' at the difference—that was my function. During those six weeks in Scotland, Wales and the English Midlands, I looked over so many country houses, castles, fortified churches, monasteries, belfries, market-place pillories, Roman remains, museums of local history, stone circles, town halls and cathedrals that my head was reeling.

We must have been around half way through the tour when, proceeding north-east out of Manchester, we headed for Leeds, a city of half a million inhabitants (a splendid place that has made no mark on the average European consciousness despite its university, its marvellous architecture and monuments). On reaching the outskirts of the city, a vaguely familiar tall, square clock tower was already visible from a long way off. As we got closer and its details became more and more distinct, my heart missed a beat. I was trembling. I burbled inarticulate cries, and I began to flail at the steering wheel, which my colleague, with his elegantly gloved hands, was hard put to make anything of.

We reached the centre, parking illegally right in front of it. I was gob-smacked, lost for words.

The thing that I had once discovered on the cover of *Architecture* on the journal racks of the secret design office on the Death Row in Budapest's Central Prison, and now just as back then. I could not take my eyes off it. The penny dropped for my companion too: he realised what I was goggling at with such a gormless, moon-eyed look, his nervous system attuned itself to my quiet frenzy, and then the senior colleague gaped at it, lost in wonder, as if he were seeing it for the first time.

Leeds Town Hall!

We gazed at the palace's 225-foot colossus of a tower (it seemed much bigger than it actually was) with the reverence that befits a masterpiece. I pushed aside the microphone that was thrust before my nose, and instead of saying something, with no thought for the BBC, the big tape-recorder on the back seat or the senior colleague, who was left floundering as he yelled after me to take care, for God's sake, I raced like a madman in the middle of the broad, mile-long busy main road that ran beside the main façade, with cars whizzing by behind and in front of me—simply to catch a view from as many angles as possible, unable to take my eyes off it.

So, this is where you are, in the flesh, Fairest of the Fair!

Here was the endless, one-storey plinth, and this was what the ten-column Corinthian colonnade looked like in reality which, supplemented by the pilasters of the side elevations, carried on round the corner and right round the building. These, then, were the ventilation shafts like French Renaissance chimneys, with jewel-like ornamental coping stones, that had been so beguiling in the photographs! This was that 'preposterous notion' of setting a square peristyle tower on massive square attic storey on top of the crowning cornice, and upon that, beneath a Baroque dome with concave sides, a clock tower that housed a bell whose chime would ring out far and wide, to all points of the compass! Flying in the face of the gentleman's agreement that rules architectural art: a 'pre-posterous notion'!

I was getting on for sixty at the time, but a nimbler sixty-year-old has never been seen. With my adolescent excitement, I more than likely cut a comic figure, but there was no stopping me; with my considerably younger English colleague huffing and puffing at my heels, for I was by now racing up the grand staircase, through the main entrance, across the oval foyer with a resounding clatter of footsteps, and into the huge central main hall.

A Baroque yawn—I sized it up at once. It was not only its sheer size as a concert hall, inferred from the immensity of its in-built organ; nor the supreme handling of form and spellbinding virtuosity of its designer's God-given talent, reminiscent of a Bernini or Borromini, but also—jumping Jehosaphat!—what was so very, so terribly English about it, such a dead give-away: its glaringly English stinginess. I couldn't get over how odd I found it, and had I not been embarrassed by it, I would have yelled down my young colleague's lughole:

"You see, my friend, *this* is the kind of thing we order differently in Hungary..."

Fortunately, tape-recorder and microphone had been left outside on the car seat. I could have offered excuses and apologies till the cows come home to no avail, had I recorded this at the time. To this day, though, I have to chuckle over it. Over the fact that this immortal plan, which from conception on cried out to be executed in Carrara marble, had been served up in shabby stucco. Moreover it had been titivated in accordance with such a tawdrily gaudy colour scheme that the likes of those maroon acanthus leaves and vermilion cornice brackets, the putti doused in shoddy piss-pot gold, done in such a provincially kitschy and flagrantly inept fashion, are only to be seen in those hideous Roman Catholic churches on Malta. In a word, I guffawed over it, though I shed a tear or two as well: I felt sorry for the genius who was not honoured by his nation as his merits deserved (even though he was barely thirty years old when he won the competition).

So, you see: that intuitive flash, my presentiment of the course my life would take, turned out to be *true*; the 'icon' had materialised on the screen of my consciousness, and all I had to do was click on it for the iconostasis of the Divine Mystery to appear in "unearthly light that is not of the Creation", and lo and behold! Willy-nilly the vow that I made to my love was fulfilled: I had fallen in love with it from a picture, and now that I found myself in its presence, having made the pilgrimage thus far, there was nothing for it but to throw myself at its feet and kiss the ground—the soil about which I wrote that poem back in 1957, squatting on a bunk bed in the gym of a Viennese hospice: *"Every vessel is my homeland."* ❧

The opening of Leeds Town Hall (1858) by Queen Victoria in the hall now named after her.

Translated by Tim Wilkinson

Gábor Gyáni

Budapest Beyond Good and Evil

It is a commonplace that a great city and its country are two different worlds. This is particularly true where the sheer quantitative proportions, or rather disproportions, are striking. Such is the case with the central territories of the Habsburg empire (later the Austro-Hungarian Empire) or rather their successor states of Austria and Hungary. After the peace treaties that concluded the Great War, Vienna, the old Imperial city, and Budapest—which had grown particularly fast after the 1867 *Ausgleich* or Compromise—became the capital cities of countries that had shrunk considerably both in size and population. Close to a third of all Austrians lived in Vienna and over a tenth of Hungarians in Budapest. No wonder that, in both countries, hydrocephaly was considered an apt metaphor. Qualitative factors only made matters worse. The empire's aristocracy, Vienna's haute-bourgeoisie and the metropolitan petty bourgeoisie who catered to their luxurious consumption did not have (nor could they have) a provincial equivalent, and neither did Budapest's élite, middle class and petty bourgeoisie have a true counterpart in Hungary's rural population. It speaks volumes that around the year 1900, the person who was bottom of the list of Budapest's top 400 taxpayers—'virilists' as they were called—paid about as much tax as someone who headed the same list for the most prosperous provincial cities.[1]

Beyond all possible doubt, Budapest and the Hungarian provinces (including provincial cities) found themselves at very different stages of development and strikingly divergent in character, in respect to their economic, social, political, cultural and intellectual milieus.

Gábor Gyáni

is Senior Research Fellow at the Institute of History of the Hungarian Academy of Sciences and Professor at the Sociology Institute of Eötvös Loránd University. He is the author of 14 books, including Women as Domestic Servants: The Case of Budapest, 1890–1940 *(1989);* Parlor and Kitchen: Housing and Domestic Culture in Budapest, 1870–1940 *(2002);* A Social History of Hungary from the Reform Era to the End of the Twentieth Century *(with co-authors, 2004) and* Identity and the Urban Experience: Fin-de-Siècle Budapest *(2004).*

The political map

Each time a general election comes round, it is noticeable just how uneven the political map of Budapest is. The distribution of votes cast in elections since 1989 shows Budapest, that most liberal of Hungarian cities, serving as one of the prime sources of support for the extreme right, particularly in the more prosperous districts on the Buda side of the Danube. The historical reasons are manifold.

Because of the votes of a substantial liberal middle class and petty bourgeoisie, Budapest was a stronghold of liberalism and social democracy between 1920 and 1939. Indeed, after 1906, during what might be called the Bárczy Era (1906–18, the tenure of Mayor István Bárczy), democratic, or what we would nowadays call socially liberal, ideals had also gained ground in municipal politics.[2] During the Twenties these political forces would have had control of the city if fair play had prevailed in the politics of the time.[3]

The overall picture is a bit more complex than that, however. In the mid-1970s, György Ránki studied the Budapest archive material covering the 1939 parliamentary election and established that the Arrow Cross movement, Hungary's home-grown fascists, largely owed their rapid rise to the support they enjoyed in working-class districts in Budapest. This finally forced people to abandon the previously unshakeable myth of the city being exclusively liberal.[4] In 1950, after half a century of lobbying from some quarters, a 'Red Belt', mainly inhabited by industrial workers, was incorporated to create a Greater Budapest at the behest of Communist party leader Mátyás Rákosi. The Left acquired an unequivocal ascendancy in the capital that could even legitimise the Communists' hold on power, should there be any necessity for such legitimation by the people's will. During the successive elections of the coalition years from 1945 to 1949, Budapest's substantial leftism really did carry weight, all the more so as extreme-right, conservative and finally liberal political factions had all been successively removed from the arena, with the social groups backing them duly intimidated and politically eliminated.

From the moment that Budapest set off on the path of modern development, a process that has been a motor for Hungary over the last century and a half, two distinct social groupings, an entrepreneurial (and managerial) segment of the middle and upper classes and an industrial working class determined its character. The civil service as the capital's working machinery also had an influence, their ethos likewise being a palpable presence in Budapest. Finally, Pest, Buda and Óbuda, separate municipalities before their unification in 1873—and later the growing belt of the suburbs—each retained something of their traditional social and intellectual ambience: Pest as primarily a commercial centre from the eighteenth century on, Buda as a municipality of government officials, and Óbuda as a settlement with strong peasant roots. Budapest the metropolis was a conglomerate of all these traditions and influences.

Budapest, the Magyarised city

Two books on Budapest's non-Magyar aspect have recently appeared.[5] Discussing the ethnic Germans and Jews of the capital, they demonstrate the once acute reality of just how divided and variegated Budapest was in its ethnic and denominational make-up. Karl Lueger, the rabidly anti-Semitic pre-Great War mayor of Vienna, used to refer to the Hungarian capital as "Judapest", but one might just as easily speak about German, Slovak, Serb and Polish, or Calvinist and Lutheran Budapests. With the exception of the Germans, they have not been properly studied yet.[6]

At the time the city was being unified in the 1870s, the tone was set by a long-standing German ethno-cultural tradition.[7] Yet, within a very short period of time, a massive tide of overwhelmingly Hungarian-speaking newcomers arrived. As a result, by the end of the First World War, Budapest boasted a population of nearly one million—more than three times what it had been at the time of unification. As István Weis, a sociologist of the inter-war period noted:

> Budapest does not have citizens in the same sense as Vienna or Paris; for, almost two thirds of the inhabitants were born outside the capital, which is to say that they have brought with them other childhood memories and customs.[8]

There is no doubt that this linguistic shift was the key to the Magyarisation of Budapest. Moreover, it is readily traceable. Until 1840, the country's official language had been Latin, though in many towns (including Pest and Buda) German was the language of local administration, in line with the fact that the residents of Hungary's urban centres (with few exceptions) were German-speakers. This started to change around the middle of the century as the ability to speak Hungarian had been a central demand of Hungarian nationalism from the 1830s onwards. However, it was only after 1867 that Hungarian became the official language.

There is a general recognition of the fact of this extraordinary linguistic, ethnic and denominational heterogeneity, and of the ensuing brisk homogenisation at the end of the nineteenth century. However, opinions differ on the nature of this process. Furthermore, after 1920, instead of looking on the Magyarisation of Budapest as a good thing, some found it partly or wholly objectionable. The slogan of the 'sinful city', which gained currency at the time, expressed this unambiguously. In March 1920, very much in line with the thinking of the zealously Christian-Nationalist regime that had installed itself after the overthrow of the revolutions of 1918–19, a Christian-Social politician declared:

> the old Masonic funny business still prevails in the capital. Freemasonry must dismantle and destroy its old stronghold... What is needed here is a new broom.[9]

He was far from alone. A submission by the chairman of one of the Budapest district branches of the Christian Social Party to the Minister of the Interior at more or less the same time was couched in similar terms:

...the capital's population [!] rightly hoped that the Christian-National course would enter within the walls of the town hall, and as evidence of that, the administration of the capital would be entrusted to a government commissioner. Today, however, when public opinion in the provinces and abroad shows a keen interest in developments in the sinful city, when the capital's Christian-National course ought to be setting an example to what course politics in Hungary as a whole should take, the town hall's doors have remained closed to the champions of the new ideas.[10]

The profound change in how Budapest was viewed was the consequence of the counter-revolutionary hysteria (and an associated virulent anti-Semitism) that swept the country after the collapse of the four-month-old Soviet Republic in the summer of 1919. This in turn determined the attitudes that the newly installed rightist and conservative political élite took to anything associated with Budapest. Horthy had given this new discourse its keynote when he was still the commander-in-chief of the national army on its entry into Budapest in November 1919. In response to being welcomed by Mayor Tivadar Bódy in front of the Gellért Hotel, he called on the city to confront its guilt:

When we were still a long way away from here and only a scintilla of hope flickered in our soul, then—let me make no bones about it—we loathed and execrated [Budapest], because we did not see the people who were suffering there, those who became martyrs, we saw only the filth of the country that had accumulated there.[11]

This was a radical re-assessment of what in fact had been an urban development of staggering proportions since the Compromise, which embraced every conceivable manifestation of being a Budapester, whether in politics, behaviour or merely language. As to the vernacular of Budapest, let me quote here a request submitted by Károly Darvassy, an engineer, to the city authorities in June 1921. In support of his claims, the petitioner even went so far as to draw up a brief compilation of linguistic anomalies:

Permit me, Your Honour, to draw your worthy attention to the particular colourlessness of the Budapest language and to some of the intolerable signs of its badness. The Budapest dialect is beginning to be completely ruined by the un-Hungarian, music-hall, hoodlum speech that is propagated by the Városliget [City Park] fairground mob and of the influence of which even untouched, well-spoken, intelligent people cannot entirely rid themselves.[12]

Darvassy's initiative swiftly and readily reached understanding ears. The council promptly forwarded his letter to the National Association of Primary and Secondary School Teachers, which subsequently reached the view that "The elimination of non-Hungarian expressions and words is an educational requirement of the first order." It accordingly set about getting rid of the linguistic shortcomings in question; in preparation for that, it called on the capital city's teaching bodies to collect examples of un-Hungarian locutions that permeated the speech of their pupils. The Association was itself planning to work up and publish the considerable material that accumulated, but in the end this did not happen.[13]

Under the impetus of this and similar experiences in schools and of the general educational ethos of the times, a public debate developed about what being a Budapester meant. We even find László Németh, an outstanding novelist and essayist passionately concerned with all matters relating to the fate of the Hungarian nation, being confronted with the reality of the 'flotsam and jetsam' of the Budapest lower classes. As a school doctor of a junior secondary school in the Water Town district of Buda, he recorded:

> Even our "colossal hall" cannot count on a more native character; for all that, the hundred-year-old Water Town has surrounded it intact until the most recent years... [For], apart from a few dozen true Water Town children, our school, too... is attended by the children of those who have been tossed this way and that in the course of the modern-day Great Migration.[14]

Separating out this 'flotsam and jetsam stratum', Németh finally concludes:

> It does not take too much intelligence to find an explanation for the Magyarisation [of schools] in the post-war (and in part, also pre-war) engulfment. The catchment area of our school in the seventies and eighties was still German-speaking, the Magyar nation supplying fifty per cent before the war and now eighty or ninety per cent (for certain).[15]

Németh arrived at this finding after an analysis of the pupils' surnames.

The continuous monitoring of the homogenisation that attended Magyarisation between the two world wars was something of a national pastime, particularly among those who were connected in some way with a school and its pupils. Sándor Karácsony, a legendary educationalist and psychologist—whose person and work divides the profession to the present day[16]—likewise considered it important to set forth his views on the hotly disputed question of a 'Hungarian Budapest' (the title he gave to his article):

> At the start of the last century, Budapest was still a German-speaking city; indeed, even in mid-nineteenth century much German speech was heard in the streets, and any Budapester who attempted to speak Hungarian did so with miserable result... These days, [however] Budapest is Hungarian. It speaks Hungarian and feels Hungarian. It may speak differently from, and not feel quite the same as, Debrecen or Dévaványa or the Bugac plain; nevertheless, it is Hungarian.

"Yet," he finally poses a thorny question, "how could this modern miracle have happened, one wonders?"[17] First and foremost, because the provincial Hungarian population found homes for itself in Budapest. "The Hungarian peasantry made Budapest Hungarian."[18] Furthermore, he adds the somewhat curious explanation that as Budapesters these Hungarian newcomers

> are all the more Hungarian [because] their souls... by a strange but understandable and natural contrariety, to their dying day feel an aching homesickness and pull towards home, to the countryside, the open air, the village, the puszta.[19]

It was precisely in this sense that, as Karácsony saw it, Budapest's Hungarianness had been "tragically Hungarian" during the years that elapsed between the

Compromise and Hungary's Millennial celebrations of 1896. Only subsequent to this did the by then Hungarian Budapest step onto a path leading to its loss of Hungarian character. The reason for that was obvious. Being an arena of intense cultural exchange, Budapest had assumed—and could assume—merely a veneer of Hungarianness, which, however, it had soon begun to propagate as a kind of yardstick across the rest of the country:

> Budapest, from the Compromise up to the Millennial Exhibition, became Hungarian; then it again turned foreign, only now this was in a Hungarian garb. It was foreign even while seeming to be Hungarian; in point of fact, it was not even aware of this.[20]

Thus, by the outbreak of the First World War, matters had degenerated to the point where Budapest's Hungarianness was nothing more than a veneer; but when the war was over, and during the revolutionary turmoil of 1919, even that thin veneer soon peeled off. Not that everything was lost, Karácsony claims, for the long-standing process of de-Magyarisation was by then over:

> At the very moment that Austria-Hungary ceased to exist, Budapest's old role also ceased to exist, and the course of its new life began. Up till then it had been the European quarter in a colony; since then it has been a self-reliant efflorescence of the life of a self-reliant people and country, nation and state.[21]

That, then, was the tone of the inter-war discourse about Budapest, with its participants seeking to suggest that the 'natural' non-Hungarianness of this cosmopolitan metropolis within Austria-Hungary was soon effaced by the Magyarising influence of a country that had now (post-Trianon) become a nation; with two-thirds of its territory taken away from the truncated country, the capital would at last be able to cast off its previously accreted sins of lacking national spirit.

Budapest as metropolis

Historians have seen all these changes in a different light. Discussing the long-term processes in the transformation of mass culture, Károly Vörös focuses not so much on the fact of linguistic homogenisation as on the co-existence of various subcultures in continual interaction and their gradual integration, albeit not entirely free of contradictions.[22]

During the decades leading up to 1900, the urban bourgeois (Biedermeier) culture of the older-established ethnic German petty bourgeoisie was living on alongside the Hungarian culture of the newly arriving Magyar petty bourgeoisie and a peasant-rooted working-class in what, already back in the 1870s, was a multi-element mass culture—and a linguistic hotchpotch as well. This was rounded out, according to Vörös, by a predominantly Germanic industrial working-class culture of other incoming foreigners (in some cases native Hungarians who had worked abroad) and the separate culture of the Jewish petty bourgeoisie that had streamed continuously into the country from the 1840s onwards. The kaleidoscopic product assembled from these elements was later on to be altered in such a way that, roughly from the Millennium onwards, it gradually transformed into a modern metropolitan bourgeois (or petty bourgeois) mass culture that was now based fundamentally on "Hungarian" (language) culture. In the meantime, a proletarian class culture was taking shape, likewise forged in Budapest.

The succeeding period, the quarter century of the inter-war years, was marked by the definitive footing that mass culture acquired in Budapest with the modernisation of the media. The social reach was spectacularly expanded, with Budapest's mass culture, which catered mainly to petty-bourgeois tastes and expectations, exerting a great hold on newcomers from the provinces, as well as on an industrial working class and urbanised petty bourgeoisie that had been established over several generations. Moreover, this mass culture increasingly undermined the distinctively working-class culture that had emerged around 1900, and which, initially, had constituted a kind of counter-culture. One of the chief motors for the irresistible spread of this commercially driven metropolitan mass culture was the cinema, which had a pivotal role in the rapid homogenisation of values and lifestyles.

Through the agency of mass culture, then, there emerged an entity that was held to be 'typically Budapestian' and which, in the end, steamrollered any resistance by the various ethnically and class-based sub- and counter-cultures. Admittedly, older traditions and local peculiarities did not completely wither away, but the earlier conspicuous diversity of codes and frameworks of reference clearly diminished.

Everything that has been touched on up to this point is virtually self-evident in the circumstances of prolonged metropolitan development. The modernisation of public spaces (using that term in the broadest sense) opened up the city once and for all to the entire population; thereby making it possible for them to be no longer restricted to their immediate neighbourhoods, but at last to take possession of the city. "Now, after centuries of life as a cluster of isolated cells, Paris was becoming a unified physical and human space" is how one historian characterises the magnificent results of the transformation wrought on the French capital by Haussmann in the mid-nineteenth century.[23] In the process, the modern metropolis, functioning as "an endless parade of strangers", changes into a ceaselessly "mobile chaos" which overturns limits of time and space to penetrate every nook and cranny of the city, and thereby imposes its remorseless pace and its own values on each and every inhabitant. It is this, and this alone, that explains the unstoppable sweep of homogenisation. Ultimately, it created the context in which the historically determined process of metropolitan transformation progressed—whether within an empire or a nation-state had little material impact.[24]

Identity crisis—a source of creativity

In influential books, John Lukacs and Péter Hanák offered two considerably diverging historical narratives of Budapest around 1900. The gist of Lukacs's book, which first appeared in English and was later translated into many other languages, including Hungarian, is that the city's lively and occasionally crude provincialism at that time sat well with a metropolitan character that sprang from the capital's indisputable cosmopolitanism.[25] This simultaneously Hungarian and cosmopolitan Budapest was captured best, in Lukacs's view, through the figure (and writings) of Gyula Krúdy, "the Hungarian Proust" who "conceals a series of dualities." To wit, "Revolutionary and conservative. Erotic and Christian. A participant in the capital's Bohemian lifestyle, yet a yearning admirer of the Biedermeier provincial Hungary of yore."[26]

Hanák, by contrast, in a book which appeared in both English and German, places the emphasis elsewhere. The Garden (as *fin-de-siècle* Vienna was portrayed by Carl Schorske) and the Workshop (the metaphor that Hanák applies to *fin-de-siècle* Budapest) stand for the two mutually distinguishable Central European alternatives of modernity and modernism. Hyperindividualistic and decadent Vienna, retreating into the psychological depths of subjectivism, is confronted by a Budapest that couples modernity with a readiness to act, and reformism with a soon-to-be-renewed nationalism.[27]

Even now that we have these two major and influential narratives on the history of Budapest, we still cannot say that we have received satisfactory answers to all the problems that crop up. In both cases, the image that these two authors outline, each in his own way, seeks to ascribe the 'essence' of the phenomenon called Budapest to some fundamental duality. It seems to me, though, that it would be more fruitful to tackle the analysis on the basis of a ternary concept. In this view, a triad of praising the city, blaming the city and negating the city would offer us a better chance of understanding the dynamic of the variable relationship of modernity and modernism.[28]

It should be made clear, however, that modernity and modernism do not fit together seamlessly and unbrokenly. Modernity may be a necessary and indispensable condition for any kind of modernism, but the latter is usually an overt and indeed vehement negation of the great project of modernity (the material result of modernisation). It may happen, therefore, that modernism as an entity does not directly reflect or articulate modernity; that is a role that for quite a long time has, in fact, been fulfilled by historicism. The reason for this conflict between modernity and modernism is something I shall be seeking to elucidate in what follows.

From the time it became a capital city (with the unification of Pest, Buda and Óbuda) right up to the Millennium, praising the city determined the conceptual universe as manifested, first and foremost, in what perception and experience saw as being 'typically Budapestian'. This decidedly liberal-national ethos was eloquently displayed in the Millennial celebrations, and Budapest figured prominently as an object of commemorative reminiscence. It was not just the thousand years of Hungary's glorious national history, supplying proof of the state's continuity, but also its achievement of modernity, culminating in the emergence of the metropolis. Its staggering pace of development since the middle of the century was presented in a separate pavilion in the City Park exhibition ground; Gusztáv

Thirring, a noted statistician, devoted a whole volume to numerically substantiating the city's dazzling achievements; and György Klösz, who ran a fashionable inner-city photographic studio, was commissioned by the city council to make a thorough photographic survey, in order to provide a lasting visual record of this splendid "modern-looking" place.[29] Meanwhile, those who proclaimed the city's magnificence seem not to have allowed their unbounded optimism to be ruffled by the least scintilla of doubt; though admittedly there was one statistician, József Kőrösi, who only shortly before had published the first data on deprivation in the Budapest slums.[30]

By 1900, that liberal optimism, which had been fostered for quite some time, was taken over and eventually 'developed' by the bourgeois radicals, the group which Péter Hanák's metaphor of a Workshop primarily fits. The city led by mayor István Bárczy (from 1906) was consumed by a fever of municipal and social reforms, in the convinction that the increasingly evident market-induced metropolitan anomalies could be moderated, indeed eventually eliminated, by stronger intervention by the authorities.

Another sort of response was offered, however, by the steadily growing and also very mixed camp of those who blamed the city—soon joined by those who sided with the anti-liberal, jingoistic and at times patently anti-Semitic 'neo-conservatives'.[31] Yet, before rushing to condemn them, let me also note that they included in their ranks (if only temporarily) individuals who, on the basis of their subsequent careers and their lives as a whole, one would not dream of accusing of violent or aggressive nationalism or an anti-urban anti-Semitism. The young Béla Bartók was so irritated by conspicuous (linguistic) cosmopolitanism in Budapest that he was prepared to take even his own mother to task for preferring on many occasions to speak German rather than Hungarian. In a 1903 letter to her, he approvingly cited a speech in which Jenő Rákosi, a noted chauvinistic journalist, had said

> "It's all the same to us whether and how anybody speaks our unique and peerless language; instead, we ourselves speak everybody else's language; we deride people who speak only Hungarian as uneducated, no matter how much they know; our girls, the mothers of future generations, we ruin at a tender age with foreign education..."

To this Bartók added as his own credo:

> For my own part, all my life, in every sphere, always and in every way I shall have one objective: the good of Hungary and the Hungarian nation.

He added that by that he meant that ordinary people should "work quietly and unobtrusively in their everyday life for everything that is Hungarian". For that reason he exhorts, "Spread and propagate the Hungarian language with word and deed and with *speech*!"[32]

That was not how things were viewed by Endre Ady, the great poet of that era, whose profound sense of identity there was truly no reason to doubt. Staunchly devoted to things 'typically Budapestian', yet he was yet acutely aware of the seamy side of life there and the concomitant sense of guilt. Lashing out at "humbug nationalists",—or in other words at those who were always ready to give preference to the peasantry and the provinces over the city—Ady declared:

> By now the manufacturers of new legends have long since said and written more than enough about the miracle and the enduring bloody sins of Budapest, with its population of almost one million. It is true that the city grew unexpectedly big out of a defiant, rash miracle, and also true that a small, awkward and crippled country has paid the price for the city's sins with bloody sacrifices. No matter, a city can only be born that way, and Budapest had to become at least the size and kind of city that it is, because otherwise woe it would have been and would be for us.[33]

Ady's passionate fulminations, for all that, do not pass over into frank contempt or rejection—sentiments that, in those days, individuals were regularly prone to voice with the pathos of exalted moral judgement.

This was the case with Ferenc Herczeg, the literary "lion" of the Horthy era, in a somewhat later volume of his memoirs that concerns the 1880s, which is the period when the writer arrived in the capital as a student:

> This was the first time I had seen Budapest... The city was not so lucky as to win my approval. It was unable to persuade me that it could be the Hungarian capital about which the provinces spoke and dreamed so much. Missing from its architecture was, above all, the national pathos that I regarded as indispensable.

He then goes on for pages on end describing the city's repellent features: the craze for duelling, the licentious lifestyle of the young and the free and easy relations between the sexes in public. "Young people intoxicated by this unfamiliar milieu," these fresh immigrants who in time were to upstage the native citizenry, "inflated boorish propensities in proportion to the size of the big city."

> They permitted themselves incredible things, and nowadays [Herczeg was writing in 1933] people cannot understand how public opinion in the eighties could have tolerated such things.

As a case in point:

> Even by day, elegant streets were teeming with ghastly females who strove with stupendous audacity to attract general attention to themselves. In Király Street, nightclubs lined up... In these places the singing was exclusively in German, there being a general belief still that it was not possible to write a popular song lyric in Hungarian.

Possibly what most disturbs the provincial (and at the same time assimilating) young man, an ethnic German by birth, as he draws up this passionate indictment is the metropolitan public space, where everything freely merges and is irretrievably diluted in the process. Even the mere sight of the looseness of interactions between the sexes fills him with disgust, for it charges the big-city atmosphere with overt sexuality. In dance-halls the ladies would throw themselves at a customer like a swarm of starved flies. A Hungarian from the provinces who strayed into such a place and ordered a modest *café au lait* would in no time at all find half a dozen women seated at his table, with the waiter setting a bottle of wine in front of each of them. In Budapest, however, Herczeg fulminated even decades later, that was normal. Anything to which the authorities or 'public opinion' raised no objection was considered to be generally accepted, "The police behaved as if they were supremely well-disposed towards the scandal-makers and especially the street women." He came to the logical conclusion, therefore, that "this city was in no way more suitable as a university town than Bret Harte's gold-mining town."[34]

Aversions to the city could also stem from quite another source, as was exemplified by the young alienated Nietzschean aesthetes. Their distinctly anti-liberal revolt, disgusted by assimilation and nationalism alike, can likewise be put down to antagonism to the city. At work behind this, as many people were well aware, was also the hugely stimulating influence that Budapest exerted. One among them, for instance, was Sándor Ferenczi, Freud's loyal disciple, who makes his pronouncements while pondering the chances of intellectual advance within Budapest's narrow psychoanalytical circles in the early 1910s. In a medium-sized city like Budapest, he argues, a person had more opportunity to observe how society becomes imbued with new ideas. These ideas, simply by virtue of their weight, blazed a trail for themselves; it was sufficient to proclaim them intelligibly *on just a single occasion*.[35]

The psychoanalysts, oddly enough, were not among the people who were ready to shed all liberal illusions in order—by way of an escape—to immerse themselves in the irrational depths of their minds. Indeed, as Ferenczi says with sincere naïvety in another letter to Freud, it was incumbent on psychoanalysts above all to rectify the neuroses of big-city inhabitants and lead them back to a normal track:

> The *sociological* significance of our analyses... is that we throw light on the *real* state of the various social strata, freeing it of all hypocrisy and conventionalism. The way that it is reflected in individual people.[36]

By contrast, there were the aesthetes such as Georg Lukács and others in the Sunday Circle, intellectuals who were alienated from society and not least from the capital's liberal vanguard—that is, the partly assimilated middle and upper-middle classes, their own class. They no longer cherished any illusions about the human values offered by modernity and the modern urban condition. For them the metropolitan world, and the bourgeois prosperity that was part of it and to which they were privy, was the very epitome of total alienation, homelessness and emptiness. From this world it was advisable to escape—insofar as there was still any way of doing so at all—just as quickly and as far away as was possible, into the pure, ethereally spiritual world of the mind (or maybe suicide). Efforts that he made in this direction during his younger days were later described as a personal war of independence by the art historian Károly Tolnay (better known as Charles de Tolnay). He "emancipated" himself from the burdens of bourgeois life in cosmopolitan Budapest by encountering the aesthete Lajos Fülep and the rest of the Sunday Circle, and eventually by studying in Germany. The manner in which he admits to this peculiar world in his autobiography is typical:

> The environment of the Lipótváros District: *nouveau riche* apartments (No. 16, then 31 Nádor Street, No. 4 Ország Square). Spacious, comfortable rooms. Cynical class-mates who believed in nothing and Polacsek garb, the importance accorded to eating (Gerbaud's confectionary)... Father's puritan attitude, severity, integrity and honesty, his hidden kindness. Mother's wobbling, laxity, semi-artistic inclinations (poetry and music), and her sentimentality.

Little wonder, then, he adds, if all the time in such a family "I felt I was a stranger...," a sense of strangeness that was incidentally of general applicability, since it also determined the relationship his parents had to the outside world:

> It would never have occurred to Father and Mother to take me with them to look at the monuments to the 'glorious past' on Castle Hill. They had no relationship to the country's past... They lived in Pest as strangers.[37]

On looking over the notions and experiences that were to form the basis for solid ideologies—or at least, enduring stances—it is fair to conclude that all, without exception, were rooted in a profound identity crisis. It would be difficult, indeed almost impossible, to make a precise and unambiguous distinction between the attitudes of a second- or third-generation member of the Jewish middle or upper-middle class and the identity crisis of young men, some of noble ancestry, who migrated to the city from the countryside but in time became modernist artists, to say nothing of the intellectual histories of those individuals who rose from the urban working class to become avant-garde artists (e. g. Lajos Kassák). All of them had the decisive experience of perceiving social impermanence as a fact of life, which was closely bound up with a severe identity crisis. Their complex and varied responses to the dramatic challenge presented by urbanisation cannot be simply explained by the widely different communities they came from. It is beyond doubt that Budapest exerted a fertilising influence on virtually everyone, this influence, however, was not exclusively due to this or that intellectual and ideological factor or choice. In the face of that extraordinary influence one can only be amazed at just how many divergent senses attach to the historical notion of what being typically Budapestian means. ❧

1 ■ See Károly Vörös: *Budapest legnagyobb adófizetői 1873–1917* (Budapest's Largest Taxpayers 1873–1917). Budapest: Akadémiai Kiadó, 1979, and Lajos Timár, "A gazdasági elit jellemzői a magyar városokban a két világháború között" (Characteristics of the Economic Élite in Hungarian Towns Between the Two World Wars). in *Tér—idő—társadalom. Huszonegy tanulmány Enyedi Györgynek* (Space—Time—Society: Twenty-One Studies for György Enyedi). Pécs, RKK, Hungarian Academy of Sciences, 1990, pp. 134–155.

2 ■ On defining the "Bárczy Era", see Gábor Gyáni: "Budapest története 1873–1945" (The History of Budapest 1873–1945), in: Vera Bácskai, Gábor Gyáni and András Kubinyi: *Budapest története a kezdetektől 1945-ig* (The History of Budapest from the Beginnings to 1945). Budapest, BFL, 2000, p. 185.

3 ■ Zsuzsa L. Nagy: *A budapesti liberális ellenzék 1919–1944* (Budapest's Liberal Opposition, 1919–1944). Budapest, Akadémiai Kiadó, 1972.

4 ■ György Ránki: "The Fascist Vote in Budapest in 1939"; in: Stein Ugelvik Larsen et al, eds., *Who Were the Fascists. Social Roots of European Fascism.* Bergen–Oslo–Tromso, Universitetsforlaget, 1980, pp. 401–418.

5 ■ Géza Komoróczy, ed.: *Jewish Budapest. Monuments, Rites, History.* Budapest, Central European University Press, 1998; Vendel Hambuch, ed.: *Németek Budapesten* (Germans in Budapest). Budapest, Fővárosi Német Kisebbségi Önkormányzat, 1998.

6 ■ László Szarka: "A budapesti szlovákság asszimilációja" (The Assimilation of Budapest Slovaks); in: Mária Demeter Zayzon, ed., *Másság–azonosság* (Otherness–Sameness). Budapest, ALFA, 1994. vol. 1, pp. 117–130; László Katus: "Szlovák politikai és társadalmi élet Budapesten a dualizmus korában" (Slovak Political and Social Life in Budapest During the Dualist Era; in: Gábor Gyáni and Gábor Pajkossy, eds.: *A pesti polgár. Tanulmányok Vörös Károly emlékére* (The Pest Bourgeois. Studies in Memory of Károly Vörös). Debrecen, Csokonai, 1999, pp. 137–153; Károly Vörös, "A reformátusság a fővárosban a dualizmus korában" (The Calvinist Church in the Capital During the Era of Dualism); in: *Kálvin téri tanulmányok* (Studies on Calvin Square). Budapest, n. p. 1983, pp. 55–63.

7 ■ Tamás Faragó: "A főváros népe: sokszínűség és beolvadás" (The Capital's Population: Diversity and Assimilation). in: Gábor Gyáni, ed.: *Az egyesített főváros. Pest, Buda, Óbuda* (The Unified Capital City: Pest, Buda, Óbuda). Budapest, Városháza, 1998, pp. 75–111.

8 ■ István Weis: *Hazánk társadalomrajza* (Ethnography of Our Country). Budapest, Országos Közoktatási Tanács, 1942, p. 47.

9 ■ Cited in Vera Bácskai, Gábor Gyáni and András Kubinyi, *op. cit.*, p. 216.

10 ■ This can be found in József Szekeres, ed.: *Források Budapest történetéhez 1919–1945* (Sources on the History of Budapest, 1919–1945). Budapest, BFL, 1972, p. 31.

11 ■ *Idem.*, p. 21.

12 ■ Cited by Gábor Gyáni: *Identity and the Urban Experience: Fin-de-Siècle Budapest.* New York, Columbia University Press, 2004, p. 193.

13 ■ *Idem.*, p. 194.

14 ■ László Németh: *A Medve utcai polgári* (The Medve Street High School). Budapest, Magyar Élet Kiadása, 1943, p. 33.

15 ■ *Idem.*, p. 35.

16 ■ On the conflicting judgements of Karácsony, see Csaba Pléh's review of Gusztáv Lányi's book about Karácsony, and Lányi's response in: *BUKSZ* (2001, Winter): pp. 380–383 and Gusztáv Lányi: "Tudományos észjárás és karizmatikus tudás. Levél Pléh Csabának" (Scholarly Thinking and Charismatic Knowledge. Letter to Csaba Pléh). *BUKSZ* (2002, Spring), pp. 5–7.

17 ■ Sándor Karácsony: *Ocsudó magyarság* (Magyars Reviving). Budapest, Exodus, 1942, p. 312.

18 ■ *Idem.*

19 ■ *Idem.*, p. 316.

20 ■ *Idem.*, p. 322.

21 ■ *Idem.*, p. 325.

22 ■ Károly Vörös: "A művelődés és a kulturális élet alakulása Budapesten (1873–1945)" (Education and Cultural Life in Budapest 1873-1945). in: *Tanulmányok Budapest Múltjából* XX. vol. Budapest: BTM, 1974, pp. 97–107.

23 ■ Marshall Bermann: *All That is Solid Melts into Air. The Experience of Modernity.* New York, Simon & Schuster, 1982, p. 151.

24■ For more on Budapest in this connection, see: Gábor Gyáni, *op. cit.* esp. pp. 25–83.

25■ John Lukacs: *Budapest, 1900. A Historical Portrait of a City and Its Culture.* New York & London, Weidenfeld & Nicolson, 1988.

26■ János [John] Lukács: "Történetírás és regényírás: avagy a múlt étvágya és íze" (Historiography and novel-writing, or the Appetite and Taste of the Past). *Történelmi Szemle,* vol. 28, no. 2 (1995) p. 287.

27■ Péter Hanák: *The Garden and the Workshop. Essays on the Cultural History of Vienna and Budapest.* Princeton, N.J., Princeton University Press, 1998.

28■ For the thinking behind this, see: Carl E. Schorske: "The Idea of the City in European Thought: Voltaire to Spengler." In: *Thinking with History. Explorations in the Passage to Modernism.* Princeton, N.J., Princeton University Press, 1998, pp. 37–56.

29■ Gusztáv Thirring: *Budapest székesfőváros a millennium idejében* (Budapest, Royal Capital at the Time of the Millennium). Budapest, Pesti Könyvnyomda Rt, 1898; *Budapest Anno... Picture Photographs in the Studio and Outside.* Budapest, Corvina, 1979.

30■ József Kőrösi: A *budapesti zsúfolt lakások állapota* (The State of Overcrowded Housing in Budapest). Budapest, Fővárosi Statisztikai Hivatal, 1893.

31■ Miklós Szabó: *Az újkonzervativizmus és a jobboldali radikalizmus története (1867–1918)* (The History of Neo-conservatism and Right-wing Radicalism, 1867–1918). Budapest, Új Mandátum Könyvkiadó, 2003.

32■ *Béla Bartók Letters.* Ed. by János Demény. Budapest, Corvina Press, 1971. Letter 12, dated September 8th, 1903, on pp. 28–31.

33■ Endre Ady: "Városos Magyarország" (Urban Hungary) in: *Ady Endre publicisztikai írásai. III. 1908–1918* (The Journalism of Endre Ady, vol. 3. 1908–1918). Budapest, Szépirodalmi Kiadó, 1977. p. 326.

34■ Ferenc Herczeg: *Emlékezései. A Várhegy. A gótikus ház* (Memoirs. Castle Hill. The Gothic House). Budapest, Szépirodalmi Kiadó, 1985, pp. 158–160.

35■ *The Correspondence of Sigmund Freud and Sándor Ferenczi,* Vol. 1, 1905–1914. Eds. E. Brabant, E. Falzecker and P. Giamperi-Deutsch. Cambridge, Mass., Harvard University Press, 1993. Letter dated January 27, 1912.

36■ *Idem,* Letter dated March 22, 1910.

37■ For pages from the "Compendium", see: Júlia Lenkei, ed.: "Tolnay Károly levelezéséből és naplófeljegyzéseiből. III." (From the Correspondence and Diary Entries of Charles de Tolnay. III.) *Holmi,* 2003, no. 3, pp. 370, 373 and 374.

Nicholas T. Parsons

Your City, My City, Their City

Reflections on Budapest Guidebooks

"Like a great many rivers, the Danube has two banks. Here, as in Paris—and many other cities, I believe—each bank is an entirely different world. As the chestnut trees close down for the night for the Buda side, the coffee-houses open up in Pest alive with music."

Antal Szerb: A Martian's Guide to Budapest *(1935)*

"Transylvanian mummy powder, Cherokee Bibles and raw sewage—where else could you hope to see such sights?"

Strapline for the Museums section of TimeOut Budapest Guide *(*1996)

The first Budapest guidebook worthy of the name seems to have been published (in German) in 1733, and there were several more German guides up to 1845, when the first in Hungarian was published. The union of the cities of Buda, Óbuda and Pest in 1873 stimulated the Vienna-based art critic, Ludwig (Lajos) Hevesi, to produce a rather sketchy guide, and in the same year Budapest at last made it into Baedeker. Other foreign series of mainline guides like Hartleben, and eventually John Murray, followed Baedeker's lead. While these early guides exhibit a natural progression from naïve local patriotism to more sophisticated and consumer-oriented analysis, the turbulent 20th century presented guidebook writers with considerably more demanding and constantly shifting challenges. It is with these modern productions that this article is concerned. Competing images of the city, some consciously, some unconsciously, reproduced by the compilers, illustrate in hindsight the framing of an urban identity, but also ideological manipulation and the creation of touristic clichés—one might say, the struggle for the city's soul and the right to project it.

Nicholas T. Parsons

has written a number of guidebooks himself, including one on Budapest. His forthcoming book is a cultural history of the guidebook as a literary genre from Pausanias to the Rough Guide.

Outsiders and insiders

In the century previous to ours, most of the mainstream modern guides covered Hungary in general and Budapest in particular until the advent of Communism. At that point, demand fell away to such an extent that producing a guide was no longer considered a paying proposition for most western publishers of guidebooks. The exception was West Germany, though even then their books mostly appeared in the late Kádár era (e.g. *Prestel's Hungary* of 1985). DuMont deserves a special mention for standing against the general trend and publishing Erika Bollweg's lively *Budapest* in its mainline *Richtig reisen* series as early as 1983, presumably a reflection of the fact that Hungary, with its more relaxed atmosphere, was a holiday destination favoured by both East and West Germans, often indeed the place where separated families could meet up. Almost the only other books for western travellers were American compendia taking in the whole of "Eastern [sic] Europe" (e.g. Fodor), an approach which inevitably tended to have a somewhat homogenising effect on very different countries and cultures. Bollweg herself presents a chatty and essentially nostalgic view of the city, in which some venerable clichés are taken from the propstore and dusted down ("the Paris of the East", "the Pearl of the Danube", "the Queen of the Bridges"). On the other hand, the book is also remarkable for being one of the very few accounts of Budapest by a foreigner who had learned Hungarian, which enables her to penetrate where others do not (e.g. in the vivid and sad cameo of an elderly Rezső Seress playing *Szomorú vasárnap* (Gloomy Sunday) in a dingy Pest nightspot).

Since the fall of Communism, there has predictably been an explosion of guidebooks dealing with Hungary and Budapest, both "stand-alone" publications and volumes in all the main series (*Frommer, Fodor, Blue Guide, Baedeker, DuMont, Rough Guide, Lonely Planet, Eyewitness* and *Insight,* besides Italian, Spanish and French offerings). It would be wearisome to describe the approaches of the various mostly well-known series, some of which (e.g. *Eyewitness*) also exist in various translations. Their markets are usually quite well-defined (backpackers are equipped with *Lonely Planets* or *Rough Guides,* sabbatical professors with *Blue Guides.*) Nowadays, publishers' marketing techniques (or lack of them), as well as the expectations of readers, have sealed the fate of most "stand-alone" guides, only a few of which make it to a second edition—something that makes the success of András Török's *Budapest: A Critical Guide* all the more laudable. Perhaps nothing so idiosyncratic has appeared on the market since the writer Antal Szerb wrote his delightful *Budapesti kalauz Marslakók számára* (A Martian's Guide to Budapest, 1935; new facsimile edition published by Officina Nova in 1991). Based on an essay Szerb originally wrote for *Nyugat,* the booklet was a whimsical and gently ironic love-letter to Budapest, qualities it shares with Török's work half a century later. [It appears in its entirety in this issue.] Both take advantage of the local patriot's privilege of mockery, whereby the *kalauz* describes the Fisherman's Bastion as *"giccs, de gyönyörű..."* ("kitsch, but wonderful"), and

Török remarks that its replica, which can be seen in the confectionery exhibition of the Museum of Catering is "only slightly more sugary than the original".

Most guides are written by outsiders for other outsiders, whatever the publishers' blurbs may claim. Török's book is that rare volume, a guide by an insider from which both insiders and outsiders can profit. On the other hand, as someone once said of Margaret Thatcher, it has the weaknesses of its strengths. Török's milieu is the coffee-house, the baths, the lecture hall, the cosy little eatery with genuine Hungarian cuisine, and all the other haunts of the intellectual urban sophisticate. Óbuda, one of the three municipalities united in 1973 to form Budapest, might just as well not exist; likewise the Roman remains of Aquincum and its surroundings, of which happily there is a long description in a rather good, but poorly distributed little guide that was published in the nineties.[1] Certain areas are of course always unfashionable for guidebooks, while those that are may be precisely what the the "insider" chooses to avoid.

Nevertheless, the sights that Török does choose to cover, always in his gossipy engaging manner, amply make up for what is omitted. My own favourite is his account of the "world-famous lavatory" in the subway of the Batthyány Square metro station, which begins with a quote from Vespasian ("a little money takes away every smell") and ends with a well-aimed dig at "privatisation" since the change. "This book," he writes in the Introduction to the First Edition, "tries to combine three types of guides with the advantages of all three: the Baedeker type, the critical guidebook and the alternative guidebook. Obviously it will not be exhaustive in all three modes."[2] Obviously. But what is actually meant by "critical" and "alternative"? Such qualities are necessarily dependent on a "point of view", which in turn means that the dominance of the authorial personality is crucial, by contrast to the studied impersonality cultivated by the formula guides. The impersonality itself is a rhetorical mode designed to create the impression of an authoritative, objective consensus of unassailable accuracy. Török's book, on the other hand, scarcely mentions a fact without also offering a subjective opinion or a comment. It is certainly no Baedeker and benefits from not being one.

Locally written specialist guides

Into this category fall a number of usually shorter books focusing on minority aspects of Budapest culture or specific topics (architecture, eating out, shopping etc.). *The Jewish Face of Budapest* by Anna Sellyei [n.d.] reflects the revival of interest in Jewish culture per se following the *rendszerváltás* (literally "system-change") in 1989. Such a topic was largely taboo under Communism, a doctrine that claimed to have superseded ethnic particularism. More comprehensive (and not actually intended as a guidebook, though it has elements of such) is *Jewish Budapest: Monuments, Rites, History,* edited by Géza Komoróczy (1999).[3] As the editor notes in his preliminary remarks, the publication of this work, or at least its title, was not uncontroversial, critics claiming that the very idea of a "Jewish

Budapest" in such an assimilated society was "ahistorical". By way of reply, Komoróczy points to the numerous books appearing at this time with titles like *Jewish Rome* (he might have added there was a particularly good guidebook to *Jewish Prague* published almost contemporaneously), as well as the German series entitled *Jüdisches Städtebild* put out by Suhrkamp. "Speaking of Jewish Budapest," he adds, "refers, on the one hand, to a distinct component in the society of Hungary, and on the other, to a Hungarian variant of the universal Jewish culture in the Diaspora."

The treatment of a culture within a culture, though often controversial, is a generally welcome departure from the monolithic approach of the total guidebook. Readers of the latter inevitably tend to experience the city as a succession of items (a Baroque church here, an Art Nouveau bank there) that have been wrenched from their period-determined and cultural context in order to become "sights." This is usually avoided in the excellent series *Our Budapest,* put out with the support of the City Hall, whereby individual architectural, environmental, cultural, social and confessional aspects of Budapest are treated in short guides written by experts, but not by bores. The knowledgeable enthusiast's perspective is quite different from that of the diligent generalist covering the "must see" items of a total guidebook, and of course it is more rewarding. Who would not warm to the late Anna Zádor's account of her beloved Classicism or to János Gerle, one of the most quixotic and selfless promoters of the city's turn of the century architectural heritage, expatiating on his favourite Art Nouveau architects? As far as I know, this is a unique experiment in officially supported, but intellectually independent, guidebook-making.

Our Budapest, modestly priced at not much more than the cost of a foreign newspaper, and published in Hungarian, German and English, has recently been revamped: the latest offerings come with highly attractive illustrations (including archival ones) and a more attractive format and layout. Apart from the fact that their editors share the Hungarian publishers' irritating and pathological aversion to indexes, it is hard to fault them. Although some titles may appear a shade whimsical ("Night Lights," "Shopfronts"), closer inspection reveals that, taken together, the series presents a mosaic of the city that is both specific and documentary, the very reverse of the homogenising clichés beloved of package tour guides. A city that is "real" and "exists in time" (to adopt Barthes' criteria) is necessarily a palimpsest, a blend of order and disorder, a mass of contradictions and parallels. This is what the series reflects by breaking down the image of Budapest into its component parts: there are books on the "Roman Catholic Churches", the "Protestant Churches" and on "Serbs in Pest-Buda"; the title on "Equestrian Statues" is complemented by that on the (Communist) "Statue Park"; essays on "The Danube Promenade" or "Parks and Forests" are counterpointed by those on "Industrial Monuments" or "Urban Transportation". What emerges indirectly from the texts is the periodisation and visual context of Gyula Krúdy's nostalgia, Antal Szerb's whimsy and Frigyes Karinthy's coffee-house culture—but also of Dezső Kosztolányi's bleak realities, where the "Palaces of Money" (as one of the volumes dealing with banks is titled) can be imagined as icons of bourgeois economic triumphalism and as affronts to the slum-dweller. The texts of *Our Budapest* imply the infrastructural and chronological reality within which the city's autobiographical or fictive visions were created.

The mainstream guidebooks, consciously or unconsciously following their historic and literary precedents in the genre, still mostly adhere to the twin track approach of self-education and self-indulgence. On the one hand they must cater to the secular pilgrim's ordained progress around the fleshpots of our materialist culture; on the other, they are obliged to offer an anxious homage to a civilisation interpreted for the casual traveller through largely decontextualised "sights". A "funky" guide like Török's stands much of this on its head, demystifying and deconstructing the icons set up by the tradition of mainstream guidebooks. The visitor using it in conjunction with *Our Budapest* is newly empowered to discover the Budapest he would like to know, not simply the one he is obliged to know. This is a liberation even for the learned and reminds me of the occasion when I was sharing a breakfast in Prague with the late and great Sir Ernst Gombrich. Our desultory coffeehousing was interrupted by the somewhat breathless arrival of a local art historian, who immediately embarked on a lengthy dithyramb concerning an exhibition of the Czech painter Kubista, which was then running and which Gombrich (he said) was on no account to miss. After enduring several minutes of this, the ancient sage raised his Hush Puppy eyes from gloomy contemplation of his half-consumed breakfast and remarked very gently, "Yes; I would like to know about Kubista. But not too much."

By the same token, a major advantage of the volumes in the *Our Budapest* series is their inherent authenticity: the authors are obliged to do no more than inform the readers about various aspects of the city, not to "sell" the usual palette of tourist sights. Dean MacCannell, in an influential work, likens tourist attractions to "the religious symbolism of primitive peoples". He identifies sightseeing as a modern quasi-religious ritual, an insight that recalls the sacral element in the first European guidebook to survive, written by the Greek Pausanias in the second century A.D.[4] MacCannell further draws attention to the way that "the rhetoric of tourism is full of manifestations of the importance of authenticity: this is a *typical* native house, this is the very place the leader fell, ...this is a *real* piece of the *true* Crown of Thorns."[5] Just as Pausanias perambulated Achæa seeking out the shrines whose rituals kept alive the essence of Greek identity under Roman occupation, so it is possible to construct a tour of Budapest and Hungary that weaves together the Magyar *lieux de mémoire* and frames a complex notion of Hungarian identity.

This is in fact what most guidebooks attempt, consciously or unconsciously. The Matthias Church, Heroes Square, the Parliament, the *Szent jobb* (the mummified right hand of King Saint Stephen) and the Hungarian Crown are the most obvious "triggers" for this expression of identity, but equally the collections of the Hungarian National Gallery, the Turkish mausoleum known as the Gül Baba

Türbe, the Calvinist Church, The Mátyás Pince restaurant, the late lamented Café New York, the Freedom Monument and the Statue Park of Socialist Realist works may also act as descant and counterpoint to the main theme. Hungarian identity is not monolithic, but many-stranded, sometimes contradictory, occasionally even schizophrenic. All these elements come together in Janus-faced Budapest, which itself has its own discrete identity or "spirit", though exactly what that is and where it resides is a matter for dispute. Nevertheless, the guidebooks are in continual search of its visual manifestation.

Creating and selling an "authentic" experience

Time is money and the tourist needs the "facts", or at any rate serviceable clichés. Instead of an accumulation of knowledge and understanding (so the accusation runs), modern tourism offers a pre-packaged ersatz experience fabricated out of marketable icons and dubious notions of "heritage". Indeed the somewhat nebulous concept of "tourism" today covers everything from a thoughtful individual's enlightened attempt at self-education to the worst excesses of sexploitation, together with the ecological devastation of desperately poor environments by visitors from phenomenally rich ones.

The guidebook writer is caught somewhere in the middle of these two extremes—at his best, a liberal spirit who opens the eyes of his readers to new cultural perspectives; at his worst, a lowly and spiritless processor of an exploitative industry. Contemporary guidebooks also exhibit tensions between a normative approach to sights that was previously symbolised by the "stars" placed against the most important ones (according to a John Murray or a Karl Baedeker) and a Post-Modern non-prescriptive approach where "anything goes." The extreme version of the latter position is adumbrated in MacCannell's remark that "anything is potentially an attraction. It simply awaits one person to take the trouble to point it out to another as something noteworthy, or worth seeing."[6] In reality, however, guidebook writers (or at least those catering to mass tourism) cannot afford to lose control of the sightseeing agenda, nor to depart significantly from a tacitly agreed list of major sights, not least because that is what their readers expect of them. The result is a compromise, whereby the *Blue Guides* have dropped their star system over the last decade, evidently feeling that such spoon-feeding patronises their readers. On the other hand, a host of mass market guides actually sell themselves on their handy lists of "must see" items, "the Top Ten Sights" of the city, or similar formulas.

One has to accept that the "cult of authenticity and place" is capable of an entire range of interpretation from the dry and scholarly to the wholly subjective and whimsical. For example, András Török, writing in *The Budapest of the Imagination* about the city's "spirit of place", cites an architect and writer who "has said that the spirit of the city of Budapest had, by 1960, retreated into the historic Castle District of Buda." He was right at the time, opines Török, "but the spirit of a city reacts to tourists like the devil to holy water: it flees for dear life. So later in the 1960's it fled ... to Gozsdu udvar (Király utca, 7th District), where one hundred years ago seven out of ten inhabitants were Jewish. However, it soon became apparent that the plans of Hong Kong businessmen to erect a trade centre on this site would force the spirit to flee from here too." (It should be said that the businessmen's claimed intention was to create a new promenade and a new community with its own stylish identity—and thus a new spirit of place.) On this reading, the "spirit of Budapest" is conservative, requiring a combination of gnosis, nostalgia, continuity and stasis to survive. Török depicts it as something whose identity is defined by what it must escape from. "Will it have anywhere left to go?" he asks with the frustrated air of a man in pursuit of the *délibáb*.[7]

The answer is: probably not. Our age is no longer appropriate for the sort of spirit of place celebrated by late Romantic writers like Lawrence Durrell or Henry Miller, if only because the "authentic" tends to become inauthentic as soon as the best-selling guidebook draws attention to it. As far as Hungary is concerned, its individual elements of supposed "authenticity"—from Gypsy music to the cowpokes of the Great Plain—are in danger of suffering the fate of native Americans on reservations; the picturesque and *völkisch* aspects of Central European national cultures are bundled into marketable packages of stereotypes for tourist groups. In the great cities, however, a somewhat different process is at work. Here, a vicarious sophistication takes the place of the naive "folk" experience in the countryside: "insider's guides" have become so ubiquitous that we are all "insiders" now, once we have absorbed the funky prose of our knowing guidebook.

A complicating factor in regard to the issue of authenticity is the increasing onus on the guidebook writer to avoid gratuitous offence to ethnic or religious sensibilities. In a secular age (at least if we are talking of Western Europe) it is something of an irony that texts for public consumption must increasingly handle articles of faith with respect, not because they are necessarily worthy of respect, but because their adherents believe in them so strongly. It is interesting to see how guidebooks now handle a cherished relic like the *Szent jobb*, bearing in mind that for several centuries in the Middle Ages relics and their associated indulgences were actually the staple ingredients of guidebooks for pilgrims. As tourist attractions, relics are the most enduring sights from the 4th century to the present, even if today's scholarly Cicerone with a secular cast of mind finds them something of an embarrassment.

A contemporary guidebook author has some difficulty in hitting exactly the right tone when dealing with the celebrated *Szent jobb*. The safest policy, one that gives offence neither to believers nor patriots, is to report without comment the claims made for it, whereby formulas like "believed to be" *(Blue Guide)*, "said to be" *(Insight Guide)* or *"angeblich"* (allegedly, *Prestel*) come in handy. On the other hand, the TimeOut guide, presumably with its laid-back young readership in mind, goes further than most in open irreverence: "The mummified fist of Szent István lies in a Matthias Church-shaped trinket box [sic]—a bit like Thing from the Addams Family. Ft20 in the slot lights up this gruesome relic."[8] Likewise the

Eyewitness Guide refers to the *Szent Jobb* as "the most bizarre relic in all Hungary". Perhaps as a distraction from the perils of commenting on the genuineness of the relic, the lighting arrangements seem especially to interest the guidebook authors. Frank Strzyżewski (op. cit. p. 254) tells his readers to put 20 forints into the box, for which they will get 118 seconds of illumination. Török (*op. cit.* p. 82) says "you drop a coin in the slot and the relic lights up. If not right away, the guard gives the case a knock, and behold, it does." The text of the *Insight Guide* stands out for being almost the only one to challenge the credentials of the *Szent Jobb* directly, remarking drily that it is "said to be [the right hand] of St Stephen... but probably dates from the 14th or even the 15th century."

Tacitly the guidebooks seem to have adopted the pragmatic line that the genuineness of the relic is not an issue; what counts is that many people have believed in the relic, or do still believe in it. This makes it a tourist "sight" that may be sacral for those who wish and simply a curiosity for the rest. In a broader sense, as MacCannell and others have pointed out, all "sights"—monuments, buildings, panoramas and relics—become part of the tourist ritual and in that sense are sacral. It is this that makes them emblematic of an individual culture, possessing what Walter Benjamin described as an "aura", but which also (according to critics of tourism) divorces them from the "real life" of that culture. It is the way in which they are used, not what they happen to be, that determines their authenticity.

Tourism and the appropiation of sights

Nevertherless, we should perhaps be as cautious about the clichés of anti-tourism as we are about the clichés of tourism itself. Interestingly, denunciation of tourism unites both reactionary writers and those who would consider themselves quite the opposite—Roland Barthes, for instance. His famous critique of the *Guide bleu* maintained that the series "answers in fact none of the questions which a modern traveller can ask himself while crossing a countryside which is real and which exists in time. To select only monuments suppresses at one stroke the reality of the land and that of its people."[9] Ironically this left-wing critique unconsciously echoes the complaints of elitist "travellers" (not "tourists"), who snobbishly object to the degradation of their private experience by mass tourism. As Hans Magnus Enzensberger tartly puts it: "The luxury they appropriate without a second thought is considered sinful when consumed by the mob."[10]

The verb "appropriate" brings us to a central paradox of tourism which guidebooks have to address in their choice and presentation of the sights. A number of scholars have drawn attention to the manner in which tourism "appropriates" its objects, an act of cultural imperialism, but also one that sets up a virtual world parallel to the society whose culture it "appropriates". To quote Enzensberger again, "today the demand for sights exceeds the supply,"[11] with the inevitable result that new sights must be created, either by inventing or by adapting them. The latter method of multiplying sights is as old as tourism itself—one thinks, for example, of the Paris morgue: in the 19th century it was featured as a gruesome spectacle even in the relatively staid *John Murray Handbooks,* although their compilers took care to distance themselves from the morbid and vulgar curiosity that doubtless prompted the visits of most of their readers. ("The painful scene," sniffs *Baedeker,* "attracts many spectators, chiefly of the lower orders.") Alternatively, "invention" of new tourist sights produces often controversial "heritage" displays, typically theme parks. The physical relic does give rise to an "experience", but it is one often detached from the (supposed) historical reality it mimics. Budapest's Statue Park represents a daring attempt to confront this problem with integrity—a "theme park" of ideology, but certainly not a "Disneyland of Communism", notwithstanding the tacky joke items available in the buffet (Molotov Cocktails, etc.), to which the guidebooks inevitably draw attention.

On the other hand, the waxworks display of Budapest history under the Castle Hill *(Budavári Labyrinthus)* helps the case for the prosecution by unrepentantly giving sensation a higher priority than knowledge. Few contemporary guidebook writers are as candid as Frank Strzyzewski in the *Reise Know-How* series: *"das Ganze ist aber eher ein Tourist-Tick",*[12] whereby one notes that his readers are expected to understand that they are not the tourists he has in mind. Of the mainstream guides, *Frommer* is even ruder ("an unimpressive tacky exhibit on the 'legends' of early Hungarian history").[13] Characteristically it is András Török who offers quirky information that is far more interesting than the somewhat dismal labyrinth itself, and indeed taps into the "reality" whose absence is lamented by Barthes. He tells us in his *Budapest: A Critical Guide* that the waxworks were a private initiative that needed a large bank loan, which is why the entrance fee was higher than for state museums; that visitors are at risk of getting lost in the caves (hence the obligatory tours); and that the humidity is 90 per cent, so the clothing of the figures tends to acquire a covering of mould. He also relates that a postman regularly came down to the caves to deliver letters to people who had taken refuge here during World War II.[14] After he had written this, the labyrinth extended its programme: brochures for the panopticon promised inter alia "authentic (sic) copies of the most celebrated cave paintings of Europe", a "night-time individual pathfinding tour for those not afraid of themselves," and a display of the "fate of our civilisation" as interpreted from the fossils of 40 million years. Such resistible attractions all add resonance to Török's dry comment on the labyrinth's main show on Hungarian history, namely that "nothing of more recent but less glorious times is shown."

Ideology and the guidebook

By contrast, one of the most thought-provoking of recently "created" sights is that of the Statue Park located on the Tétényi Plateau near the garden city of Érd. Uniquely in post-Communist countries, the city fathers decided to display Budapest's now undesired Socialist Realist monuments as a way of symbolising democracy's capacity to accept and integrate even an inconvenient past, in contradistinction to totalitarianism's desire to obliterate it. As the project's architect (Ákos Elő d) put it: "This park is about dictatorship, and in the moment when it becomes possible to express, to describe and display that [dictatorship], in the same moment the park becomes something that is about democracy!"[15]

This statement has a subtlety that the guidebook seems to have difficulty in mediating. Despite the Statue Park being one of the most interesting (and delicate) experiments in the representation of a defeated ideology by a victorious one, several guides (*Baedeker,* 2000 Edition, *Reise Know-How,* 1998 Edition, and others) find no space for it. The more politically savvy guides, especially those aimed at younger readers, seem to realise it has significance, but are muddled about what that is ("A truly mind-blowing experience," says *Lonely Planet;* "One of Europe's most unique museums," opines *TimeOut,* albeit ungrammatically.) The recent *Budapest Bradt City Guide* (2004), one of the liveliest of the smaller guidebook series, devotes a whole page to the park, but seems somewhat to misunderstand the genesis of the display: "When Communism fell, this wasn't intended as a memorial; by contrast it was a dumping ground for beacons of the socialist period, an insignificant place 15 km from the centre, a country's act of closure." "Dumping ground" is a phrase that infects *TimeOut*'s description as well, while others make play with "graveyard" associations.

It is left to Bob Dent's excellent *Blue Guide* to give a detailed and measured description of the park's origin and contents. More importantly, he dispassionately draws attention to the controversies aroused by including in the display a memorial to the Hungarian members of the International Brigades who fought against Franco, and one to volunteers who fought against the retreating Germans in 1944–45. This last arouses the ire of *Budapest Week's Insider's Hungary,* which describes the inclusion of this particular monument in the park as "not only cheap, but downright insulting." The remark touches a neuralgic point, but also illustrates the difficulty of producing a text for the ignorant that adequately reflects the complex struggle for a nation's soul expressed in offical iconology. The visitor would need to turn to the *Unser Budapest* guide to the Statue Park, written by Géza Boros and published in 2002 by the City Hall, to gain more understanding of why such monuments landed here—whether or not he would agree with the decision that was made. A clue is also provided by Dent's shrewd highlighting of the fact that most of the park's 40 statues were actually erected "in the 1960's, 1970's and even 1980's, the more liberal years of the Kádár era". (For example, the monument to the Hungarian fighters in the Spanish Civil War was erected only in 1970.)

Apart from outright historical misrepresentation, e.g. of the circumstances surrounding the deaths of Captain Steinmetz and Captain Ostiapenko, whose monuments achieved a certain notoriety despite the best efforts of the Kádár government's ideologues, the Communist regime was also concerned to monopolise the martyrdom of the anti-Nazi / anti-Fascist struggle. A conscious reversal of the attempted Communist takeover of history therefore lies behind some of these controversial decisions regarding the Statue park. You won't fully understand that from the guides that merely talk of "dumping grounds" and "graveyards" and do not appear to have grasped the extent of the Communist instrumentalisation of "martyrdom". The visitor will be most likely to grasp what is going on if he has Boros's guide in his hand, where he can read on page 43 that Agamemnon Makris's monument to the Hungarian fighters in the International Brigade was removed from its site in the city in 1993—and replaced by a monument to the Hungarian victims of the Soviet labour camps. Invaluably Boros also supplies the outline of the discussions that took place regarding several of the individual items placed in the park, as well as illuminating the thinking behind the whole project, in particular its architect's vision for the (as yet unfinished) whole.

The exploitation of "martyrdom" is a political and ideological tool of mass-manipulation that has many contexts ranging from the crucifixion of Christ to the Iraqi or Palestinian suicide bombers of today. The authorities who set up monuments to "heroes" or "martyrs" have naturally wished such works to be taken at face value; traditionally, guidebooks have tended to oblige them (for example, eschewing ironic comment when respectfully listing the ubiquitous Soviet "Liberation Monuments" in Central Europe). The rise and fall of contentious monuments is a recurrent phenomenon in Budapest's turbulent history and includes a few celebrated (or notorious) examples. One thinks of the Neo-Gothic monument to General Hentzi, commander of the Austrian garrison in 1848, which Franz Joseph caused to be erected on Szent György Square in a doomed attempt to memorialise a martyr for the regime. Its location was designed to reinforce the Habsburg claim to legitimacy—and give maximum offence to the Hungarians who saw 1848 as a "lawful revolution". Its removal in 1899, fifty years after Hentzi's death, marked the end of a long ideological struggle and was thus redolent with symbolism, a conscious attempt to replace the image of Hungary as an occupied territory with that of Hungary as an equal partner. (Out of sight, out of mind: no modern guidebook I have seen—not even Török—so much as mentions Hentzi.)

A more topical example is the equestrian statue to General Görgey, a figure who epitomises a major fault line that still runs through Hungarian society and historiography. Condemned as a traitor by Kossuth for sparing his Hungarian troops from further slaughter when he surrendered to a Russian army in 1849, the General was for long a disgraced figure. However, he was rehabilitated with a monument designed by György Vastagh Jnr. and erected (1935) during the Horthy era. Damaged by a shell in the 1945 siege of Buda, this statue was reputedly melted down by the Communists, who probably used its bronze for the 1951 Stalin monument. Official Stalinist historiography backed the Kossuth line on Görgey, who was therefore once again *persona non grata* and accordingly airbrushed out of the national pantheon. After the fall of Communism, a replica of Vastagh's original work was erected (1998) on the bastion opposite the Korona coffee-house on Castle Hill. Clearly some of the most revealing aspects of Hungarian history and society could be dealt with in a discussion of this statue and of the extraordinary fate of its subject, yet you will search the Budapest guidebooks in vain for any mention of the man or his monument. It is only the 1997 volume on *Equestrian Statues* by László Prohászka in the *Our Budapest* series that gives a full account of the Görgey monument with an interesting aesthetic commentary—but these volumes do not appear to be available outside Hungary.

Suppressio veri

The guidebooks to Budapest and Hungary published under Communism were often quite good in a formulaic sort of way, but unsurprisingly they left out anything regarded as "sensitive." Nevertheless, they were certainly a great deal better than the Intourist type of production, hilariously satirised by the British novelist, Malcolm Bradbury, in his burlesque *Why Come to Slaka?* (1986). Written in a perfectly attuned parody of the mangled English of the tourist brochure, this guidebook to the "People's Republic of Slaka" caricatures the tone of such works, complete with their linguistic slips that accidentally reveal the truth. For example, the section on Slaka's "Achievements and Political System", graciously written by the Minister of Culture himself, lauds the "National Assemblage of the Fatherland", which is composed of "representatives of all groups: the committee for State Security, the Counsel of Ministers, our military leaders and even elected representatives. These give their advises to the *Supreme Counsel* ('Politburo'), which decides on executions." The page where this helpful text occurs is illustrated with a characteristically shabby black and white photograph featuring what appears to be a Hungarian *csikós* driving a herd of wild horses towards an electricity pylon. The caption reads: "Slakan shepherd urges into the future his flock."

While this would be grossly overstated as a parody of the Hungarian guides produced for foreigners under the Kádár regime, the shadow of the dictatorship does of course fall across the history section, e.g. of Corvina's 1967 German guide to Budapest. Its final three paragraphs present the period from 1947 up to the date of publication as a triumph of five-year plans, prosperity and progress, all as a result of "the people" taking command in every sphere of life. In the comparatively restrained boasting of this Corvina guide (*"Die strahlenden Kaufläden beleben nicht mehr allein die zentralen Stadtteile, sondern auch die Außenbezirke."*—"Glittering shops enliven not only the town centre, but also the suburbs.") one hears a muted echo of Bradbury's *Why Come to Slaka?,* where we read "The advanced watercress industry is a miracle of aggro-organization. Our nuclear technology is proud of its piles, and our RMBK Kiev-type reactor, with its spectacular emissions, offers the means of electrifying our entire people."

There is a notable exception to the general dearth of British guides to Hungary in the sixties and seventies, namely Alan Ryalls' *Your Guide to Hungary,* published by the small firm of Alvin Redman in 1967. A decade after the Revolution, and boasting a Foreword by the President of the National Office of Tourism, this guidebook generally reflects the image that the Kádár regime sought to project of a land wisely ruled by five-year plans, helpful officials and smiling traffic policemen (the author seems particularly enamoured of the last named). "The Hungarian People's Republic," we are told at the end of the History section, "is carrying on a consistent, firm policy for peace to protect its own achievements and to promote peaceful co-existence and co-operation amongst all people." If this sounds like His Master's Voice speaking, the author volunteers his own assessment as follows: "I have been asked quite seriously by Britons and Americans whether the 'hordes of Soviet troops' stationed in Hungary interfered with my holiday in any way. I can honestly say that throughout my travels in Hungary, I have never come across these 'hordes of Soviet troops', though I have occasionally seen a couple strolling in the streets, apparently in harmony with the Hungarians around them."

Ryalls' book, which is full of useful and practical information but offers minimal coverage of architecture and cultural artefacts, faithfully transmits the Kádár regime's decision to eschew the earlier threatening attitudes of Stalinism ("those who are not with us are against us") in favour of the disarming and reasonable-sounding tone of "those who are not against us are with us." One's impression of the author, derived from the somewhat breathless and occasionally naïve tone of the book, is that of an idealistic English leftie of the caravanning and camp fire variety. There is no reason to doubt the genuineness of his enthusiasm for Hungary and Hungarians. While he seems a little over-eager to toe the official line in places, it would be wrong to dismiss such a thoroughly useful book as mere propaganda. Rather, it conjures exactly the air of "normality" that Kádárism liked to project, and for which, after all, evidence could be adduced if you were ideologically so inclined. By ironically putting the phrase "hordes of Soviet troops" in inverted commas (twice!), the text also manages to imply that their numbers were greatly exaggerated by ill-informed and possibly ill-intentioned persons, without risking any confrontation with the actual figures.

However, most of the mainstream guide publishers steered clear of the Communist countries before 1989, not so much out of ethical concern as out of a correct perception that not many westerners wanted to go to them. This of course generally left the field clear for the bland local guidebooks, produced also in some foreign languages. All credit, therefore, to Eugene Fodor (himself of Hungarian extraction), whose *Fodor's Hungary* (1987—abridged from an earlier edition of *Fodor's Eastern Europe*) contains an excellent and candid *Overview of Contemporary Eastern Europe* by Fodor's compatriot George Schöpflin. The latter's paragraph on mid-eighties Hungary is not only a model of fairness, but dryly punctures the clichés about the "happiest barracks in the Soviet camp", for example, "Hungarians ... do believe they are better off than their neighbours —the regime encourages this belief tacitly as a way of promoting complacency— but they also have to work extremely hard for the privilege. A majority of Hungarians will do two jobs: they have to, to make ends meet."

Telling "the truth" about contemporary Hungary (2005)—or any other free country—is, in a sense, a more complex and difficult business than writing about a country where you know that most official information is designed to mislead. At the most banal level, several guides have struggled to put the incidence of crime into perspective for anxious package tourists, whose ignorance of European geography and relative "civilisation" is legendary. It is not in dispute that crime increased sharply in Budapest in the period after 1989, since the ordinary police were both under-equipped and unprepared for the abuse of new freedoms. Indirectly the tourist might experience this by visiting restaurants in control of the local mafia, or from street muggings. The *Rough Guide* is surely right, however, when it states that, although the city is "no longer utterly safe at night, [it is still] far less risky than any western capital". *TimeOut,* though it adds extensive advice on what and where is safe, is equally forthright in its overall view: "Budapest is one of safest cities you could visit."

This needs saying, especially when you consider that *Fielding's The World's Most Dangerous Places,* an American-published antidote to the verbal slurry of travel brochures, gives prominence to the publisher's homeland (along with Russia and Zaire) in its listing of alarmingly "Criminal Places". The first edition featured one of those informative little boxes beloved of modern guidebook designers: a table of statistics on the New York police. In a single year (we are told) they discharged their weapons 928 times at suspected criminals, although unfortunately 755 of these shots missed the target. 155 shots were fired at dogs, achieving rather more satisfactory results (only 44 misses); the accuracy of suicides was even more impressive.[16] And Americans are nervous of downtown Budapest…?

Another area where candour has broken out is in the treatment of those Turkish baths used as homosexual pick-up joints, formerly a completely taboo subject for guidebook writers. Until very recently, no hint of this appeared, even in the surviving English language paper, *The Budapest Sun.* Its recurrent articles about the baths's architecture, usually written by a rather solemn art historical lady, had long been a source of mirth to the cognoscenti. Eventually a reader wrote in to suggest that a health warning should in future be attached to these aesthetic disquisitions, in view of the fact that the regulars at the two most notorious baths evidently went there "to inspect each others' architecture rather than that of the building..." Several of the guides now allude to the gay and lesbian scene at the Király baths, but pronounce it harmless. ("Not much actually goes on, except for some intensive cruising,"—*Lonely Planet,* "harmless strutting on male days"—*Bradt.*)

While there is greater transparency regarding such individual aspects of the city since the changeover, it could be argued that many guidebooks for visitors to Budapest have been just as uncritically gung-ho about the joys of capitalist transformation as the Communist guides were about their system. For example, the authors of the generally excellent *Visible Cities: Budapest* (Third Edition 2004) evidently do not see it as their brief to discuss the social and economic fall-out from the transition, even though both of them are foreigners long resident in Budapest.[17] The history section of the text ends with a relentlessly upbeat paragraph headed "Into the Future" that paints a picture of a virtually seamless transition from Kádárism to the market economy. Yet, to be fair to the authors, it is probably true that the average tourist, at whom their highly readable tome is aimed, wants an escape from reality, not a confrontation with it, so a guidebook that keeps telling them that the people who are serving them on their holiday are slaves to poverty or exploitative employers is unlikely to sell many copies. Nevertheless, and as one would expect, the more radical guides like *TimeOut* do point out that "the standard of living for many, particularly pensioners, dropped below Communist-era levels," and that the expected post-rendszerváltás boom "turned out, in the hands of the MDF, to be a bust" (1996 edition).

Ethnic generalisations and political slants

The proto-sociology and ethnography of the Enlightenment trickled down into the 19th century guidebooks' generalisations and clichés about national traits or the characteristics of "Venetians", "Parisians" etc. Antal Szerb gives a humorous twist to this tendency at the beginning of *A Martian's Guide,* when he tells the man from Mars: "First and foremost, honoured visitor, I must urge you to ignore news-papers and other egregious pundits who tell you that the citizens of Budapest are like this or that. The people they are talking about are no different from any other commercially oriented folk in need of cash. How should such creatures be of interest to a Martian? Indeed, how important are the inhabitants of any town? In Paris, it is only the people who are dull and unattractive. I shall acquaint you with a city where, in my opinion, the beings that really matter are the houses."

Szerb's playful inverted chauvinism draws attention to a recurrent contradiction in the practice of tourism, usually expressed in the clichéd joke that "Paris would be just fine without the Parisians". Karl Baedeker himself once came very close to saying just that: "I do not think that [a Handbook to France] would find a rewarding market in Germany," he wrote to John Murray III in 1844.[18] "My countrymen... journey little in France, with perhaps the exception of Paris. In any case I do not feel inclined to such an enterprise. I do not like France. I have not been to Paris myself, and do not feel moved to do so."[19] Indeed *Handbooks* to both *Switzerland* (1844) and *Germany and the Austrian Empire* (1842) appeared before Baedeker's western neighbour was grudgingly given its due. Vienna thus featured in the series thirteen years before Paris (1855).

Once Hungary was definitely on the tourist map, the pseudo-ethnographic generalisations were not slow in coming. Romantic images of *barack*-drinking, *paprika*-loving, intensely patriotic Magyar men jostled with those of the mysterious Magyar beauties or feisty Piroskas. The 19th century invented the tourist iconology of "*Puszta, Paprika* and Gypsy Music" (still a chapter heading in *Baedeker's Hungary,* 2000 Edition), while the metropolis developed its own operetta-like mythology of a brilliant coffee-house culture and a Proustian big city nostalgia, whose source lay primarily in the bon-vivant exploits of Gyula Krúdy. At the same time, much was made of the Magyars' inherent melancholy, stemming from centuries of oppression. Melding these two elements produced the "laughter in tears" *(sírva vigad)* that the Hungarians decided was characteristic of themselves. After Trianon, this image was reinforced by that of the "land of three million beggars", of a sombre pessimistic folk mourning past greatness and lost lands.

Nevertheless some guides seemed to remain rooted in the *belle époque:* an example is the untruthfully titled *Was nicht im 'Baedeker' steht: Ungarn und Budapest* (What Baedeker Misses: Hungary and Budapest) by Géza Herczeg, a gossipy tour of the city, heavily orientated to entertainments and published in 1928. In Herczeg's picture of Hungary, her inhabitants still seem to be playing roles in operetta, rather than opera. Perhaps, however, it is significant that this guide appeared in the year before the Wall Street Crash, after which the taste for the *belle époque* seemed increasingly inappropriate, in Hungary as everywhere else. It is all the more surprising, therefore, that a contemporary guidebook should still be retailing what is really an outdated image of Hungary, though of course it makes for good copy. *Budapest: The Bradt City Guide* (2004) begins its section on "People" with an amusing quote from H. Ellen Browning (1897); "When a Hungarian enjoys himself, he will cast himself on to a bench, lean his arms on the table amidst the bottles and glasses, put his his head down on them and sob audibly... But this is only when he is having a good time and thoroughly enjoying himself." The text pursues this idea, remarking that Hungarians notice a cloud from afar "but develop myopia when it comes to its lining." It then moves on to describe the divisions between the "fiercely patriotic" Hungarians, whereby some are "westward facing Europeans" and others are "fervent nationalists who believe in a Greater Hungary." Finally, having rehearsed a few of them, the author admits that the "Hungarian character evades simple stereotypes."

Bradt's lively text brings out one rather interesting contrast between Budapest guidebooks today and those written up to the Second World War, namely that they are now almost all written from a liberal or left-liberal standpoint. Even the *Blue Guide to Hungary* (by the same author who wrote the *Blue Guide to Budapest*) was described by one reviewer as probably the first ever to be written from the left of centre, though in reality this simply means the text is not as obviously and donnishly conservative as others in the series. This trend doubtless has its source in the young(ish) backpacker's flexible, free-wheeling attitudes that are catered to by *Lonely Planet* (which has a reputation for lambasting fading tourist resorts), and in the youthful radicalism of *TimeOut's* parent magazine, the bible of trendy London. Often it would appear that the left-liberal leanings of guidebook authors are entirely unconscious, perhaps because they are derived from their informants in the milieu where they felt most at home during their visit. (Of course exactly the same could have been said of the earlier conservative guidebook writers.)

Bradt's guide, for example, painstakingly charts Fidesz's (the Alliance of Young Democrats) shift to the right, remarking of the party's dispute with Mayor Demszky over various Budapest projects that Fidesz saw the city as "the embodiment of dangerous, non-Magyar forces of cosmopolitanism and liberalism" (p.14).

Lest this should seem unnecessarily opaque, it explains a few pages later that "liberal cosmopolitanism ... usually means 'Jewishness'" (p. 21). It also adds that Fidesz "refused to accept the result" of the 2002 election (p.16). While some, or all, of these remarks would doubtless give offence to Fidesz supporters, they undoubtedly represent widely held views which it is surely legitimate to mention. Yet the authors of the guide, fearless in their deconstruction of the current opposition, are suddenly discreet when it comes to dealing with Fidesz's mortal foes. It describes Prime Minister Péter Meggyessy laconically as "a banker and former finance minister" (p.16) without mentioning that he was, after all, a high official in the Kádár era and finance minister in the last Communist regime. Moreover, he was a self-confessed former informant for the security services.

Arguably an opinionated guidebook is more stimulating than an objective one, and anyway most "objective" ones turn out remarkably like that familiar sort of English person who loudly proclaims that he is "apolitical", but somehow always happens to vote Conservative. But if politics can look after itself, generalisations about national character can be a hostage to fortune, at least when they venture beyond the customary banalities. Even thoroughly well-informed and well-written guidebooks can be overtaken by events that must make the author wish he had phrased an opinion differently. J. A. Cuddon's mostly excellent *Companion Guide to Jugoslavia* (Revised edition 1974, US Edition 1984) gives us a romantic picture of the South Slavs, who, he says, are "intelligent, passionate, individualistic, devoted to principle (to the point of obduracy), impulsive, capable of being very gay and also very sad and reflective. Sometimes they are really sombre. At times they are very devious and impenetrable, at others implacably bloody-minded. They are morally and sexually healthy and they usually have beautiful unfussy manners."[20]

This is hardly a description that accommodates such phenomena as ethnic cleansing and its accompanying atrocities. In fact it unintentionally recalls a hilarious passage concerning the Slav soul in George Mikes's humorous classic, *How To Be An Alien.*[21] And as for the assertion that the Southern Slavs are "morally and sexually healthy," one does wonder about the sort of field research the author must have undertaken to establish this. Such excesses are the romantic conservative's obverse of the left-liberal's "political correctness"—both end up by patronising the "side" they imagine they are supporting. The then general editor of the *Companion Guides* insisted that his authors should eschew (a vaguely defined) "politics" altogether. If one were to obey this direction literally in writing a contemporary guide to Budapest, one could not even mention, for example, the highly controversial Terror Háza (House of Terror). Unsurprisingly, Bradt's *Budapest* does give it substantial coverage, this time with rather more emphasis on the Communist terror than on its Horthyist and Arrow Cross precedents. It refrains from comment on the political disputes that have swirled around the museum, merely observing that the display is "more about atmosphere than artefacts". To get at least a hint of the controversies you must turn again to Török, who highlights the fact that some of the same left-wing activists who were tortured here by the Communists had already suffered in the same cells when they were run by the "secret police of the ultra-right-wing inter-war regime". "Some people," he adds darkly, "would like to turn it into a museum of Stalinism."

Epilogue: looking to the future

Much of publishing consists of updating and repackaging existing information, putting new wine into old bottles—and this is more true of guidebooks than of most other genres. Great ingenuity is expended on devising new, hopefully bestselling formulas to present what has been presented a hundred times before, but to do so more effectively and spectacularly. The *Eyewitness* series (British, with translations into major European languages) most obviously moved the genre forward in terms of production values, with its excessively semiotic approach to communicating information and its sophisticated axonometric plans of major buildings. Virtually no latitude is allowed to its writers, whose contributions often read like soundbites to accompany the illustrations. It is a highly successful formula, but can seem somewhat sterile for the reader who still likes an evocative text with occasional idiosyncracy.

Despite the huge marketing clout of big series like *Eyewitness, Insight, Rough Guide, TimeOut* and *Lonely Planet,* most of which have deservedly capitalised on their ability to update at ever shorter intervals and to provide slickly comprehensive "Practical Information", it is encouraging that smaller guides still enter the market. *Budapest: The Bradt City Guide* and Török's *Budapest: A Critical Guide* are refreshing for their irreverence and occasional recklessness. Bradt's description of Petőfi as "the eloquent James Dean of his age" is pretty rich when you actually think of comparing Dean's career with Petőfi's, but at least it shakes up the solemn and stale images of "Hungary's national poet" to be found in most guides. Török meanwhile has achieved the near impossible feat of producing a bestselling stand-alone guide from his homebase, a book that has not been taken hostage by a series "formula". Another recent entry into the market is the more conventional *Budapest* from the Buda-based publisher of the *Visible Cities* titles. This takes a leaf out of the *Eyewitness* series with superb illustrations and plans. Its strength lies in the clarity of the text and the well-designed integration of the illustrations with the same.

Mark Twain famously remarked that rumours of his death had been "greatly exaggerated", and the same could be said of the rumours concerning the death of the book. In fact, production of books has increased at the same time as alternatives to it have multiplied. This suggests that the experience of reading a book is neither one that can be satisfactorily replicated, nor one that at least a sizeable minority wish to give up. For this reason, it is hard to believe that the guidebook has had its day, despite the ever more ubiquitous DVD, and soon (no doubt) satellite guided tours by means of text messages on mobile phones. I doubt that any of these inventions will supplant or enhance the experience of curling up in an egghead Pest cafè with Török's *Critical Guide.* ❧

NOTES

1 ■ Pp. 41–70 of *Pannonia Hungaria Antiqua* edited by Gyula Hajnóczi, Tamás Mezős, Mihály Nagy, Zsolt Visy; in the *Itinerarium Hungaricum* series, Archaeolingua Foundation, Budapest, 1998. The poor availability of this excellent series is a sad reflection on the continuing deviousness of Hungarian book distribution.

1 ■ Török, op cit. p. 6.

3 ■ First published in Hungarian as *A zsidó Budapest* in 1995 (Városháza és MTA Judaisztikai Kutatócsoport, Budapest). The English translation appeared as part of the "Atlantic Studies on Society in Change" (No. 101) and was published by the CEU Press in 1999.

4 ■ Dean MacCannell: *The Tourist: A New Theory of the Leisure Class* (New York, 1976, p. 2).

5 ■ MacCannell, op cit. p. 14.

6 ■ MacCannell, op cit. Second Edition (N.Y. 1999) p. 192.

7 ■ In *Matrix,* Number 34, Summer 1991, pp. 64–65. This whole issue of the periodical is devoted to *The Budapest of the Imagination,* edited by Linda Leith and published by *Matrix:* c.p. 100, St-Anne-de-Bellevue, Quebec, Canada. Interestingly, in the third revised edition of his insider's guide to Budapest published seven years later, Török makes no such claims about the Gozsdu Court (*Budapest: A Critical Guide*—Corvina, Budapest, 1998, pp. 169–70), merely observing that "the area was at the heart of the former Jewish quarter, and has preserved something of its atmosphere". The controversy is brought up to date in a fascinating article by György Szegő in *The Hungarian Quarterly* (Volume 45, No. 176, Winter 2004—"The Gozsdu Court in the Jewish Triangle," pp. 108–116).

8 ■ *Time Out Budapest Guide,* Various authors, Penguin Books, London, 1996. p. 46.

9 ■ Roland Barthes: *"The Blue Guide"* in *Mythologies*. Translated by Annette Lavers (New York, 1972) pp. 75—76.

10■ Hans Magnus Enzensberger: *A Theory of Tourism* in *New German Critique,* No. 68, Special Issue on Literature (Spring-Summer, 1996) p. 121.

11■ Enzensberger, op cit. pp. 127 and 130.

12■ Frank Strzyżewski: *Budapest und Umgebung,* Reise Know-How Verlag Peter Rump GmbH, Bielefeld / Brackwede. Second updated edition 1998, p.223.

13■ *Frommer's Budapest and the Best of Hungary,* Second Edition; New York, 1998, p. 139.

14■ András Török: *Budapest: A Critical Guide,* Third Edition, 1998. Corvina, Budapest. p. 63.

15■ Quoted in: Géza Boros: *Statuenpark*—"Unser Budapest" guide series, Budapest 2002, p. 6.

16■ Quoted in Jeremy Harding: "Best Remain Seated." *London Review of Books.* Volume 20. No.1. 1st of January, 1998. pp. 29–30. In fairness it should be said that the situation in New York dramatically improved subsequently as a result of Mayor Giuliani getting a grip on the city.

17■ Annabel Barber and Emma Roper-Evans.

18■ John Murray III was the founder—and first author—of the famous British rivals to *Baedeker, John Murray's Handbooks.*

19■ Quoted in Roger Clark: "Threading the Maze: Nineteenth Century Guides for British Travellers in Paris" in: Michael Sheringham (Ed.): *Parisian Fields* (London, 1996). p. 21. It is an irony that both Karl Baedeker himself and one of his descendants died while at work on a *Baedeker Handbook to Paris.* The revenge of *civilisation* over *Kultur*?

20■ J. A. Cuddon: *The Companion Guide to Jugoslavia.* Prentice Hall edition, Englewood Cliffs N.J. 1984. p. 120.

21■ George Mikes: *How To Be An Alien* (London, 1946, Thirty-second Impression, 1965) p. 24.

Edit Sasvári

Pauer 2005

Retrospective at the Műcsarnok

The year 2005 has brought Gyula Pauer major accolades. He was honoured with the Kossuth Prize for over four decades of achievement; his memorial to the victims of the Holocaust was installed by the Danube;[1] over the summer, Hungary's premier art exhibition hall, Budapest's Műcsarnok, mounted a retrospective on his oeuvre.[2] For Pauer, once one of the 'wild men' of the Hungarian neo-avantgarde, this serial acclaim must have a special connotation: it can all be put down to the tardy recognition of a body of work that, being utterly incompatible with the dogmas laid down by the official tsars of artistic taste in the Kádár era, often had to contend with very tight constraints.

Pauer's early work unfolded in an indoctrinated society on whose members the authorities imposed the very terms of the language in which they were expected to express themselves. Some successful artists sincerely believed in the communicative potential of that Kádár-era discourse and even managed to stir the sensibilities of people who had a hard time with it. That its narrow-mindedness was designed precisely to cover up the truth, many came to realise only after they had escaped the penumbra of its authority. Pauer never belonged to that category, being one of a number of artists who all along maintained a presence outside officially approved channels. He was an active participant in the underground manifestations of the Sixties, a member of the Szürenon group,[3] and

1 ■ *Shoes on the Danube Bank*. Holocaust Memorial, 2005.

2 ■ Budapest, 15 July–28 August 2005. Curated by János Rauschenberger, Marianna Mayer and Péter Orosz under the direction of Tamás Oszvald; texts provided by Annamária Szőke.

3 ■ The label—a word-play on *'sur et non'*—implied both an avowal of surrealism and its repudiation and was used for a series of exhibitions in the late 1960s and early 70s by artists like Attila Csáji, Sándor Csutoros and Gábor Karátson.

Edit Sasvári
is deputy director of the Kiscell Museum of the History Museum of the City of Budapest. She has published widely on contemporary art.

Can Togay & Gellért Pauer

Gyula Pauer: Shoes on the Danube Bank, *2005. A memorial to citizens of Budapest shot and thrown into the Danube at the time of the Arrow Cross terror. Budapest, Széchenyi Quai.*

in the early Seventies, one of the young avant-garde Budapest artists who showed their works in György Galántai's Balatonboglár Chapel gallery before it was shut down in 1973. That same year, Pauer found himself at the receiving end of a three-year prison sentence (subsequently commuted to a fine) on a trumped-up charge of defying lawful authority; then, in the latter half of the decade, his monumental work *Protest-Sign Forest,* installed in the village of Nagyatád, was officially ordered to be destroyed. Other artists, too, were to find out over the succeeding years how this type of conceptual art had become a serious irritant to the authorities and how the artists, under pressure, lost their footing in both human and moral terms. Some chose to leave the country, with a few returning only after the 1989–90 change in régime, while others were obliged to look for fresh pastures to work in. Pauer plumped for the theatre, but he never deserted the visual arts; indeed, those years in the theatre did the visual artist in him a power of good. He was an innovative and highly regarded designer of scenery and costumes for many celebrated productions by directors such as

Gábor Zsámbéki, Tamás Ascher and Péter Gothár at the Csiky Gergely Theatre in Kaposvár in its heyday, before going on to work for the National Theatre and its then affiliated workshop, the Katona József Theatre in Budapest.

The cornerstone of Pauer's artistic philosophy is the 'pseudo' principle, which can be interpreted as a metaphor for the make-believe realm of Kádárism, for its social manipulation of the individual. He 'unmasked' Kádárism's bogus discourse well before this language had lost all credibility. Pauer's sharp insights assumed artistic and sculptural form. The prototype for this was the 'pseudo-cube'—a crumpled surface applied to a minimal form by means of a photographic process and an airbrush. The surface—a central element in subsequent works—was itself truly the 'mask'.

Coming as it did a decade and a half after Hungary's democratic transformation, this Műcsarnok exhibition threw light in a paradigmic way on the problems and issues involved in presenting art of the recent past. Pauer and his former creative partner, the exhibition's curator János Rauschenberger, can lay claim to the concept of the show. They came up with an original exhibition strategy for the occasion and marshalled a vast body of material to implement this. They did not aim to put together a strictly biographical or historical cross-section of the oeuvre, but opted for illustrating its chief themes instead. Rather than setting the emphasis on faithfully recapturing the atmosphere of the times, the old works were firmly drawn into the present day. Indicators of this were not only the professional way in which sponsorship and back-room support staff were used, or even the series of ancillary events that were mounted on a 'Pseudo Stage' erected in the exhibition space, which featured big names from the other arts.[4] A major consideration in Pauer's conception was the harnessing of a multimedia approach to recycle a group of his old works from a viewpoint that was centred on the present.

Any retrospective exhibition imposes a burden on artist, art historian and curator alike. Its debatable character as a platform stems primarily from the fact that it is bound to touch on and take on board a host of issues that are complex in their own right, such as how to treat the past and present, to say nothing of how to interpret and handle the oeuvre itself as a totality of consecutive

4 ■ Films: Béla Tarr: *Autumn Almanach, Satantango, Damnation, Werckmeister Harmonies;* Róbert Koltai: *We Never Die;* György Fehér: *Twilight, Passion;* Géza Bereményi: *El Dorado, Bridgeman, The Disciples;* Dr. Putyi Horváth, Sebestyén Kodolányi & Péter Forgács: *Pauer Sixty, A Pseudo-Pauer Evening in the Kossuth Club;* András Jeles: *Dream-Brigade;* Frigyes Gödrös: *Glamour;* Frigyes Gödrös & Péter Kornai: *Da Capo;* Can Togay: *The Summer Guest;* János Rózsa: *The Witches' Sabbath;* Frigyes Gödrös & Dr. Putyi Horváth: *Private Horváth & His Friend, Friar Wolfram;* Péter Gothár: *Time;* Sándor Sőth: *The Great Mail Robbery.* Performances such as *The Evening is Pseudo in the Name of Eat Art* with Gyula Pauer as Didactor, Endre Paksi Lehel as Typewriter, Béla Tarr and others; János Vető's interesting performance of *Snippets, or Smarmed-Down. PSEUDO Music for 12 voices* with accompaniment; performance of György Kemény's *Eat or...;* performance of Géza Bereményi's *Mihály Víg and the Balaton;* performance by András Szirtes; a performance of *Bada Dada.* Poetry readings and talks with film and theatre directors, talks with artists, book launches, etc.

components. Perhaps the most noticeable element in the Műcsarnok exhibition was Pauer's distinctive take on the past, his ties to the older works of his oeuvre. He came up with a witty alternative to how an artist can handle his own history, or how he can absolutise the still living, active and continuously creative indi-vidual at the 'expense' of his historicalness. In terms of its results, the broadly overarching concept of presenting an oeuvre that filled all of that huge exhibition space was effective and thought-provoking, with the accent falling on its 'organisation'. A key factor was Pauer and Rauschenberger's approach as theatre and film-world professionals. Ultimately, the main thrust was the visual impact of the various topics, thereby providing a unifying frame that was meaningful.

The organising principle was simple enough: one room—one subject, so to say. The series of rooms to the left of the entrance hall displayed Pauer's early works (the pre-Pseudo creations), including in a 'Subjective Room' pieces commemorating close relatives who have died (his son Henrik and a twin brother who was an amateur painter), then the Eighties work *Beauty Samples.* The output of paintings and the conceptual compositions of the Seventies were located in the central body of the gallery, with the two transverse rooms accommodating facing statues of *The Shroud of Turin* and the veiled *Maya.* These esoterically allusive statues were both separated by a huge tulle curtain from the gallery's apse, in the middle of which stood the Pseudo Theatre and on whose back wall was projected an enormous photograph of that major Pauer work, the aforementioned radically political *Protest-Sign Forest.* The line of rooms on the right-hand side, proceeding back towards the entrance, were occupied by the mysterious compositions making up the set of the so-called 'Puci Péry' landscapes[5] and in what was dubbed the 'Finale' Room, the designs for theatre and film.

On passing an 'Exit' sign visitors would most likely have assumed that the exhibition was over, but they were in for a surprise. Pauer's parting joke was that this did not lead to the way out but into a darkened empty room in a dim corner of which a horrendously snoring attendant was "guarding" nothing at all. *The Silence of the Attendant* it was entitled.

Returning to the rooms on the left, the subjects that were lined up there were the embodiments of some sort of a memento. Thus, the very first room covered the beginnings, with Pauer taking a somewhat nostalgic, yet detached look at his young self, the tyro sculptor, making what was little more than a token selection from the works that he produced during the Sixties. The private remembrances, the illusory and the restrained (but not restraining) emotions culminated in the room that invoked Pauer's son and brother. *Beauty Samples* in the next room evoked yet another aspect of memory. This set of plaster casts, which was pro-

5 ■ Behind the name is the creative trio of Pauer, Rauschenberger & Zoltán Érmezei, who died at a young age.

Big Pseudocube (Pseudo I.), aluminium, foil, enamel 24,5 x 24.5 x 29.5 cm, Janus Pannonius Museum, Pécs.

Marx–Lenin, 1971, Műcsarnok retrospective (detail).

István Dabi

Maya, 1978, oak, silk, paint, height 210 cm. Hungarian National Gallery, Budapest.

Ferenc Gelencsér

Protest-Sign Forest (fragment), 1978, wood, sawdust, paint, 60 x 60 cm.
King Stephen Museum, Székesfehérvár.

Gyula Pauer

Protest-Sign Forest, 1978, 131 boards with inscriptions, on wooden poles (destroyed).

István Dabi

The "*Beauty Sample*" room, Műcsarnok retrospective (detail).

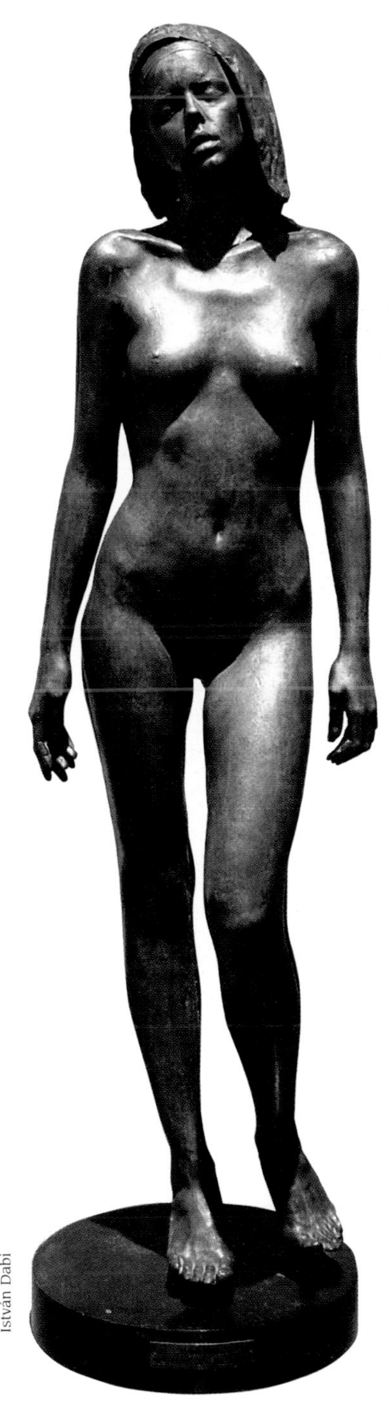

István Dabi

Miss Hungary, 1985, bronze, 197 cm. Hungarian National Gallery, Budapest.

Finale, photo-sculptures for Sławomir Mrożek's play *Vatzlav,* 1995,
Műcsarnok retrospective (detail).

The Silence of the Attendant, environment, 1998 (reconstruction), Műcsarnok retrospective (detail).

The Statue of the Shroud of Turin, 1991,
Műcsarnok retrospective (detail).

duced to mark the staging of Hungary's first beauty contest, faithfully preserves the imprints of the individual lineaments and bodies of the contestants. The huge, baroque composition that was constructed from the casts completely abolishes that individuality, however, because it no longer raises a 'monument' to the memory of the individual but to an event that ultimately ended in tragedy with the death of the beauty queen herself.[6] Also displayed in the room was an enormous photograph of the composition produced from the casts of the women's bodies.[7] That presumably had the purpose of serving as a record or illustration of *Beauty Samples* and, more particularly, of the large group of statues, but it became more than that. The photograph, with the forest of bodies, engaged the imagination more than the actual composition, even though the latter dominated the room as one of the central works. The casts, strong as the impact each one had separately, nevertheless gave the impression of being present merely as illustrations that belonged to the group of statues. The photograph and the casts were subordinated to the larger composition, despite the fact that they were recording the original (or, in the case of the photograph, an earlier) state of affairs. It was not quite clear whether Pauer was prompted by design or arbitrary choice to 'downgrade' the original works to illustrations.

The re-processing of certain other conceptual works—their enlargement, that is—confirmed, on the other hand, that Pauer intended the original object to play a sort of walk-on role in relation to the 'copy'. That applied particularly to some pieces, including photographs and textual compositions that emerged in the Seventies. Faithfully reflecting the era, their small size and tentative execution constituted a readily identifiable artistic endeavour that, at the time, reached only a rather limited circle. These were not strident works; they demanded a decidedly intimate relation with the viewer, who was forced to bend over close to inspect them. For this setting, though, they were just too small, and a means should have been found that packed enough communicative punch to win over a modern public. To put it another way, Pauer here did not document a particular moment in history or his artistic development, but rather sought an answer to the serious question of what his former works would be able to say to the public with the aid of modern technology and means of communication. The results 'vindicated' the earlier achievements, and it was truly this discrepancy that made the exhibition interesting and original.

Except at the start of his career, Pauer always employed photography as a resource in his sculptural work. It thus seemed self-evident that, true to his medium, he should resort to the simple 'dodge' of enlarging his earlier works. The 'replicas', visually distinct from the originals placed alongside them, redressed the 'unspectacular' nature of the originals. Hence, while the visitor could scan an enlargement of the composition *Marx–Lenin,* the picture-postcard-sized

6 ■ The winner of the contest, Csilla Molnár, a student from Siófok, took her own life not long afterwards.

7 ■ The work is currently the property of the local gallery in Körmend.

original sat on a modest nearby pedestal. The historical/art-historical authenticity meant to evoke a faithful period atmosphere was almost totally obscured by the new. This manoeuver enabled Pauer to transfer some of his works to 'up-to-date' media and thereby re-create them for this occasion. This went mainly for the conceptual works of the Seventies and those monumental compositions that were destined to perish physically, thanks partly to the nature of their medium, partly to the cultural politics of their day, and not least to the vicissitudes of time.

During the Seventies, Pauer was also working as a set and costume designer for the theatre and for films. This undoubtedly encouraged his feel for monumentality. It was during his years at Kaposvár that his first large-scale work for a public space—in the nearby village of Nagyatád—saw the light of day in 1978. *Protest-Sign Forest* was bulldozed by the local authority, but not before it had made the point, beyond dispute, that the idea for the most original large-scale work of that period had been realised, as it happened, in a location far from the capital city. *The Tree's Memorial,* created in the same place and at the same time, met a fate similar to that of *Villany Pseudo-Relief* seven years before: being outdoor works, both were destroyed by the ravages wrought by the weather. These two latter works were reconstructed on their original scale for this exhibition, along with a room-sized pseudo-environment that was created for the 'Pseudo Exhibition' of 1970 but dismantled at the end of it.[8] There may have been diverse reasons why the above-listed works did not survive the passage of time, but one thing they had in common was their insistence on the grand scale at a time when monumentality was a privilege reserved for sculptors who tamely complied with the régime.

The photograph that Pauer took at the time to document *Protest-Sign Forest* was projected in giant scale onto a back wall at a central spot in the exhibition. The sole surviving fragment of the composition, which was originally made up of 131 pieces, was the caption and was here placed on a small pedestal at the centre of the same apsidal room.[9] Nevertheless, it struck this viewer how much greater an impact the projected photograph had than that fragment, which even in its fragmentary state bore moving testimony to the doomed fate and afterlife of *Protest-Sign Forest.* One reason why the photograph seemed visually more powerful was its summoning up in the viewer a sensuality linked to remembering. Through enlargement, the image is expanded but also slightly

8 ■ *Pseudo-Wainscotting,* 1970, one-off environment for the József Attila House of Culture, Budapest, 3–5 October 1970 (see: *Catalogue of Gyula Pauer's Works,* compiled and edited by Annamária Szőke, Műcsarnok, Budapest).

9 ■ This was a caption bearing the following text: *"The sculptures I would like / to make, Clothilde, are such that if they were to be excavated, / they would eventually incubate by themselves / without needing a bulldozer or archaeology. / From underground, they would shape and form / the space in their environs by their own laws."* The work is currently the property of the King Stephen Museum, Székesfehérvár.

diluted, a process similar to the way in which memory operates by enlarging the stuff of the past and simultaneously toning it down. That sense of frailty and crushed greyness endowed the work with a poetic quality; the nebulous aesthetics of enlargement conjured up the intellectual memorial of an achievement that has disappeared.

The exhibition's main point of interest lay in Pauer's eschewal of a historicising approach to his life's work in favour of starting from the viewpoint of how to install his material creatively in the huge space at his disposal. That attitude made it possible to treat each and every element of the works—to implement, augment, reduce, transform and re-create them at will. This is a basic model that corresponds to the somewhat simplistic and commonplace notion that what matters in conceptual art is a work's idea, because the execution will always be 'lame'. The authentic vehicle of those conceptual works, a still very much alive and mentally active Gyula Pauer, is able to adapt them to the occasion. In this case, Pauer, together with his team, had the entire gallery space of one of the largest old-style exhibition halls in Central Europe at their disposal, one which in its time has overwhelmed more than one artist. They treated it as if it were a mere doll's house. ❧

Tamás Szőnyei

Palaces on the Danube

The area south of Pest's tourist-favoured centre is hardly recognisable from its appearance of some ten years ago. At that time, south of streamlined Elizabeth Bridge, the Art Nouveau splendour of Freedom Bridge and south of the less impressive Petőfi Bridge, a high-potential but unexploited area stretched along the riverbank, for many decades a virtual no-man's-land. While opposite on the Buda side the modern blocks of the University of Technology slowly began to emerge, the Pest side remained a dreary symbol of post-Socialist neglect. Between the tracks of the suburban railway running along the river and those of the number 2 tram line further off-shore, there rested an empty stretch of land—or rather, not completely empty. It was overgrown with grass and weeds; here and there a couple of decrepit storage buildings or an occasional truck appeared. The site was fenced in, indicating an owner, but what activity all that suggested was hardly in keeping with such a prime location.

Back in the early 1990s, it all seemed very different. Budapest was proposed as a host for a World Fair, and the abandoned tract in Pest, along with a tract on the facing Buda bank, were earmarked as the Fair's site. Such a project, however, would have required heavy investment. The then new (1994) Socialist–Free Democrat coalition government opposed it, arguing that an Expo would be too costly and the money for it was needed elsewhere. This, in turn, was seen on the Right as a sign of defeatism—a lack of faith in the strength of the nation. Hence, the area remained as it was, neglected and unused. In the meantime, Budapest witnessed a frenzy of property development. In vacant inner city lots—remnants of the Second World War—office buildings were erected in quick succession; further out there emerged gigantic shopping malls and landscaped residential

---

Tamás Szőnyei
is a journalist on the weekly Magyar Narancs. *His most recent book is* Nyilván tartottak. Titkos szolgák a magyar rock körül *1960–1990 (Kept on File: The Secret Service and the Hungarian Rock Scene,1960–1990),* 2005.

housing developments conceived with the expected wealth of the rising well-to-do upper middle classes in mind. Ancient factory buildings were demolished, their surroundings were cleared and transformed, and some of the city's slums were rehabilitated. It was easy to see that this unexploited site in Pest, some 55,000 square meters, could not escape this flurry of development.

Still, it was not the logic of property-development which decided its fate. The skirmishes of Hungarian politics after the changeover in 1989–90 had their effect. The antecedents of this story are to be found in the depths of the "socialist" decades.

In Blaha Lujza Square, one of the busiest traffic junctions in Budapest, there is a memorial stone marking the spot where the National Theatre once stood. The building was knocked down in 1965; the sad moment when the demolition charges went off was captured on film by a news crew. The official reason was that it was an obstacle to the construction of a new underground train line; up to this day, many still believe that by destroying an institution symbolising Hungarian national culture, Communist hardliners aimed to assert their hegemony and break the spirit of the Hungarian nation. The theatre company moved "temporarily" into a different building, hastily renamed the National Theatre despite its lacklustre appearance. From that time on, there was constant and prominent discussion on the need for a National Theatre worthy of the name. One of the most popular and influential members of the company, the actress Hilda Gobbi, even launched a public subscription for its sake. The author of this article still has a 3-forint (!) memorial stamp that features one of the award-winning designs submitted in the competition for the new building.

For decades nothing happened. Finally, in 1996, the Socialist–Free Democrat coalition government decided that it would build the new National Theatre on one of the most expensive sites, in downtown Erzsébet (pre-transition Engels) Square, then functioning as a bus terminal and a parking lot. In the spring of 1997, Ferenc Bán's design, judged unanimously to be the best, won the competition. That winter, also through a competition, the director of the future company was appointed—András Bálint, a widely acclaimed actor and director who had for years been running one of the best and most successful theatre companies in Budapest. The foundation stone of the theatre was laid in March 1998, and the building was scheduled to open in October 2000. Then, in 1998, the right-of-centre opposition won the general elections. Normally, it would seem, such a political change would have no effect on this type of project. But, in Hungary, events do not necessarily follow a "normal" course. In the autumn of 1998, the coalition government headed by Viktor Orbán halted construction. The rationale for the halt was that the project was too expensive, and that the National Theatre could be built elsewhere, at less cost, with a different design. However, the real message was unmistakable: other changes were coming. The appointed director resigned, and the abruptly ended project was tussled over by the cabinet and the

Budapest municipal government, which remained in the hands of the Socialists and the Free Democrats. The pit dug in Erzsébet Square as the groundwork of the theatre became a memento of senseless and petty political revenge. Its fate was debated for years. In the end, an underground garage was constructed below the square, while a public park was developed at ground level. No proper function has been found for the underground structure, and now a rock club called appropriately Gödör (The Pit) (which has become popular in the meantime) operates out of it. As for the location of the National Theatre, the Orbán cabinet picked the section of the Pest Danube bank, between the Petőfi Bridge and the Lágymányos Bridge (built in 1998), which had stood vacant since the aborted World Fair project. The earlier Horn government had invited international bids for the site; the deal with the winner, a property-developing consortium operating mainly on Canadian capital, was signed by the Orbán government. The Hungarian state kept the site selected for the National Theatre, while the Trigránit consortium swept up the rest with Sándor Demján at its head—a highly efficient company manager before the changeover, who emerged as one of the most successful businessmen following it. Trigránit projected the building of a conference centre, hotels and residential buildings on the property and, via another company it owned, it also took part in the construction of the new National Theatre.

The circumstances of the construction of the new National Theatre were nothing short of scandalous. In the end, it was not the competition winner György Vadász who designed the new theatre, but Mária Siklós, who was then expelled from the Chamber of Architects, because she undertook the job as a commission without entering the competition. The inaugural performance in March 2002 turned into a campaign event (It was an election year.), and the building was metaphorically demolished by architectural critics. In 2004, the State Audit Office formally reported the predictable, that construction was by no means cheaper but, on the contrary, substantially more expensive than the cost of the original design in Erzsébet Square would have been. The difference ran to several billion forints—estimates varied according to whether the funds spent on restoring the Erzsébet Square pit (which were public funds, too) were to be included.

The depressing effect of the harsh, eclectic exterior of the new National Theatre was only made worse by the theatre's placement at the corner of the otherwise empty construction site. There was nowhere to go for a stroll, a drink or a meal before or after a performance—you could only jump into your car or onto the first tram and leave as soon as possible. The situation is still the same today; the only improvement is the new Palace of Arts which stands between the theatre and the Lágymányos Bridge, almost leaning on the bridge. The two new residential buildings erected on the opposite end of the site and the office building being constructed in its centre, however, hold out hope that eventually there will be people using this vacant space. In the developers' conception, the heart of the area will be a conference centre which, if it functions properly, will fill the planned hotel rooms with big-spending visitors from abroad all the year round. Conference tourists will be ready and willing to spend on culture, especially if it is close at hand. The cultural "shop" appealing to them would be represented not so much by a Hungarian-speaking National Theatre, but by the Palace of Arts, featuring a concert hall and a theatre auditorium as well as a museum.

The Palace of Arts, the largest cultural investment project for many decades, was initiated by the Orbán government, as they sensed the isolation of the National Theatre. At first a new museum of modern Hungarian art seemed an option, but the lack of specifics regarding a plan threw art historians into an uproar. The competition for the architectural design was announced all the same and was won at the end of 2000 by Zoboki, Demeter & Associates. The short gestation period for planning was repeatedly interrupted by disputes amongst architects and changes in design. To mention but one, there had been a great deal of hesitation over what to put into the new museum—an issue to which art historians were far from indifferent.

The final outcome, a multifunctional art palace, was inaugurated in March 2005. (Public testing of the concert hall had begun in January.) No new museum was established; instead, the Budapest branch of the Ludwig Collection was moved from its previous home in the Royal Palace on Castle Hill. Conditions in the Palace may not have been ideal, but one can claim that at least the collection was located in a tourist epicenter, easily accessible and also attracting the casual visitor. Against the loss of the Castle Hill location, the shows can now be viewed in the kind of high-standard space familiar to anyone visiting the best museums in Europe. The permanent exhibition of this contemporary art museum, with a display area of 4500 square meters, is located on the second and third floors, the latter receiving natural light. Temporary shows are mounted on the first floor. (Exhibitions were devoted, for instance, to Gerhard Richter, an outstanding contemporary German artist, and to Tibor Hajas, an early representative of the Hungarian Neo-avant-garde, who died young in 1980.)

For a considerable period, it seemed that the House of Traditions, an institution documenting and preserving folk art, was going to move its headquarters to the Palace of Arts. Ultimately, however, it did not seize the opportunity and stayed where it was. Filling the space it would have occupied is the National Dance Theatre, which at the same time keeps its old venue on Castle Hill. The 450-seat auditorium in the Palace of Arts, named the Festival Theatre, is theirs and hosts theatre productions and concerts as well.

The third new inhabitant of the Palace of Arts is the National Philharmonic Orchestra, headed by pianist and conductor Zoltán Kocsis. The Orchestra spent long decades in a nondescript modern building demolished this year and has at last been able to move into a satisfactory home. The 1900-seat National Concert Hall offered a star-studded Spring 2005 season with the Budapest Festival Orchestra conducted by Iván Fischer, the London Symphony Orchestra conducted by John Eliot Gardiner, the Chicago Symphony Orchestra with Pierre Boulez and Daniel Barenboim, the Milano Giuseppe Verdi Orchestra with Riccardo Chailly and, at the other end of the spectrum, Cesaria Evora, Madredeus and Ibrahim Ferrer (who sang in Budapest only weeks before his death).

The acoustic design of the hall is the work of Russell Johnson. A concert hall of this size and quality had been sorely missing from the music life of Budapest. The concert hall housed by the beautiful Art Nouveau building of the Academy of Music has fine acoustics, but is too small for the performance of works requiring a large orchestra. The far larger stage and auditorium of the Budapest Congress Centre, everyone agrees, fails to meet the acoustic requirements that were expected of it. Significantly, Zoltán Kocsis, not a man known for hiding his critical opinions or mincing his words, wrote of the National Concert Hall in terms of the highest praise. The world-class names picked from the programme of the Palace of Arts (www.mupa.hu) indicate the high quality of what is being offered, worthy of a modern, cosmopolitan metropolis.

Acknowledgement of this high quality is as widespread as has been the controversy surrounding the genesis of the facilities. There was a cost over-run. For this reason, the Orbán government took on a cash payment guarantee worth 52 billion forints for the construction of what was at the time still being called a "Cultural Block". On the strength of that guarantee, the job was undertaken by the same consortium which owned the property—the consortium that had also built the National Theatre. This was the public-private partnership that brought the term PPP into Hungarian public discourse—with private capital providing credit for the construction, and the government paying the money back over a ten-year period. No matter how indignantly the opposition objected that this financial setup would leave a huge sum of money, unprecedented where cultural investments were concerned, totally uncovered by the binding public procurement process, the work got under way. In the end, the Socialist–Liberal coalition which won the 2002 elections preferred to go ahead with the project. The still empty pit in Erzsébet Square was an all too vivid reminder. They didn't want to fall into a "pit" of their own making.

Thus, between August 2002 and January 2005, the Palace of Arts was completed, covering an external area of no less than two thousand square meters and an inner space of sixty-four thousand square meters. It has been functioning smoothly ever since. The building itself, with its neon lights glimmering in the evening, received more disapproval than praise from critics. Nevertheless, the criticism was far less scathing than in the case of the National Theatre. Even if it is not looked on with favour by everyone, it is beyond doubt that Budapest at last has a high-standard, state-of-the-art cultural facility, impressive in dimensions and housing a museum of contemporary art and an absolutely magnificent concert hall. For a long time to come it will be our companion, and for a long time we will also be paying for it. The post-2002 government amended the contract signed by its predecessors. The terms for repaying the debt have been extended from ten to thirty years, and the original 52 billion forint figure pledged for the building of the palace, which cost 31 billion, is now almost 100 billion. ❧

Tamás Torma

Three in One

The National Concert Hall, the Festival Theatre and the Ludwig Museum

The Palace of Arts is Central Europe's most modern arts centre. It is the dimensions of Gábor Zoboki's block-shaped building that first catch the eye. Geometrically cool and elegant, it provides a favourable background to the over-decorated National Theatre into which it seems to blend when viewed from a distance. Immense and intimate spaces are at times combined with remarkable originality. The Palace of Arts can take on as many aspects as it has sides. While the National Theatre unfortunately does not "look on to" anything in particular and appears to harmonise neither with the river nor with the city, the Palace of Arts clearly coheres with the Danube embankments at the Lágymányos Bridge. The Palace's porticoed-pillared museum entrance opens out towards the space defined by the two buildings and the Danube. The "house within a house" concept owes its origins to the constant modifications of plan and function; these eventually crystallised into uniting the Concert Hall, the Ludwig Museum and the Festival Theatre under one common roof within the glassed-in lobby, while retaining their separateness within the connecting cube.

Arcadom, one of the best firms in the business, unfortunately chose to put together the glass sheeting that constitutes the "vesture" of the building out of two and three metre sheets. Technical problems with bridging can be the only explanation for the concrete column that so conspicuously mars the magnificent panorama of the river from the wing of the building closest to the Danube: there is a slight bend in the river here and it is as if we were looking back at the famous view of the bridges and Gellért Hill from an island. The many glass rasters and the mottled flagstones take something away from what should be a grandiose experience. A building of this size, catering to several functions, has several faces. For me, the least successful is the side facing the freeway of the bridge, it most resembles a hospital, or the service side of a shopping mall.

Tamás Torma

is an editor of arts programmes at Hungarian Public Television.

The trendy strip-lights have been criticised but I for one like them as they glitter cheerfully on the floodlit building.

Inside, the functions that were finally decided on (and at the last minute) have been assembled in a dynamic and venturesome way. Zoboki built from within, making the inner functions his starting point: the concert hall, ultimately the most important unit, projects spectacularly and roundly into the rectangular world of horizontal and perpendicular lines. The lobby may sometimes give off the strange feeling that we have arrived at a logistics centre, but that is quickly dispelled by the attendants, who politely usher us onwards.

The heart of the building is the National Concert Hall, 25 metres high, 25 metres wide and 52 metres long, home to the National Philharmonic Orchestra led by Zoltán Kocsis, the National Choir and the Music Library. It has a total capacity of 1900, including room for 136 standing. A further 160 seats can be placed on the stage if needed. The shoebox shape defines the architectural character of the building, yet it does not seem angular: gentle inclines and elevations lend the hall variety: what it most resembles is the nave of a church. The orchestral podium is located in the open auditorium, mobile units allow for the stage to be arranged in three different sizes, as well as an orchestra pit if required. An acoustic canopy extends over the auditorium, with mobile wings which can be raised, lowered or revolved as required. Similarly mobile are the 84 adjustable reverberation chambers on three levels, which embrace the Hall. Their plaster reliefs—painted in the "trecento" colours of blue, brown, green, red and yellow—are the work of the sculptor György Jovánovics, who worked with Russel Johnson to create a design that would not interfere with the acoustics. The hall can also be curtained off for piano recitals or pop concerts, when minimum reverberation is best. The close care and attention to acoustics have definitely paid off and the Hall comes to life when the music starts to play.

The Hall's focal point is the organ designed by Hungary's Pécs Organ-building Ltd. with Germany's Mühleisen. The massive instrument has 7,700 pipes and cost 600 million forints (almost EUR 2.5 million). Between the organ and the stage, the orchestra seating clearly displays the full range of pale green velvet covers on the cherry wood seats. The flooring of the Hall is in Chilean cherry wood, the balcony fronts and ceilings in Canadian maple. State-of-the-art audio-visual systems for film projection and special lighting effects are also provided; CD and DVD recordings can be made in the adjacent studios.

The National Concert Hall. Auditorium

The Ludwig Museum has the prime location in the building, overlooking the Danube. Its entrance area includes an Internet café with a view all the way up the river to Gellért Hill and the Liberty Statue. The museum's design, which incorporates the work of specialised consultants such as the Austro-Hungarian CCC+Bogner and the UK's Lord Consulting, includes illuminating ceilings, which are a type of suspended ceiling that diffuses light across the whole surface. The first floor houses temporary exhibitions, the second and third floors permanent exhibitions from the museum's own collection. Adjoining the exhibition areas are projection rooms and interactive demonstration rooms equipped with computers, as well as a reference library.

The eastern third of the building holds the Festival Theatre with a capacity of 450. Its technical facilities make it suitable for classical and jazz concerts, dance productions and fashion shows as well as drama productions. The Festival Theatre comes complete with a stage floor that includes a rotating disc, within which are two smaller circles that can be raised or lowered. It is also equipped with a complete flying system for set flats and an adjustable stage opening that can be widened or narrowed, depending on the specific needs of the production. ❧

PERSONAL

George Szirtes

Foreign Laughter

My first translation commissions for novels came from Hungary and it was my task to interest some British or American publisher. So it was with two twentieth century classics: Dezső Kosztolányi's *Édes Anna* (*Anna Édes,* Quartet/New Directions) and with Gyula Krúdy's book of Sindbad stories, *The Adventures of Sindbad* (CEU Press). I had read the first in Hungarian and had heard so much about the second that I read some quarter of it and straightaway got started. It seemed to work well not having read it all. There was a lovely sense of freshness and discovery in the process. I was the first-time reader in two languages simultaneously. I enjoyed this. So when Quartet asked me to undertake the translation of László Krasznahorkai's *Az ellenállás melankóliája (The Melancholy of Resistance),* I did not read it through: I merely glanced at it. My internal translation engine, I thought, seemed to work best through a kind of visual scratch and sniff method. What I actually saw looked daunting, the tone hard to gauge. There were no paragraphs at all. The sentences were very long, too, the first occupying half a page— the others often longer, rarely shorter. First, I had to work out the structure of that first sentence, seeking out the main verb, feeling the structure grow like some strange plant that seemed to be putting out several branches in various directions all at once, the sense constantly and wilfully qualifying itself to build its picture of chaos, a chaos that would prove to be the keynote of the book. What seemed obvious was that the working through of that chaos would involve some dark irony whose precise degree of darkness was not yet established.

George Szirtes

won the foremost British poetry award, the T.S. Eliot Prize, in 2005 for his book of poems Reel. *An outstanding translator of Hungarian fiction and poetry, he has also translated the novels of László Krasznahorkai, Sándor Márai and fiction by Krúdy and Kosztolányi. His version of Krasznahorkai's* Háború és Háború *(War and War) will be published by New Directions (USA) in 2006. He is currently working on a group of novels by Sándor Márai including* A Zendülők *(The Rebels) for Knopf/Viking–Penguin.*

How seriously dark was the dark? I knew that a number of Hungarian readers regarded Krasznahorkai's work as unremittingly bleak and depressing. But there seemed to me to be a kind of comedy at play in it too, a dark comedy whose visual compulsiveness produced its own poetry.

Pace was everything in the book. The pace was inevitable, the vision tragic-comic, but the comedy, if comedy it was, changed in the course of its passage through English. It was as if English did not tolerate such monumental slow-paced Hungarian bleaknesses without a certain irony, an irony that was implicit in the Hungarian text but grew a little in translation. The very notion of order was different. Order in Hungary means something rather Prussian or Soviet. There is a national fear of disorder, a fear the book itself shared while distancing itself from the Prussian and semi-fascist form. Notions of order and its opposite are clearly conditioned by historical experience and the weight of that experience varies across societies and nations. The two central characters, or heroes of the book, seek some sort of higher order that is so far out of reach that the very attempt seems grotesque and absurd. As with the notion of order, so with the grotesque and absurd elements of the book: given these historical differences, grotesque and absurd tend to mean something slightly different in English.

There is a marvellous scene where Valuska is in a pub at closing time, persuading the drunken customers to act out a full eclipse of the sun. Béla Tarr's film version of the book, *The Werckmeister Harmonies,* employs only part of the story and begins with this scene, concentrating on the desolate symbolism of the spinning and lurching figures: the text moves more slowly and deliberately, leaving space for comedy.

> Some of them, those stuck in the corner nearest the fireplace, or under the coat rack, or laid out across the bar, were suddenly smitten with the desire for a sleep so deep that not even a volley of cannon would have woken them, nor could he [Valuska] look for comprehension among those who, having lost the thread of conversation about the monster due to arrive on the morrow, remained standing but glassy-eyed, though, doubtless, having regard to the miserable innkeeper staring pointedly at his watch, both the horizontal and vertical among them would have agreed upon a common course of action, even if only one of their company, a purple-faced baker's apprentice, was capable of giving it form by means of a sharp nod of the head. Naturally Valuska construed the onset of silence as an undoubted sign of the attention about to be concentrated on him, and, with the help of the house-painter (a fellow covered from head to foot in lime) who had invited his intervention in the first place, employed what remained of his sense of direction to clear a space in the middle of the smoky bar: they pushed back the two chest-high drink stands that were anyhow in the way, and when the forceful if vain entreaties of his erstwhile assistant ("G'won, squeeze up to th' wall a bit, willya!") met the unsteady resistance of those clinging vaguely to their glasses and showing a few faint signs of life, they were constrained to employ the same methods on them so that after the minor kerfuffle caused by all that shuffling and involuntary backward stepping, a space did in fact open, and Valuska, hungry by now for the limelight, stepped into it, and picked for his immediate audience those

standing closest to him, who happened to be a lanky driver with a pronounced squint, and a great lump of a warehouseman, referred to for now simply as 'Sergei'.

The miracle of the book seemed to lie as much in the self-deflating grandiosity of those long periods as in the obsessive comprehensiveness of its vision. Human beings, it tells us, are hapless in the face of stars and railway timetables, comically inept when confronted with the forces of decomposition and ruin. Their suffering is terrible, unremitting yet absurd. It is as if Pa Ubu had entered Kafka's Castle. It is Joyce with the lights off, Flann O'Brien locked into a cellar. It may be difficult to decide at what point the alarm turns to tears of laughter or grief, but then that is the point.

The book rolled slowly over and through me for four years. Four years was two and a half years longer than it ought to have been. They were four years of frustration, exhaustion and cursing. I cursed the endless sentences, the lack of landmarks that paragraphs might have offered, the wilful manner and cosmic ambition, as it sometimes seemed to me, of the author. At times the book seemed to be a particularly terrifying example of the kind of elephantiasis that afflicts Hungarian fiction. The smaller the country, I thought to myself, the greater the ambition. You make up for the lack of language territory by offering sheer verbiage as compensation. Hungary was a small country locked into its isolated language, its authors' prolific energy and ironic earnestness battered down the doors to the outside world.

The Melancholy of Resistance was published by Quartet at the beginning of 1999. Asked by Quartet as to who might provide a suitable endorsement of the book, I gave the name of W.G. Sebald, then forgot to mention it to the man himself; so when he rang up one day to announce he had received the typescript I was full of apologies. He was not at all put out: he thought it was a marvellous book and was pleased to provide a few sentences. From Quartet in the UK it passed to New Directions in the USA. New Directions had already published one of my earlier translations (*Anna Édes* by Dezső Kosztolányi, also first published by Quartet). New Directions then passed the book to Susan Sontag, who had herself written at length in praise of W.G. Sebald. She too was more than prepared to provide enthusiastic copy for the book jacket. Though little reviewed in England (that is to say it was reviewed briefly, albeit with intense pleasure) Sontag and Sebald had put their imprimatura on *The Melancholy of Resistance* and the critical response in America was henceforth considerably more powerful. The worst that reviewers could find to say about *Melancholy* was that marvellous as the book was it took a little determination to discover that fact. Personally I was enormously relieved to be rid of it, but I found it grew in my head as time went by. It lost its wilfulness, its association with headaches, exhaustion and fury and, while I needed considerable persuasion to set out on a second book by Krasznahorkai, I was certain that the pain would be worth it.

It was after I had begun that second book, *War and War,* that Knopf approached me to translate Sándor Márai's novel about Casanova, *Vendégjáték Bolzanóban,* literally, 'Guest Performance in Bolzano'. Márai was, by then, far better known than Krasznahorkai, almost entirely on the basis of the worldwide success of his novel *A gyertyák csonkig égnek* literally, 'The Candles Burn down to Stumps', but published in English as *Embers.* Márai was born in 1900 and had been a leading writer in Hungary between the wars. a virtuoso among virtuosos, but had gone into exile in 1948 when the Communists took over, and his books subsequently disappeared off the lists of Hungarian publishers. He was *persona non grata,* a self-confessed bourgeois poet, playwright and novelist—not of the political Right but not sufficiently of the Left for the new Soviet regime to allow him to continue. He left, taking with him his magnificent diaries, and never returned to Hungary, dying by suicide in San Diego in 1989, the very year of the Communist collapse. His beloved wife was dead, their adopted son was dead—everyone around him had died, and he lived in obscurity. Could he have waited a year or so he would have seen the tide turn hugely in his favour. He became an icon in his homeland, a touchstone, a banner, though it is not always clear who should be waving that banner or what it might stand for.

Márai never wrote in English—Hungarian was his loved instrument. His tragic, exemplary story is twisted at the core by exile. The discovery and publication of *Embers* is part of that twisted story. This, briefly, is how it is said to have gone. Roberto Calasso, the writer, publisher and translator, was browsing through a French publisher's backlist when he found an obscure book by an obscure Hungarian writer, took away a copy, read it, loved it, and decided it was a forgotten masterpiece. He called a meeting of other major world publishers so that he could sing its virtues, and published it himself in Italian, with enormous success. Other languages followed. The English text, published by Knopf in 2001, however elegantly rendered by the head of Knopf, Carol Brown Janeway, was translated from the German version, with Janeway referring to the earlier French edition for support. Janeway read no Hungarian and, as a publisher, trusted none of the available translators. That was what she said in public at any rate. Some suspected she was none too sure of who they were. Possibly there was no time to find one: the iron needed striking while it was hot. There were fierce letters to *The New York Times* and rumbles of protests in correspondence, but by then the book was a triumph in English. Tragic and exemplary, Márai's Hungarian remained in the shadows. The luminous triumph was the translation of a translation. The faithfulness of the English version continues to be debated, but the name of Sándor Márai, however mispronounced, was pronounced frequently and with great respect.

Janeway came to me by way of Barbara Epler of New Directions, who had, I think, been praising my translation of Krasznahorkai to her. I assume Janeway went on to read *The Melancholy of Resistance* and became convinced I was the man for Márai too. In any case I had a message to meet her at Claridges Hotel in London on 10 January 2003. The night before, I gave a reading near Liverpool.

The reading was fine, if a little desolate, but nowhere near as desolate as the boarding house the organizers had found for me. Everything was broken: there was flex hanging off the walls the door could not be locked the handle having been smashed, there was no hot water the toilet bowl leaked, there was a plastic incontinence sheet on the bed and a group of skinheads were partying down the hall. I slept very little, couldn't shower or shave, and arrived at Claridges the next day dirty, with rings under my eyes. Janeway was crisp, tidy and businesslike. She quizzed me on Márai and other Hungarian novelists, checked me out, then asked if I could undertake the next Márai novel as quickly as possible. Having started a second Krasznahorkai for New Directions, it meant translating two novels at the same time. I had no idea then that I would also be ushered into co-editing with Miklós Vajda a 400-page anthology of Hungarian writing the next year for the year-long festival of Hungarian culture in Britain. Eighteen months of productive madness was about to begin. I left bedraggled, with a sympathetic smile from the doorman. It had been a strange, exhausting, hallucinatory experience made all the stranger by the fact that Janeway's glasses were distinctly askew during the entire course of our meeting.

The success of *Embers* still puzzles me: the degree of its success, that is. Márai was declared a rediscovered master of world literature on a par with... well, anyone you care to think of. It couldn't all be put down to marketing, nostalgia and romance, though these played their part. But nostalgia for what? Written in 1944, the book is set in the long dead ashes of the Austro-Hungarian empire: aristocrats, hunting lodges, cadet schools, wet nurses, concepts of honour. Few readers would have known the world to which they were subscribing in their imaginations, nor would they have wanted it back. They wouldn't vote for it. The nostalgia, I imagined, was less to do with location than with pace, reassurance and stable values, any stable values at all. There was, I felt, a touch of Ruritania and Anthony Hope about *Embers.* But, that couldn't be all.

Nor is it. *Embers* is a fascinating mixture of luxuriant writing, razor-sharp psychological perception, theatrical tricks and one vast dramatic twist. Underlying the mechanics of plot and prose there is an intense, unremitting curiosity about the way the conditions of life play themselves out in action and imagination. In the book it is about 1940. A long-retired army officer is waiting for his old friend to reappear after decades of absence. The officer's childhood wet-nurse is still with him, otherwise he is alone. The wife whom he had loved is dead. He tells the nurse, now the maidservant, that he has many vital questions to ask the returning friend, but when the friend appears it is the officer himself who does all the talking. That is the twist. The major theme is the honour code: the conflict between friendship and desire. Most of the book could be a stage play (and has been a stage play in France and Germany, shortly to be so in England, too, adapted by Christopher Hampton), with some flashbacks and one vivid piece of action set years earlier in the nearby forest.

The key to the book is not so much the plot, the theatrical tricks, the characters or the location: it is the way in which luxuriant writing is put at the service of a fiercely enquiring philosophical mind that peels away layer after layer of human consciousness until, however perfectly uniformed the body, the soul is revealed to be naked and lost in forests of its own.

The key to *Embers* is also the key to the Bolzano book, published in 2004 in Britain as *Conversations in Bolzano,* in the USA as *Casanova in Bolzano.* It is the story of an episode in the life of Casanova following his escape from the Leads prison in Venice. Casanova arrives in Bolzano accompanied by Balbi, a defrocked friar, and hangs about in a hotel doing this or that until the arrival of the Duke of Parma, who has married Francesca, the only woman Casanova has ever really been in love with, and for whose hand he fought a losing duel with the much older Duke. It is only once the Duke appears, well over halfway through the book, that the story leaps into action, and eventually a confrontation with Francesca takes place, concluding the book. I was aware that some people regarded the book as a masterpiece ("Ah, Bolzano," a Hungarian friend had said. "My favourite!") but I wasn't always sure this was the case from the point of view of shape or narrative device, but, maybe because I am a poet rather than a novelist, the book held me throughout, much in the manner of an ancient mariner, through sheer eye and voice. As with *Embers,* the mechanics and occasional melodramatics of the plot are mostly a magnificent excuse for the exercise of Márai's desperate curiosity. The book is an enquiry conducted chiefly through monologues.

I first thought of these monologues as the equivalent of the musical cadenza, but a speaker at a Márai conference put it better: he referred to them as arias. A cadenza is a kind of decorative excess in which the souls of the instrument and instrumentalist are driven through a gap in the music. To compare them to cadenzas would suggest that Márai's monologues, however rich and dense, were interruptions to the fabric of the narrative. That is not the case. Márai's monologues are structural: in fact they are the structure. In an aria the very spirit of the character becomes a central element in the architecture of the work. In Márai's novel it does not matter very much whether the monologue-aria is spoken by the character or the narrator, for the essence of the work is the single project of enquiry. It is Márai we hear all the way through: that luxuriant, ironic and yearning prose is his way of framing the question the book is there to answer. In *Embers* the question is primarily about an ethos of friendship and loyalty under the stress of desire. In *Bolzano* it is about spirit and gender: what, asks the book, is physical and psychological desire, and what has that desire to do with love and sacrifice?

The first and most vital task of the translator of Márai is to render that luxuriant but sharp prose into English, to take stock of whatever flourishes (cadenzas within arias?) are lodged in the text and to find a natural place for them. These flourishes might include stock characters: there is a Jewish money lender and a gay barber in Bolzano, not to mention a range of landlords and Shakespearian mechanicals—the sidekick corrupt priest, market women, traders, policemen, a queue of lovesick gullible types—who comprise the operetta element of the book. Although the book has received handsome reviews in both Britain and the US, no one has dealt with the operetta aspect of the structure. Translating those operetta characters, the moneylender and the barber, is a tricky and delicate task. One step too far and they become hostile parodies; one step too short and they become timid wastes of space.

The hairdresser is "a pretty, rosy-cheeked, blond, blue-eyed boy", who speaks in "a singing slightly effeminate voice, lisping slightly", and Mensch, the money lender, is pure stage Jew:

> A short, scrawny creature, he was sitting in a dressing-gown at a long narrow table, the fingernails of his delicate, yellow hands grown sharp and curling, so that he appeared to grasp things the way a bird of prey seizes its quarry, his lank grey locks hanging over his brow, and his small, bright, intelligent eyes, eyes that glowed from beneath deep wrinkled lids, staring with burning curiosity at the stranger. He greeted Giacomo in his dirty kaftan, lisping and bowing stiffly without rising from his chair, mixing French, Italian and German words in his speech but mumbling all the while, as if not quite taking him seriously but thinking of something else, not really listening to his guest. "Ah!" he said, once the visitor had given his name, and raised his eyebrows until they met the dirty locks above them. He blinked rapidly, like a monkey hunting for fleas. "Have these old ears heard correctly? Is an invalid to trust these poor ears of his?" He spoke of himself in the third person, with a kind of tender intimacy, as if he were his own nephew. "Mensch is a very old man," he lisped ingratiatingly. "No-one visits him nowadays, old and poor as he is, " he mumbled. "But here is a stranger come to call," he concluded and fell silent.

It might seem unlikely that the author could transcend these apparently lazy stereotypes, but Shakespeare does, and so does the operatic analogy best suited to Márai, which is not operetta in the end, but something grander and more substantial. Out of second-hand frills and period lace comes a furious masked discourse in which Casanova's one true female love, dressed as a man for the masked-ball, pays a visit to the great seducer, who is dressed as a woman for the same occasion. The longest and most intense of the arias belongs to Francesca, who first proffers then discards layer after layer of the courtesies of female love to leave a mass of fierce and brutal energy, at which point the theatrical costume she is wearing makes a spectacular and complex counterpoint to the visionary content of her speech. This aria has been prepared for by some equally powerful short ones, particularly that of her aged but still dangerous husband, the Duke of Parma. It is in these passages that Márai may be seen as occupying the same literary culture as Krasznahorkai: paragraphs disappear, sentences stretch and there is only the semi-comic darkness where the ignorant armies of human logic and human passion clash by night.

A small excerpt from the Duke of Parma's monologue might help suggest this. The old man has arrived at Casanova's room and produces a secret letter, from his young wife to Casanova, that he has intercepted. He has already threatened to kill Casanova if he ever encountered him again as a rival. The letter, written by the barely literate young woman, consists of only four words that he proceeds to analyse with a dangerously ironic close reading.

> "This, then, is the letter," he declared with a peculiar satisfaction, dropping the parchment together with his spectacles into his lap and leaning back in the chair. "What do you think of the style? I am absolutely bowled over by it. Whatever Francesca does is done perfectly: that's how she is, she can do no other. I am bowled over by the letter, and I hope it has had an equally powerful impact on you, that it has shaken you to the core and made its mark on your soul and character the way all true literature marks a complete human being. After years of reading it is only now, this afternoon, when I first read Francesca's letter, that I truly realized the absolute power of words. Like emperors, popes and everyone else, I discovered in them a power sharper and more ruthless than swords or spears. And now, more than anything, I want your opinion, a writer's opinion, of the style, of the expressive talent of this beginner. I should tell you that I felt the same on a second reading—and now, having glanced over Francesca's letter for a third time, my opinion has not changed at all. The style is perfect! Please excuse my shortcomings as a critic, do not dismiss the enthusiasm of a mere family member from your lofty professional height—but I know you will admit that this is not the work of a dilettante. There are four words and one initial only, but consider the conditions that forced these four words onto paper, consider that their author, even a year ago, had no acquaintance with the written word: turn the order of the words over in your mind, see how each follows the other, like links in a chain hammered out on a blacksmith's anvil. Talent must be self-generating. Francesca has not read the works of either Dante or Virgil, she has no concept of subject or predicate, and yet, all by herself, without even thinking about it, she has discovered the essentials of a correct, graceful style. Surely it is impossible to express oneself more concisely, more precisely, than this letter. Shall we analyse it? *'I must see you.'* In the first place I admire the concentrated power of the utterance. This line, which might be carved in stone, contains no superfluous element. Note the prominence of the verb...

...and so on for three remorseless pages, expending a ridiculous amount of energy on each of the four vital words. This furious, precise, but pointless exegesis is produced by excess: excess of love, jealousy and fear of death. The Duke's remorselessness is what Casanova is up against. It is such remorselessness that makes Márai such an unlikely great writer for a contemporary audience. The conventions he works with are subjected to far greater strain than they are intended for and are thus transformed in his hands into something mould-breaking and strikingly relevant to contemporary concerns about love, desire and possession.

The translator enters the book like a member of the chorus. He joins his voice to one of the available melody lines and does what is necessary to amplify the music of the mind that moves through the language or score before him. Just how ironic is the Duke of Parma? How serious? How accurate? How perceptive? How dangerous? And if he is all these things to various degrees, how do these degrees and proportions play themselves out in English? Where are the echoes? There is no difficulty in finding echoes for the gay barber or the Jewish moneylender. These are tunes everyone knows by heart. A Jonathan Miller production of *Rigoletto* had the Duke singing the famous air *La donna e mobile,* by dropping a coin into a jukebox. A cheap sentiment to a cheap tune, said the production. The production subsumed and ironised the cheapness. Miller had bigger fish to fry.

And so does Márai. As with Krasznahorkai, the devil is in the detail, but the detail is part of a project. The Duke of Parma is a little like the Grand Inquisitor in Dostoevsky, a little like Iago in Shakespeare, but mostly he is a voice in Márai's head. When Francesca enters, she is even greater than the Duke. After she finishes her monologue, the reader feels there can be little left to say on the subject of passion. Her voice, like the Duke's, arises out of Márai's desire to know and understand. That desire employs luxuriant prose but it understands the effect of such prose and knows how deep it cuts. A book that appears to be fribbling and grandstanding by turns explodes at the end. The jukebox blows up. Casanova, who is himself something of a jukebox, but is also portrayed as a force of nature, is doomed to carry the tunes of that jukebox through the rest of his life.

There is in Hungarian writing, whether poetry or prose, a precarious balance between weight and lightness, between despair and laughter. It is compressed and landlocked, occasionally a touch provincial in imagination, booby-trapped with anxieties and melancholy. It is forever pressing against the limits set on it by circumstances. That is why its laughter always seems a little edgy and nervous. Ears trained exclusively on the twentieth-century English novel may occasionally find it hard to place this laughter and this music, but it is available in English too, though the translator has to stretch a little, taking a step forward in one place, a step back in another. The translator has to adapt the text because language is not to be bullied into submission. The translator has to be a little sly, a little brazen and a little rakish, all the while observing the customs of the place. Both Krasznahorkai and Márai expand the horizons of English-language writing: they are semi-familiar strangers who know their manners but are visibly straining at the leashes. It is the translator's job to see that they pass through border controls, take their places in the street and become part of the landscape. ❧

Miklós Györffy

The Short-Sighted Seer

György Spiró: *Fogság* (Captivity). Budapest, Magvető, 2005, 770 pp.

György Spiró has been publishing plays, novels, short stories and essays since 1974. Despite frequent political hiccups before 1989, he has won himself a recognised position in contemporary Hungarian literature, and yet, though his plays are very successful and in regular production, he has not found his real place in the current literary canon. For the past twenty years, this canon has been dominated by post-modern text literature, and Spiró has not been a follower of the post-modern. Nor has he belonged to any of the literary camps here. Canon-setting literary criticism will, how-ever, find it hard to ignore *Fogság* (Captivity), a monumental historical adventure story, his fifth historical novel.

Captivity presents a challenge to the critic in that it contains none of the ingredients that suit the post-modern palate. Indeed, for quite some time the historical novel had seemed to have run its course—until recently that is, when quite a few post-modernist authors, such as László Márton, László Darvasi, János Háy, Zsolt Láng, have produced what appeared to be historical novels. These works, however, all happen to subscribe to the idea that history has come to an end; that all historical narratives which project a trend, or set a direction, or postulate that something of substance may have existed amid the current of events, are abstract castles-in-the-air. In fact, you cannot even say this with any certainty, since there is no reliable evidence that any event can be deemed as historical. The towering originality of *Captivity* arises less from its plausibility than from the bold ambitiousness of its fictitious elements. The superimposition of present and past, personal and historical experience, has proven itself a fertile notion and has yielded a monumental novel unparallelled in its scope, technical novelty and view of history as ongoing drama, in which even the thinking individual is but a helpless plaything. *Captivity,* however, is set in an easily definable historical period—at least according to current authoritative chronology. The setting is the Roman Empire in its first century, from about 35 AD to the 70s of that century. The locales—Rome, Jerusalem, Alexandria and others—can also be clearly identified. Not only are they

---

Miklós Györffy
reviews new fiction for this journal.

named, there is also the clear intention to reconstruct them as they were (to the extent the available sources will allow).

Captivity is also a straight narrative with a central figure. From this angle, Spiró's novel is less an historical novel than a story of adventure or an *Entwicklungsroman*. His protagonist is Uri, a sickly, clumsy, short-sighted, ugly Jewish boy in Rome. Of not much use to his merchant father and unable to find his niche, he is more or less allowed to follow his own instincts. He reads whatever he can lay his hands on and acquires an imposing knowledge of literature and philosophy. In addition to Latin, he also learns Greek and Aramaic. He explores Rome thoroughly, becoming familiar with every quarter of the city. One day he is unexpectedly chosen to be a member of a seven-man mission that will take the annual tax paid by the Jews of Rome to Jerusalem. Uri fails to understand why he, a nobody, has been chosen for this great honour and serious duty. The fact, unknown to him, that his father had lent two hundred thousand sesterces, a substantial sum way beyond his means, to one of the most influential of the Jews in Rome, Agrippa, grandson of Herod the Great, may have something to do with it.

This lengthy (770 pages) novel is divided into four parts of largely equal length. The first, "From Rome to Jerusalem", describes the journey on foot through Italy to Syracuse in Sicily, where they take ship. From Caesarea in Judea, they set off on foot again to Jerusalem, where they join the many Jews flocking to the city to celebrate the Passover. Toughened by the journey, Uri has learned from experience to accommodate himself to his companions, despite their mistrust of him. Then, quite unexpectedly, at the gates of Jerusalem, he is knocked down by the Jewish guards and thrown into prison.

At this point readers accustomed to historical adventures set in antiquity will expect that, with this lengthy and detailed exposition behind them, they have now reached the turning point (an expectation reinforced by the novel's title). Uri has been taken captive, so this is what the story will be about—possibly how he escapes, how he is pursued, and perhaps how he becomes the centre of an intrigue. Though *Captivity* may not be a post-modern novel, it does not follow the patterns of classical or conventional historical novels either. It is this irregularity which, among other things, makes it extraordinary. Yet, the novel displays an outlook on history that brings it close to the post-modern. In point of fact, Uri finds himself set free as unexpectedly (and apparently without explanation) as he had been seized. Not only are we left in the dark about why he had been cast into prison in the first place, there now follow further unexpected, or seemingly unexpected, twists and turns. He is received by Pontius Pilate, Procurator of Judea, in the company of Matthew (leader of the delegation and possibly responsible for Uri's two or three weeks in captivity) and that of Herod Antipas, King of Galilee. This is the time of Christ's crucifixion, to which we find another reference in the novel—this one even more direct than that to Pontius Pilate, though readers may not grasp it immediately. Into the cell that Uri is cast with two other prisoners, comes a third, for a single night. An older, balding, fat man with an unkempt beard, notorious for chasing out cheating merchants from the temple. If not at once, then towards the end of the novel, it becomes clear that, despite an appearance totally different from the traditional iconography, he is none other than Jesus of Nazareth.

The brief appearance of Jesus (for three pages) in Uri's story is a bold, almost presumptuous idea, but it is in accord with traditional narrative. It provides an exposition of something later to be elaborated in greater detail—namely, the birth of Christianity. There are other motifs in *Captivity* that are handled and expounded in keeping with similar structural principles. In contrast, several turns in Uri's story (including his reception by Pontius Pilate) are more or less arbitrary narratives. Some events and turning points are also introduced without apparent motivation and remain unexplained later in the novel. They are shown as happenstance, the random working of fate. One example is how, when Uri thinks he is free at last, the authorities put an end to his first stay of two or so weeks in Jerusalem by banishing him to a small village in Judea for an unspecified period of time. We never learn why he was sent there under armed escort, unless it is for the same reason that prompted his arrest: he is believed to be an agent (or a spy?) of Agrippa's.

There are more unclear changes in Uri's life. Shortly after all the fatigue and excitement of the journey, and the shock of his arrest and abrupt release, Uri suddenly behaves as an experienced and witty man of the world when he is received by Pilate; he converses with ease, and his smalltalk is studded with quotes from the classic authors. Somewhat later, in the village he has been exiled to, he puts up with misery and physical tribulations with composure and serenity. As unexpectedly as he found himself banished, he is summoned back to Jerusalem and sent on to Alexandria. There is something in all this and in further events that compelled one critic to comment that the reader is expected to volunteer a greater amount of co-operation with the narrator's intentions than is usual. In other words, whatever takes place and how it takes place has to be accepted. This is the only way the novel works, but thus it also becomes truly accessible, intriguing and highly enjoyable. There are two easily graspable reasons whichg made Spiró shape his plot in this way. One is his view of history, to which I shall come back later. For now, suffice it to point out that *Captivity* demonstrates the senselessness of individual lives and the defencelessness of individuals caught up in historical events. It does turn out that there is some motivation behind the twists and turns of fate Uri is subjected to—such as his alleged connection with Agrippa. Yet, since this does not exist (and if it did, it could hardly justify what happens to him), the story of his life is an experience of the absurd. How Uri finds himself dispatched here and there by this or that set of authority is almost Kafkaesque.

Another, less structural reason seems to be Spiró's intention to make us see certain scenes and milieus through Uri's eyes—what is more, with the utmost historical accuracy. It is as if Spiró has delved into a vast amount of source material that he feels reluctant to waste. This is a consideration in the Judean "detour" that lasts around one hundred pages. Similar digressions occur later, though not independently of Uri's merely being a helpless individual in the upheavals of history, a *donné* we have to take at the author's word. The wealth of ethnographical, religious and cultural material, in whose epic current Spiró's protagonist is immersed, is indeed stunning. In the Judean digression, this method is justified, since it shows how the hero's character and thinking develop. The idle Roman Jewish "intellectual" is confronted with the miserable, ancient peasant life of the Jews and is immersed in it for a time. In the Jerusalem and Alexandria passages, Uri's eyes work like a film camera recording the townscapes. These highly evocative descriptions eventually bring readers close to Uri.

With him, they feel more at home and move with greater confidence through the ancient streets and public buildings.

A brief word should be said here on the relationship between historical authenticity and fiction. The author of a historical novel necessarily prepares by thoroughly researching the given period; in Spiró's case, the task must have been daunting. The locales take in the whole eastern half of the Mediterranean, in all its ethnic, cultural and religious diversity. Uri comes into contact, in a multitude of localities, with the almost endless variety of life in the Roman Empire—from politics and commerce, through literature, philosophy, finance, strategy, navigation, arts and crafts and peasant husbandry to religious doctrines and superstitions. Only the few classical scholars among us would be able to recognise the sources Spiró has used and be able to judge how reliable they are. The average reader is hardly likely to be able to judge which details are well-documented, which are pure invention or guesswork, or how credibly the invented is adjusted to the authentic. One gets the impression through Spiró's handling of his sources that Jerusalem or Rome probably looked like that, more or less, in the 1st century AD. A Roman Jewish boy like Uri may well have experienced the situations he is drawn into in the way he does, and the novel indeed makes you believe this quite powerfully. The questions of authenticity are often swept aside by the sheer power of the narrative.

Captivity may, of course, remind one of Thomas Mann's great historical novel, *Joseph and his Brethren,* in which the vast amount of scholarly material Mann employs simply serves a story about which we are sure of one fact—that it has never happened. Or, it never happened that way. Mann was arbitrary in his selection of sources, being primarily interested in what provided ideological or aesthetic inspiration for him or simply helped depict the milieu. Thomas Mann's *Joseph* abounds in anachronisms, both ostentatiously obvious and disguised—and this is part of its irony. In Spiró's novel, there is one ostentatiously obvious, fundamental anachronism, and this is its language. Spiró uses an almost impertinently contemporary idiom in *Captivity.* It is not only the narrator's voice that is devoid of all archaisms, stylisation, elevation or decoration, so too are those of all the other characters. In places their speech is offhand and cocky, the way their supposed contemporary counterparts would speak. There is thus a tension between the language of the novel and its apparent authenticity, since we can be certain that neither the fictitious nor the historical characters could have spoken this way. Because of this fertile tension, we read Uri's story as a story of today, despite all the historical detail it is wrapped up in.

A similar tension arises between the historical and the adventurous. Though the historical background to Uri's story is clear and is made even clearer through the introduction of Pilate and (in the first two parts) through references to the Emperor Tiberius, in essence this is a story which focuses on everyday events unconnected to history in the traditional sense. The most captivating sections are those in which the historical background is of secondary importance. In the brilliant Alexandrian section, the book's long drawn-out climax, one is hardly aware of reading a work of historical fiction. One reason, external to the novel, might be that we know much less about late Hellenistic Alexandria than we do about the Jerusalem of the New Testament or about the Rome of Tiberius and Caligula. A second reason, intrinsic to the novel, is that Spiró and his protagonist feel that here, in a world of intellectual skirmishing and political machination, they are in their real element. The pogrom of the Jews of Alexandria is appallingly contemporary rather than historical—perhaps here the reader would like to know if this is in compliance with the known authoritative sources. We want to know if it had really been like its twentieth-century counterpart.

The relationship of private adventure and imperial history which prevails in the first three parts is relaxed in the fourth and last part. This has something to do with the change in the time scale. The first three parts, roughly three-quarters of the whole, recount the events of just three years—the last two of Tiberius's reign and the first of Caligula's, Uri's *Wanderjahre* that is—while the last part spans almost forty years.

Who, then, is Uri, and what is his story? He encounters various turns in his fortunes, unexpected or implausible in terms of the plot or the development of character. One of these is the way he ends up in Alexandria—as a "moon messenger", taking astronomical calculations from the astronomers of Jerusalem to those in Alexandria. This appears merely to be a pretext to link him with perhaps the best portrayed character of all—Philo, the renowned, actual Jewish philosopher—and through him, to connect Uri with Alexander the Alabarch, the highest of the Alexandrian Jews. In Judea, Uri was viewed with suspicion as Agrippa's supposed agent; here he is liked, indeed cherished, for the same reason. Treated as equal to the talented sons of the Alabarch and as the disciple of Philo, he finds himself at the centre of social and scholarly life, with his own rooms in the Alabarch's palace and provided with servants and money. Despite being a Jew, he attends the *gymnasium* for the privileged. His poor eyesight is all that remains of the old reticent, awkward Uri. On political issues he soon proves to be an oracle and elicits the envy of the Alabarch's sons with his wit and erudition. Then the pogrom breaks out, and he is left in the lurch by all his rich and influential patrons in their scramble to save their own skins. Uri almost starves to death in the closed ghetto called The Zone. When the danger ceases, he returns to Rome.

His adventures could just as well end here. With the final part "Rome" running to some 250 pages still to come, readers may wonder how Uri's story can possibly go on. In a sense, *Captivity* begins all over again and, as I have said, with a new narrative technique. After the years of wandering and study, Uri has children, but has little affection for his ever-growing family—except for his first-born son, a handsome, intelligent, gifted child who, Uri hopes, will be able to achieve everything he was unable to. Uri now spends most of his time with the Roman political and social elite. He also engages in various commercial ventures. His father had died while he was away; he now has to pay off the debts his father had incurred in order to lend money to Agrippa—that Agrippa himself might repay the debt is out of the question. Though Uri's reputation as Agrippa's protégé, favourable or otherwise, is still left unexplained, at least the background to the loan is finally clarified. This happens when Uri finds himself at a feast with Agrippa, now King of Galilee. As a lower-ranking guest, Uri is called upon to use a feather to help the king vomit. Once done, Uri takes the opportunity to ask Agrippa to relieve him of his debts. The overindulgent king, who mistakes Uri for his long-deceased father, informs him that the debt had been repaid a long time ago when "I got your son a place in the delegation which delivered the sacred money." Uri realises that this was how his father, who loved him after all, wanted to secure his future. He ought to have have found himself aprofession, a fortune, a position in Judea or Alexandria, and he should never have returned to Rome.

This realisation is, however, relative—Uri is getting on fairly well in imperial Rome, though his various commercial ventures and diplomatic tasks cannot really be gratifying. The Alabarch arrives in Rome with his son and Philo, and Uri becomes something of a secretary and interpreter for them. He has entrée to the meeting-place of the élite of Rome, the house of Claudius, is received by Claudius on several occasions after he has become emperor, and he is present in the theatre when Caligula is murdered. A succession of emperors follow—Nero, Claudius, Vespasian —and decades later, Uri is branded a Nazarene with just as little reason as his exposure to other absurd haphazards throughout his life. He and his family are banished from Rome. Ten years later he is recalled and receives an apology. While in exile, his favourite son Theo is carried off by slave-merchants, and Uri has almost forgotten him when he accidentally comes across him, a castrated and parasitic wreck. His second son Marcellus is indeed a Nazarene, a follower of Christ, of whose religion Uri has a withering opinion. True, he thinks no better of any religion; as he becomes older, he tires more or less of everything—family, politics, books, the lot. His last passion is collecting books, but when his collection perishes, he takes it with equanimity. As his days pass, more and more news crops up, increasingly mechanically and unemotionally, of various purges, political murders and even massacres.

"This frenzy may have resulted from a general lack of belief," he thinks of the new creed Christianity. Is this Uri or the author speaking? Who speaks in *Captivity,* and on whose behalf? What is the message this narrator intends to send through Uri's story? The narrator speaks the language of today, sees things from today's perspective, which must surely be the author's own personal and intellectual perspective too. Still, for narrative purposes, Spiró uses his protagonist's angle from within the ancient world all the time; we learn about everything through Uri's impressions, experience and information. Credibility is thus somewhat impaired. There is some discrepancy between Uri's personal angle and the author's accu-mulated knowledge of the period. In this light, the question of Spiró's gloomy view of history is of secondary importance. He does not suggest, I believe, what post-modernist authors do—that there is no history and it has never existed—nor does he project an abstracted essence of history as he sees it. If anything, he offers something that is no novelty at all, but a gut-felt experience. "This century, the 20th, is like an execution squad incessantly on duty," the Nobel Prize winning novelist Imre Kertész wrote in his *Diary on the Galley.* Kertész also said, "We live in a world in which neither belief nor negation exists, and action manifests itself in its own particularity and singularity, without any sort of value order." Spiró shares Kertész's views on our age. The protagonist of *Captivity* lives in a world in which the one-off person and the one-off action not only fail to fit into a world order, but also lose all rationality in the eternal circulation of murderous power games. All Uri wants to do is live, no more. Why is he not left alone? Could this be the "captivity" no human can escape? ❧

Gábor Csepregi

Music as an Ethical Force

Alan Walker: *Reflections on Liszt*. Ithaca, Cornell University Press, 2005, 277 pp.

Even if you have read Alan Walker's magisterial biography, you still have not yet learned everything about Liszt. Liszt's activities and relations were so wide-ranging and numerous that some had to receive lesser attention in this three-volume book. Liszt achieved pioneering results as a pianist, conductor, composer, teacher and administrator. His private life was marked by fascinating events and painful family afflictions. These fresh reflections not only throw additional lights on an extraordinary life and work, but also help to further eliminate some of the misunderstandings and misinterpretations that still surround, and hurt, this towering figure of 19th-century music.

Walker makes clear that false statements spring from a misplaced scholarship that prefers doubt and slander to fact. Liszt neither wrote an autobiography nor discussed systematically his creative work. Fortunately, his voluminous personal correspondence provides us with invaluable insights into his daily activities, theoretical views, and above all, his true motives and beliefs. To solve puzzles and invalidate unjustified claims, Walker often turns to this substitute self-portrait.

Although informative and, in some chapters, highly analytical, the biography could not do full justice to Liszt's life-long attachment to Beethoven's music, partly because the course of the narrative could not follow a single path. In the essay on Liszt and the Beethoven symphonies, the reader is better able to grasp and appreciate the nature of this intimate and steadfast bond. Liszt was fascinated by the symphonies, and he felt that they could never be studied enough. While he was still a young pianist, he transcribed three of them. Much later, while living in the Dominican convent of the Madonna del Rosario near Rome, he returned to these, as well as to the other six. In an austere setting—his room was furnished with a bed, a writing desk, and an upright piano with a missing D-natural—he set out to transfer the finest details of the score to the piano. He took care to indicate the name of

---

Gábor Csepregi

is Professor of Philosophy and President at the Dominican University College of Ottawa, Canada. His book, The Clever Body, *will be published later this year.*
He is editor of the scholarly journal Science et Esprit.

the instrument to imitate, so the pianist understood exactly what colour had to be drawn out of the keyboard. He knew that when the imagination is at work, the hands succeed in approximating the desired sonority. They are able to evoke a particular atmosphere as well. Once, at the Villa d'Este, Liszt drew his student to the window and pointed to the peaceful countryside. "Play that," he said. There are your evening harmonies." The challenge he continuously faced consisted in reproducing for ten fingers the content of an entire orchestral score, so that the music was both playable and faithful to the composer's intention.

In this essay, more so than in the biography, focus is placed on the significant challenges Liszt had to face. Where the faithful reproduction of the notes was no longer possible, Liszt attempted to "capture Beethoven's orchestral effect". The notes have been *translated* rather than *transcribed.* What mattered to him was coming as close as possible to the spirit of the work and not so much to its letters. To respect obediently the demands of the composer, rather than to give free rein to one's own fantasy, required exceptional gifts. Hence the paradox that, according to Walker, characterises much of Liszt's approach to transcription: "Only the greatest master is capable of becoming the perfect slave."

Liszt looked upon Schubert songs with the same humility and loving care as he studied Beethoven's symphonies. He sought to secure a wider recognition for Schubert's music and, by solving some arduous technical problems, wanted to advance the field of piano technique. One of his difficulties consisted in bringing into a harmonious whole the details of the song and the already highly demanding accompaniments. The transcription of the well-known *Erlkönig* excellently illustrates Liszt's ability to flawlessly integrate the vocal line to a judiciously altered pianistic part. In the *Ave Maria,* Liszt distributes the melody between alternating hands, thus creating a greater physical space on the keyboard and leaving more room for the "melodic fingers".

The many transcriptions Liszt made allowed him to enlarge his repertoire. Amidst the frequent travels and numerous successful recitals—in Berlin, in 1841, he gave twenty-one recitals in ten weeks and played eighty works—he kept working on various transcriptions. What motivated him? Certainly not the desire to show off his uncommon skills, as some might still believe. Liszt considered his phenomenal musical abilities as a medium through which music could reach sensitive ears. He felt morally obliged to promote the musical works of the great composers of both former and present times. Hidden behind his virtuosity was a sense of duty. Nature bestowed gifts on him that must be put in the service of both music and humanity. "In his day," notes Walker, "there were no gramophone records, no radios, no real interest in preserving the music of the past. Liszt's answer was to enshrine it in the piano (or as much of it as ten fingers and one lifetime enabled him to do)." Therefore, he kept creating remarkable pieces, the value of which is not mere utility. In some cases, the copy was better than the original.

The principles that guided his transcriptions also presided over his editing activities—another fleetingly mentioned topic in the biography. The editor, he alleged, must "fully and carefully" present the original music and add his own "tentative" way of playing it. Once again, the spirit of the music prevailed over the letters. Liszt claimed that music is an ongoing dialogue between an object—the notes and a subject—and the musician, who brings the notes to life in concrete circumstances. While fully respecting the composer's indications, the performer should also free himself of the text. A neutral and anonymous attitude is unacceptable in music. The sum of the notes does not make the piece. Only the artist's personality and passionate engagement bring the music to life and induce resonances in the listeners, notwithstanding a few missing notes.

Liszt never imposed his solutions upon the pianists. Since he was not excessively concerned with literal accuracy, he encouraged his students to find out what sounded better, or even what appeared to them the most convenient solution. While the Russian diplomat Wilhelm von Lenz played Weber's Sonata in A-flat Major op. 39, Liszt pushed him away from the piano and began experimenting with different effects. There is no great artist, at least in the modern era, without a creative criticism of masterpieces. Whether the result is an entirely new work (the symphonic poem *Hamlet*) or a variant (the alternative versions of Schubert's Impromptus), the creative genius is energised by such interactive processes. If we carefully follow these metamorphoses, we might come to a better understanding of their sources. Is art's secret not best unlocked by art itself?

The same moral obligation that Liszt owed to his masters, he felt for his numerous pupils. The teacher, he argued, is merely the means through which the proper understanding of musical works are achieved. The few pages Walker devotes to presenting Liszt's principles, as well as his own ideas on education, should be read aloud in every music department. Piano students, Liszt insisted, must get acquainted with the techniques of composition, improvisation and transposition. Music is indivisible, and the practice of an art cannot be confined to specific abilities. Today, notes Walker, the tendency to divide the discipline into separate compartments leads to unfortunate consequences. "The age of specialisation came to invade every aspect of our musical lives, but it did not make us more musical." To be musical also means to come to identify oneself with music, instead of relating to it in a cold and detached manner. To create and nurture this symbiotic relationship, correct teaching is not sufficient. What is needed is a teacher who, in addition to his knowledge and technique, has passion and personality. It was admiration and love that brought most of the students to Liszt's masterclasses in Weimar. They feverishly prepared the pieces for the next lesson and even paid the three-mark fine when they were caught practising with open windows.

Walker recounts the lives of three outstanding students. Because of the unbounded zeal with which he promoted Liszt's music, Walter Bache, the *English Disciple,* was labelled dangerous. Or worse, he was ignored. When he called upon a famous critic of his time, the maid returned with the following message, "Mr Davidson says he is not at home." The concerts he organized and recitals he gave invariably resulted in financial plight. In one of his letters, he wrote about a crucial decision: should he think more about his financial comfort or lose a third of his income in one evening? He would not have been a Liszt pupil if he had been leaning towards the first option. Bache's portrait, for this reviewer at least, is the most moving and uplifting in this book. If today there were two or three Baches in every major city, the future of classical music would be much more promising.

According to Liszt, Carl Tausig, the *Polish Wunderkind,* did not need a teacher. Besides his inborn talent, he possessed the most important ingredient of pianistic proficiency, the rare ability to tackle increasing technical difficulties with the outmost relaxation. The "pianist of the pianists", as Walker calls him, played the most strenuous passages with Olympian calm and ease. Unfortunately, this marvellous artist was unable to transfer his elegance, balance and refinement into other areas of his life. A reluctant teacher, he was prone to lose his temper, uttering insults when the student fell short of the desired perfection. Still, his rather impatient and cold way of teaching had its own virtue—the most energetic refusal to condone *Spektakel,* which means playing to the gallery with faked emotions. He knew, from his own experience, that nothing is more alluring to an artist than acting out a role on stage.

Hans von Bülow's divorce from Cosima, Liszt's daughter, has been widely publicised. What is much less known, and convincingly brought out here, is the nobility of Bülow's character. He recognised Isolde—his wife's third child, though fathered by Wagner—as his own legitimate offspring. Together with Liszt, he placed art above personal injury and kept conducting Wagner's music. After the break-up of his marriage, he wrote, "It is really terrible that the second half of one's life should have no other object than to repair the follies of the first." But he did much more than to amend his blunders. He gave nearly perfect recitals—perfection was beyond the reach of the performer, it was only in a work—creating sensations not only with his playing, but also by his repeated scolding of the audience if disturbances were caused. Once, while conducting Liszt's music, he lectured a group of men in Ohio for keeping their hats on. Alas, today we seldom witness such a strong demand for reverence and attention. Yet, in some concert halls, educating the public about the proper way of listening to classical music seems to me a pressing need.

All the great and small battles that this extraordinary man fought in the service of music deserve to be better known by a wider public. Bülow secured international recognition and financial stability for the Berlin Philharmonic Orchestra. All subsequent conductors of this ensemble owe him a great debt. Beyond the high standard that he set for each player, he devoted much care to programme building. His forceful conducting on the podium was just as spectacular as his rendering of the classics at the piano. "His arm gestures were wide, and his baton swished with military precision. His body would sway back and forth as he attempted to capture that elusive quality called tempo rubato (elusive, that is, to orchestras). He darted here and there, attending to the shape of every phrase, piercing the players with his gaze and drawing from them music of unimaginable intensity. And of course everything was performed, and even rehearsed, from memory."

Pianists who intend to study and play Liszt's works would draw great benefit from reading the essay on the Sonata in B minor. In fact, it has been written mainly for them. Walker rightly contends that musical analysis cannot ignore the players who "must turn shadow into substance, silence into sound." He aptly presents the structure of the sonata by highlighting the main themes, their metamorphoses, and the numerous subtleties without which the hidden beauties of music cannot come alive. The novelty in this essay is the specific recommendations that Walker gives to the performers. His approach here is more direct and insistent. He tells them, for instance, where the tonal centre unambiguously appears and, much later, returns in order to underscore it; what kind of reading the beautiful Grandioso theme requires; where the temptation to linger must be resisted; what the choice of a particular key (the "beatific F-sharp") in the Andante movement evokes; why pedal markings must be taken seriously; and where the chief climax of the piece occurs. He also explains why the three-part Fugato remarkably displays Liszt's penchant for irony. To make this audible, the pianist must play, as it were, without feeling, but certainly not without energy and adequate technical preparation. Walker forewarns that, in the recapitulation, the fast play of the octaves will bring only "cheap applause" at the cost of betraying the composer's intention. What matters at this point is the thematic integrity of the passage and not the desire to shine with empty brilliance.

All these useful observations lead to a central question, "What sort of player does the B minor Sonata require?" One of the requirements is the thorough knowledge of the works of all those composers who influenced Liszt in one way or another. Liszt is best played by performers with a rich repertoire. His music calls for the generalist's breadth of knowledge. It also demands that close attention be paid to the many fine details. Much harm is done by pianists who, by playing the music loud and fast and without a sense of delicacy, seek only to elicit admiration for their physical skills.

Several decades passed before the true greatness of the Sonata was understood and recognized. While Liszt was playing it, Brahms fell asleep. The critic Hanslick deemed the enthusiastic listener "beyond help". Even Busoni, Bartók and Dohnányi needed time to gain insight into its magnificent depths. Today it has become one of the oft-performed solo works for piano. The world of art provides us with plentiful examples of misjudgement, and the story of the Sonata serves as a salutary warning against hasty dismissals. To read music with scholarly knowledge is not enough. Understanding takes time and patience, and a great work "slowly-slowly" (Bartók's expression) yields its formal beauties and emotional range to those who treat it with reverence.

Time was also what the biographer Alan Walker needed to express his personal views. In *An Open Letter to Franz Liszt,* composed with respect and admiration, he presents a brilliant assessment of the master's character. Several aspects of Liszt's life are examined—his relation to his children, women and critics; his advanced ideas on social issues; and his devotion to the cause of modern music. The portrait is particularly valuable in showing how, in some instances, virtues lead to vices, and amazing gifts yielded unfortunate results. Liszt's proverbial generosity and self-effacement caused as much harm as good. The exuberance of his creativity produced both masterpieces and works of lesser value. Walker repeatedly raises the question "Why?" and, by giving enough details about Liszt's actions, helps the reader to conjecture the answers in his head.

The mainspring of Liszt's diverse activities was the conviction that the musician is marked by a sacred predestination and, as a priest, is entrusted by God to accomplish his mission. However, being chosen implies the ethical duty of giving something back. It is perhaps in light of this vision that we should read the very last words of this remarkable collection of essays, a biography "may even reveal some

Péter Laki

Forty Years with Bartók

János Kárpáti: *Bartók-analitika* (Bartók Analysis)
Budapest, Rózsavölgyi és Társa. 2004, 272 pp.

In his 1928 essay "The Folk Songs of Hungary", published in the New York journal *Pro Musica,* Béla Bartók explained that "the peasant's art [was] a phenomenon of Nature" and therefore new Hungarian art music, which was based on peasant music, was itself created "through Nature" and was fundamentally natural in its character.

Let us not dwell on whether or not peasant music is really a phenomenon of Nature. However, since Bartók himself claimed to have created his own style "through Nature", one *naturally* wonders if it is possible to find any laws (similar to the laws of nature) that reveal the structural properties of Bartók's music. This question, which has occupied Bartók scholarship from the very beginning, has some broader theoretical implications. At issue is whether the twentieth century was able to produce a universal musical grammar along the lines of classical harmony, or whether it even attempted to create such a construct. We can go even further and ask whether it is possible at all to explain twentieth-century music, or any music for that matter, through structural rules.

It is hardly surprising that over the years there has been a wide variety of answers to these questions. János Kárpáti's approach differs from other schools of thought in its primary focus on musical *hearing.* This eminent Hungarian musicologist built his harmonic theory on an observation made by his former teacher, Bence Szabolcsi. Szabolcsi had been the first to use the term "mistuning" to describe certain sonorities in which some tones in traditional chords were replaced by their immediate neighbours, a half-step higher or lower. Kárpáti has greatly expanded on the idea of mistuning, showing that this extremely simple concept expresses a profound truth and captures something essential about Bartók's music.

Yet, Kárpáti has never become a slave to his own theory. He has been almost alone among Bartók analysts in remaining open to other approaches. His new collection of articles on Bartók is characterised by a wide intellectual horizon, profound understanding, and above all, a host of funda-

---

Péter Laki
is Visiting Associate Professor at the Oberlin Conservatory of Music. His books include Bartók and His World *(ed., 1995).*

mental and illuminating observations. The fifteen articles reflect four decades of Bartók studies and were selected from a much larger body of work. A complete bibliography of Kárpáti's writings on Bartók may be found in the appendix. One article ("Bartók Analyses from Overseas") appears here for the first time; many others have been rescued from hard-to-find periodicals.

In several works of Bartók (for instance, his String Quartets Nos. 4 and 5) we find five movements arranged in a symmetrical order. The two inner (Nos. 2 and 4) and the two outer movements (Nos. 1 and 5), arranged around a central movement, form two pairs that correspond to one another in some way.

Whether consciously or not, Kárpáti adopted this structural principle for his book. The central portion is taken up by four articles joined under the heading "Analysis", echoing the title of the entire book. It is here that we find Kárpáti's treatise on mistuning as well as his critical reactions to the theories of other scholars. It is both refreshing and uplifting to see the sobriety Kárpáti brings to his arguments. His criticism is never dogmatic. Rather, he subjects all theoretical hypotheses to the test of the ear before passing judgment.

No Bartók analyst can avoid taking a position concerning the work of Ernő Lendvai. This highly influential Hungarian theorist introduced the mathematical notion of the golden section into his discussion of Bartók's music. In the 1950s, when Lendvai first developed his theories[1], they were attacked for political reasons. Some people found the use of "cold" mathematical ratios incompatible with the image of Bartók as a "populist" composer. Western analysts later found fault with Lendvai on purely musical grounds.

Kárpáti is cautious to a fault as he approaches this hornet's nest. He refrains from discussing the political dimension, although it is delusory to think that the musical notes themselves tell the entire story in this case. Writing in 1999, Kárpáti provides an overview of this complex issue that is more complete and more nuanced than any previous treatment has been. Without engaging in polemics, he simply examines the facts in a completely unbiased way.

He is equally circumspect when it comes to commenting on recent American Bartók scholarship. With astonishing ease, he navigates these complicated theoretical systems (which he was one of the first in Hungary to understand in depth). He summarises their main ideas for the uninitiated reader and, armed with his forty-year experience in Bartók analysis shows the merits and shortcomings of the new works.

Two groups of articles form the pair of "inner movements" arranged around the analytical studies in the book's centre of symmetry. One of these groups is labelled "Case Studies"; here Kárpáti discusses individual works by Bartók. The label would also fit the other group, where the focus is on individual geographical regions studied by the composer in his capacity as ethnomusicologist. Kárpáti was the first in post-war Hungary to study Arab and Far Eastern musical cultures, and therefore, he is supremely qualified to speak on Bartók's connections to them. He has visited the same site in North Africa where Bartók had conducted fieldwork in 1913; thus, he has first-hand knowledge of the area. Years

1 ■ Lendvai's first Bartók analysis, which Kárpáti does not cite in this book, was published as early as 1947. "Bartók *Improvisations* sorozatáról, 1920" ["On Bartók's 1920 *Improvisations* Cycle], *Zenei Szemle* III: pp. 151–167.

later, Kárpáti visited Japan and Korea and published a valuable study on *The Music of the Orient.*[2] Thus, we get much more than the documented facts on Bartók's field trip to North Africa, facts that would be available to anyone. Based on his own original research, Kárpáti adds some very important new data to our knowledge.

In "Béla Bartók and the Orient", he ventures into virgin territory, showing the influence of certain Indonesian and Chinese scales in Bartók's music, especially in the piano piece "On the Island of Bali" from the *Microcosmos* series. Although Kárpáti's argumentation is convincing as always, one wishes he had discussed the sources from which Bartók may have known the music of the Far East. This article was written in 1964, before Kárpáti began his Oriental music studies. We would like to read an updated version that would synthesise information from Kárpáti's different research interests in the same way as in the North African study.

For many years, Kárpáti's studies concentrated on the composer's chamber music.[3] The three "case studies" of the present volume reflect this particular line of inquiry, with essays on the trio *Contrasts,* String Quartet No.1 and what he calls "dramatic turns"—a special compositional strategy observed, once again, through the string quartets. In each instance, the "case study" concerns a specific phenomenon found in the music. The First Quartet, for example, is seen, most interestingly, in the light of contemporaneous *art nouveau.* Kárpáti shows how the visual arts can provide a new conceptual framework for what Bartók himself considered one of his first mature compositions.

Studies of a more general nature may be found at the beginning and the end of the book. Two opening chapters—one on the relationship between Bartók and Beethoven, the other on Bartók and Schoenberg—assess Bartók's place in the history of music; together with the ethnomusicological studies elsewhere in the book, these articles provide a panoply of different contexts for the study of Bartók's work. The piece on Schoenberg is particularly important, in part because of its sheer length, but also because here is another topic Kárpáti has explored independently from Bartók. Let us not forget that he wrote the first, and to this day only, Hungarian-language monograph on the founder of the Second Viennese School. His Bartók/Schoenberg study, written in 1963, is still fresh today; its observations are cogent, its structure logical, and its argumentation compelling.

The volume closes with three reviews of Bartók monographs by Tibor Tallián, László Somfai and László Vikárius. Once again, Kárpáti proves to be a sensitive and keen-eyed reader who sees the virtues of each work even when he expresses occasional disagreement on certain issues. His well-balanced treatment turns the reviews into valuable scholarly contributions in their own right. In the last entry of the book, Professor Kárpáti confers "knighthood" on his former student László Vikárius. Even the title of his review emphasises that Kárpáti considers his younger colleague's work a "new direction" in Bartók studies. (Incidentally, it is here that the book's symmetrical arrangement becomes complete. Vikárius's book addresses the concept of influence in Bartók's music, creating bridges between

2 ■ *A Kelet zenéje* (The Music of the East). Budapest: Editio Musica, 1981.

3 ■ See his *Bartók's String Quartets,* Budapest: Corvina, 1975, expanded and revised as *Bartók's Chamber Music,* Stuyvesant, New York: Pendragon Press, 1994.

Bartók and other composers just as the first two essays of this Kárpáti volume do. Of course, this does not contradict Kárpáti's claim about Vikárius's "new direction".)

The conclusion of the book thus becomes a new beginning. The experienced scholar announces the arrival of a new generation, ready to carry the torch. Yet, in his introduction, Kárpáti asks us not to consider this book to be his last word on Bartók. I don't know who would be capable of making such a mistake. Since the book came out in 2003, there has been a new Bartók paper by Kárpáti, and we can only wish for a whole new volume of writings by this outstanding, indefatigable and versatile scholar. ❧

Ferenc Bónis

"I Am Not Too Talkative..."

Zoltán Kodály: *Letters in English, French, German, Italian, Latin.* Edited by Dezső Legány and Dénes Legány, Argumentum—Kodály Archívum, Budapest, 2002, 525 pp.

Zoltán Kodály's correspondence is an important part of the composer's papers. Amounting to more than a thousand letters, it may be safely regarded as complementing what he wrote on music for publication (totalling some two thousand printed pages) and the notebooks published posthumously in two volumes. These latter, without any discernible attempt at being put in a formalised shape, record the ideas that were on Kodály's mind at any given time and were jotted down for his own use. The letters, however, cast light on his ordinary working days, whether they deal with publishing matters, travels, pupils, helping others or personal relationships. Fragments as they are, their publication completes and authenticates the intellectual portrait of Kodály.

The letters written to British and American addressees are mostly directed to various organizations, or persons representing them, with whom he had contact. They include the Oxford University Press, which played an important role in the propagation of Kodály's works in the English-speaking world. Professor Edward J. Dent of Cambridge University, the founding president of the International Society for Contemporary Music, was the English translator of the text of *Psalmus Hungaricus,* Kodály's *chef d'oeuvre.* As a conductor and composer, Kodály came into contact with the music department of the BBC early on, and that relationship is amply documented by the letters in this volume. His contacts with Maud Karpeles, the Secretary of the International Folk Music Council, focussed on scholarly topics or on the organization of research, for Merton College in Oxford, he wrote a late composition at the behest of the college. The Three Choirs Festival in Gloucester, where Kodály's great works were conducted by the composer himself, was another major contribution to their achieving popularity in Britain. Percy Young was the first biographer of Kodály in the English language, so their exchanges concentrated on the book he was working on.

Kodály corresponded in various languages. His exchanges with Professor Dent were in German, and he corresponded with the musicologist Cecil Gray and

---

Ferenc Bónis
is a musicologist, editor of Kodály's collected writings Visszatekintés *(Retrospection) and author of several books on Béla Bartók and Zoltán Kodály.*

with the Oxford University Press in French. From the end of the 1920s onwards he began to write in English, sporadically at first; following the Second World War, all his correspondence with English-speaking addressees was in English. His correspondence with Dr Ernst Roth, the head of his London publishing company, Boosey & Hawkes, is in German; while, curiously, the language of the letters he sent to Hungarian pupils of his who had settled in Britain and America, such as Mátyás Seiber or Tibor Serly, was English. To the young pianist Tamás Vásáry he wrote mixed letters, partly in English, partly in French.

In a letter to Percy Young, the otherwise laconic composer wrote at remarkable length about his own evolution and his relationship with British music. This letter was used by his biographer as a preface to his book:

[30 June 1962]

Up to my 40th I lived the life of an average musician, without taking particular interest in school singing.

In collecting folksongs, however, I became soon aware that country schoolboys still sing many good songs, which are unknown to town-people, and that the few songs taught in the schools were anything but Hungarian or beautiful. To introduce folksongs in schools then ran against the practice of pedantry.

In 1923 on the occasion of the first performance of "Psalmus hungaricus" I found our only chorus so weakened (it was a few years after the war)—that I decided to add a boy's chorus. Their fine singing inspired me to write some short pieces for them, like "See the Roma", "Straw Guy", and in a couple of years with the collaboration of my pupils a little literature came into being. But it turned out that only the best teachers could produce results and it seemed most urgent to educate good teachers and to work out good methods.

In the course of a number of visits into England since 1927 I observed the highly developed singing in schools, and to this I am indebted for much stimulation, which helped me gradually to complete my work for children.

I am now very pleased to return to the English, what I learned from them, and was able to adapt to our needs in Hungary. Because after warm reception of my previous choruses I hope that my young English-speaking friends will accept Bi[cinia] Hung[arica] in the same way.

Z.K.

The letter to Maud Karpeles gives an interesting insight into Kodály's ambivalent relationship with the authorities in Hungary at the time.

2 June, 1962.

Dear Miss Karpeles,
just before leaving for Galyatető (for a week, back the 11th, 16th trip to Rome) I got your letter from 28th.

We shall be at Gottwaldov (unless some unforeseen event) but not going to Rumania.

As to Unesco, I would prefer to write personally in my name, directly. Our National Commission would perhaps not like my propositions, whereas Unesco-people knows me, years before they wished to have me in Paris for a year, then for the Music Council. Since we (i.e. "democratic" countries) "stepped out" in those times from Unesco, I could not accept. (Later we "stepped in" again.)

Now we can discuss the matter in Gottwaldov.

Yours truly

Z. Kodály

Kodály maintained personal contacts with the younger English composer Benjamin Britten. A letter he wrote to Britten on 8 September 1964 is a good example of his whole style of correspondence: "I am not very talkative," he wrote.

Dear Mr Britten,

many thanks for your kind letter from 15th August, which I was unable to answer before the stormy conference of the IFMC was over.

It wants no persuasion for us to go to Aldeburgh, from which we heard so many attractive reports. It seems to be even lightly possible in 1965, since I had an invitation to the U.S. for the summer, and we could pass over England.

I am not very talkative, but an introduction to the concert of the chorus you wish to invite, makes me some pleasure.

Mr Riss may write 1. to the conductor (Ilona Andor, Budapest, IX. Tóth Kálmán u. 25.); 2. to the Directrice of her school for permission (Dr Mrs Jenő Dénes, Budapest, IX. Vendel u. l.); 3. to the Institute of Cultural Relations (Dr Endre Rosta, Director. Budapest, V. Dorottya u. 2.) This Institute is able to support such excursions covering partly the costs of transport. The date of 19. June would be quite suitable. The schools being finished a few days before.

With the hope, that all ideas will come true, and with repeated thanks for your kind invitation, and with warmest greetings to you and Mr Peter Pears from us both,

Yours very sincerely,
8.9.64.

Zoltán Kodály

Finally one of his German letters which, however, concerns England and was written to Dr Ernst Roth of Boosey & Hawkes, Kodály's British publisher. In 1938, just after the *Anschluss* when Austria had been annexed by the German Reich, Kodály (similarly to Bartók) broke off relations with his Viennese publisher and settled on a British company for the publication of his works. Shy and reticent and wary of friendships, Kodály found a trusted intimate friend in Dr Roth toward the end of his life. Still, despite their close relationship, his letters to Dr Roth are brief, terse and objective; almost every word is directed at some specific business. Let me add some information that may be relevant regarding the works and facts mentioned in the letter. "Veni Em. [manuel]" refers to Kodály's choral piece *Advent Song,* his expression of solidarity with the persecuted and intended as encouragement for them. Kodály published the first edition of this work in 1944, at the time when the persecution of Jews in Hungary was at its height. "66" is the composer's work "66 Singing Exercises for Two Voices", one of the volumes (and published in a separate booklet) of the work *Choral Method,* which Boosey & Hawkes published. "Mountain Night V" is the closing piece of a choral cycle without words for female voices. In Jerusalem, Kodály (accompanied by his wife) took part in a congress of the International Folk Music Council in 1963. Curiously, while Kodály was not particularly impressed by Stravinsky's music, he nevertheless asked Dr Roth for the orchestral score of the revised version of *Petrushka.*

25 May [1963]

My Dear Friend,

Thank you for your letter as well as the greetings via Tardos, received in good order yesterday.

As regards "Veni Em"[manuel], I would advise a double Engl(ish)-Lat(in) text for the publication, in which case it would be sung in many more Prot(estant) churches, where there is no Latin singing.

Hopefully, you have already received "66". A single piece has words, but for the sake of unity it can be left out.

Mountain Night V ought to be finished already; it is eagerly awaited here (for a local reprinting).

Our summer plans are now reduced to Jerusalem, where we are going to see each other at the beginning of August.

In October I must travel to Copenhagen for a conference.

I hope the summer will bring you genuine rest and increased strength for the next working year.

With all good wishes

Yours

Z.K.

A substantial volume of Kodály's letters was published in the centenary year of his birth, in 1982, by Dezső Legány. The current book of letters was also edited by him and his multitalented musician son, Dénes Legány, who died tragically young. This dedicated and meticulous work, devoted to the letters written in foreign languages, has done great service to Hungarian and international Kodály research.

The editors have remained true to the editorial principles of the 1982 volume. They have published every single letter in its original language and have given a serial number to those letters whose existence can only be presumed (and whose actual text is obviously missing from the volume). This reviewer does not agree with this method. Only those texts should be published which evidently exist, which are accessible and whose publication is permitted. The situation is best described by a saying attributed to Leó Weiner, the legendary professor of chamber music and a contemporary of Kodály: "a pianissimo that cannot be heard is not there." From the aspect of publication, the assumption that a letter whose existence can only be suspected may be well-grounded or less well-grounded, and the editor's guess at the number of those "latent" letters is either correct or not. It would make more sense if these "suspected letters", instead of being assigned serial numbers within the main body of letters, were placed in an appendix.

Somewhat questionable, too, is publishing those letters written in English, French, German, Italian and Latin in a single volume without translations. English-speaking readers are quite unlikely to understand letters in German (and the language skills of the average Hungarian reader are best not mentioned). Archival purposes may, of course, be satisfied by such a compilation, but the publication of the letters, one would think, is ultimately to make the ideas they contain as widely known as possible.

The blurb mentions "some 1100" letters written in languages other than Hungarian, as letters the editors know about. 1045 letters are registered by them in the main body of the text. The result of an investigation of the last 250 items in the publication shows that 54, that is, 20 per cent, are only assumed to exist by the editors. Their texts are completely missing. Thus, to refer to 1045 letters is misleading.

The publication method is lopsided in the sense that only Kodály's letters or replies are included, and we are left in the dark about what the other party may have said. That makes some letters quite difficult to interpret. The notes are also open to criticism, being sometimes too prolix, sometimes far too brief. Readers are quite likely to know that William Shakespeare was an English playwright and poet. On the other hand, it may be much more relevant to be told who in 1965 was the secretary of the Gesellschaft der Musikfreunde in Vienna, that Kilián Szigeti was a Benedictine teacher and musicologist, that the German musician Heinrich Möller "lectured" Bartók, then fifty, on the "essence" of Hungarian folk music, that Péter Csobádi, one-time secretary of the conductor Ferenc Fricsay, was also the author of a short book on Bartók and the editor of a large collection of studies on Mozart, that the French writer André Malraux was a Minister of Culture under de Gaulle, or that Alicia Elschekova was the co-editor of Bartók's collection of Slovak folk music. These are facts that are a great deal less well known and would have deserved to have been noted.

Kodály used a great many abbreviations in his letters. These abbreviations are regularly resolved by the editors within brackets in the main body of the text—sometimes superfluously, as when they resolve the same abbreviation used for the same institution three times in one and the same letter, a clumsy procedure.

So there is quite a lot to be criticized from a professional point of view in this edition of Kodály's non-Hungarian letters. Nevertheless, we can only welcome the fact that so many of them have been made accessible, revealing an abundance of hitherto unknown autobiographical facts. For that, the two editors deserve credit without reservations. ❧

Rudolf Paksa

Justice or Political Retribution?

Pál Pritz: *The War Crimes Trial of Hungarian Prime Minister László Bárdossy.* Boulder Co., East European Monographs, 2004, 221 pp.

After the cataclysm of the Second World War, so-called People's Tribunals, committees investigating accountability for war crimes, were formed all over Hungary. The tribunals concentrated their efforts on seeking out, charging and sentencing politicians, office holders and bureaucrats who had played a national or local role in the Horthy era—summarily branded "fascist"—particularly in the war years. Naturally, trials in which the former leaders of the country featured as defendants drew the greatest attention. It was following a trial of this kind that László Bárdossy, prime minister between 3 April 1941 and 7 March 1942, was sentenced to death. Although Bárdossy's was not a show trial based on trumped-up charges (the evidence was real and not prefabricated), the outcome was clear from the start. Bárdossy would be found guilty as a major war criminal, as in his person the Horthy regime itself would be placed in the dock.

The trial was not free of procedural errors and oddities. Constitutionally, only Parliament was entitled to examine the prime minister's political responsibility, yet the court rejected the defendant's objections. The prosecution committed numerous errors, referring to laws that were no longer valid, misquoting documents and using them one-sidedly. Even the judge openly displayed passion. All of this provided ammunition for those who maintained, not without foundation, that the real purpose of the Communists who organised the tribunals (and were still one of the many parties in the new multi-party democratic republic) was not to serve justice, but to judge and seek revenge for political crimes. That may be one of the reasons why, in the eyes of some, Bárdossy took on the image of a uniquely evil war criminal, while others saw him as a martyr executed for political reasons. In fact, what a thorough historical analysis of the compelling political forces of the time and the decision-making mechanisms then in force demonstrates is that László Bárdossy was neither of the two.

Pál Pritz is a professor of 20th-century Hungarian history at Eötvös Loránd University in Budapest. His speciality is Hungarian political and diplomatic history between the two World Wars; his book

Rudolf Paksa

is a member of the History Workshop of the Eötvös Loránd University.
He is one of the founders of the Eötvös College Oral History Archives.

The War Crimes Trial of Hungarian Prime Minister László Bárdossy summarises many years of research and teaching. Pritz previously published the documents of the trial. Here, by following the main junctures of the political biography of László Bárdossy, he provides a view of the diplomatic history of a country that found itself on a track allowing less and less freedom of movement as time went on. The book also includes two major documents pertaining to the trial: the first indictment submitted to the court and the speech Bárdossy planned to deliver as his last plea. The volume comes complete with ample notes, a selected bibliography, maps displaying the territorial changes of Hungary under the Horthy regime and a full index of names and subjects.

László Bárdossy was born in 1890. His father, Jenő Bárdossy, was a ministerial counsellor. Following family tradition, the young Bárdossy studied law in Budapest, Berlin and Paris. His command of foreign languages, broad perspective, acute mind and brilliant debating talent distinguished him from his peers. In 1913, fresh out of law school, he joined the staff of the Ministry of Education. After the collapse of the Austro-Hungarian Monarchy in 1918, the Hungarian government sought out experienced civil servants loyal to the newly-independent Hungarian state to serve on the staff of its newly organised Foreign Ministry. Thus, in 1922, Bárdossy came to join the Press Department of the Foreign Ministry, from where he moved on to become number two in the Hungarian legation in London in 1930. In 1934, he was appointed Minister Plenipotentiary in Bucharest. In January 1941, Prime Minister Pál Teleki asked him to join his cabinet, to fill the office vacated by the death of Foreign Minister Pál Csáky. From his beginnings as a humble official, László Bárdossy had reached the peak of his career. In April 1941, following Pál Teleki's suicide, Regent Miklós Horthy appointed Bárdossy prime minister.

After a distinguished diplomatic career, Bárdossy's premiership was anything but glorious. Neither is the balance sheet of the Bárdossy cabinet, a depressing chapter in twentieth-century Hungarian history. During Bárdossy's term in office, which lasted hardly more than a year, Hungary took part in the occupation of Yugoslavia and went to war with, among others, the Soviet Union, Great Britain and the United States. Nor do the scales tip in his favour if we judge his domestic policies. Parliament passed the so-called Third Jewish Law, which outlawed sexual relations between Jews and Gentiles as "criminal miscegenation" and banned intermarriage.

Bárdossy's record as prime minister was marred not only by discrimination, but by atrocities that claimed thousands of lives. Several thousand civilians of Jewish and Serbian origin in the southern region annexed by Hungary from Yugoslavia were murdered by Hungarian gendarmes and soldiers. At the same time, the deportation of Jews seeking refuge in Hungary from Poland and Czechoslovakia—the majority were, in fact, Hungarians—indirectly led to a massacre of more than ten thousand. All this occurred despite Bárdossy's sharp rejection of the servility of the pro-German military clique (especially that of Chief-of-Staff Henrik Werth), and despite the fact that, given the political spectrum of the times, Bárdossy could not be regarded as an advocate of extremist views. A gifted and skilful diplomat with a broad outlook, Bárdossy, succeeding as prime minister after Count Teleki's death by suicide, promised to be the right person to ensure successful tacking between German demands and British expectations.

This was not to be. The new prime minister must have felt that he had little choice, not only because of the pressures exerted by the great powers, but also because the blind anti-Bolshevism of Regent Horthy and the general staff, coupled with a longing for a revisions of the Trianon-imposed frontiers, led inevitably to a pro-German stance. All this made it impossible for Bárdossy to dampen demanding voices with the help of subtle diplomatic moves and his noted charm. He doubtless knew that he was coming into a heavy legacy when he accepted the role assigned to him—the odious move of taking part in the German occupation of Yugoslavia despite the non-aggression pact the two countries had signed not long before. However, he could not have foreseen that within two months Germany would attack the Soviet Union, and in order not to appear a disloyal ally, Hungary would have to enter the war like other countries within the German sphere of influence. On top of this, members of the government took an unequivocally anti-Communist stance.

The dream of territorial revision (the partial recovery of regions which the country lost through the Trianon peace settlement) and the spectacular initial successes of the Wehrmacht determined the pro-war sentiments. The Hungarian army general staff believed the Soviet Union was a Golem with feet of clay, to be crushed in a six-week war. German victory hinged upon whether the German military would be able to force the Soviet giant to its knees in a *Blitzkrieg.* Hence, rational politics would have prompted the Hungarian government to wait until it became clear whether the German thrust forward on the battlefield proved successful or else ended up in a prolonged life-and-death struggle. It was decided at the 23 June cabinet meeting to sever diplomatic relations with the Soviet Union. Following this decision, a bombing raid on Kassa (Košice) by aircraft (whose provenance has not been clarified up to this day) was interpreted by the Hungarian army leadership as a Soviet provocation. As soon as Chief-of-Staff Werth informed Regent Horthy of it, the Regent without reflection declared war on the Soviet Union. The decision was made known to Bárdossy that very afternoon. All that remained for him to do was to report the situation to the government and Parliament. It is Bárdossy's historical responsibility that he failed to check this unwarranted zeal or to resist the Regent's decision. It must be noted, however, that to do so in a political climate completely at odds with such an action, Bárdossy would have needed much more wisdom, foresight and courage. Nor must it be forgotten that Bárdossy always lacked the political prestige that would allow him to turn against the Regent in a way that would have forced Horthy to rethink. The inevitable result of any resistance would have been the dismissal of the prime minister.

It characterises the contemporary mood well that when Bárdossy informed Parliament of Hungary's entry into the war, the deputies cheered. No one expressed the least criticism. By early September, Bárdossy managed to shake the Regent's confidence in the unwaveringly pro-German Werth, an opponent of the prime minister. He was replaced as chief-of-staff by Ferenc Szombathelyi. Nevertheless, this achievement is dwarfed by the consequences of entering the war, which soon took on catastrophic dimensions.

It was on 29 November that Bárdossy was handed the British ultimatum via the minister of the United States. It demanded the withdrawal of the Hungarian army from the war against the Soviet Union within a week. Faced with such a demand, which was impossible to meet, Bárdossy was able to elicit some sympathy on the part of the US envoy. This, however, did not change one whit the fact that, once the deadline passed, Hungary was at war with Great Britain as well.

It is fairly obvious that Bárdossy could not have guessed that after Pearl Harbour, Germany would unexpectedly declare war on the United States, thus forcing Hungary to move again. Hungary's response to this new challenge, however, once again points the finger at the prime minister's weakness. Although the Hungarian government at first only expressed "solidarity with" Germany and cut diplomatic ties with the United States; a German expression of disapproval was enough to make Bárdossy declare war on the United States, with the previous approval of the council of ministers, the very next day.

By Christmas 1941, Bárdossy became totally isolated politically. By then, many public figures of some standing had raised their voices in disapproval of the way the country had drifted into war and of the growing commitment to Germany. The only hope that remained was a new prime minister whose reputation was less eroded and not yet compromised. Thus, Bárdossy failed to fulfil the hopes invested in his personality. He proved incapable of reducing the double pressure weighing on the country by retaining or perhaps widening its scope for diplomatic manoeuvring. Instead, he drove the nation along an ever-narrower track leading in one direction only. Soon it became clear that this was not only a track that brooked no deviation, but a slippery slope leading irrevocably to catastrophe.

It cannot be denied that Bárdossy's culpability regarding the country's role in the war does not not extend beyond carrying out the Regent's wishes without opposing them. Viewed this way, one might say that Bárdossy did the job he was meant to do and was then dismissed. That may well have been the reason why the only person really surprised when the Regent withdrew his confidence from him in March 1942, appointing the pro-British Miklós Kállay to replace him, was the ever obedient Bárdossy himself. He had always performed his duties in an exemplary way, accepting responsibility even where he was not responsible.

Afterwards, Bárdossy would only play a secondary role in Hungarian political life. He increasingly became captive to his own previous decisions; he remained firmly committed to continuing the war on Germany's side and opposed any disengagement from the Germans, which he interpreted as abandoning them when they were in trouble.

In the indictment, Bárdossy was charged with having committed grievous crimes and unconstitutional acts that are unparalleled not only in Hungarian history, but in the history of the whole world" (p. 99). The charges included his role in the occupation of Yugoslavia, his personal responsibility in the attack against the Soviet Union, co-operation with the Hungarian National Socialists (the Arrow Cross), putting obstacles in the way of the attempted armistice with the Soviets in October 1944, responsibility for the atrocities committed during his premiership in the country's annexed southern regions (Újvidék/Novi Sad in the Voivodina), his speeches "inciting" participation in the war and the anti-Jewish measures taken while he was in office. According to the indictment, he personally unconstitutionally initiated and carried through the country's entry into the war with both the Soviet Union and the United States, deceiving members of the government who were coopted when the decision was taken.

When exercising the right of the accused to have the last word, Bárdossy accepted that all necessary sacrifices must be made to restore the nation's spiritual peace. Thus, he was reconciled with being called to account although he objected to the irregularities of the trial. He emphasised that the purpose of his speech was not to make excuses, but to explain his views in the interests of historical truth. He noted that the court disregarded the revisionist mood predominant in Hungary at the time, as well as German pressure upon the country. He explained that his political steps were motivated by his intention to fulfill German demands to the minimum and to prevent the greater evil of German occupation at the cost of lesser ones. With respect to the taking of personal responsibility, he underscored that he had the opportunity to save his own skin by rejecting the prime minister's office, but in his view this would not have served the country's best interests, since it was very likely that the prime minister coming after him would have meekly met German demands. In his speech he made a clear distinction between crime and responsibility; he accepted his personal responsibility for his policies, causing tremendous damage and immeasurable suffering to the country, but protested against being depicted as someone who had committed crimes in bad faith.

Pritz's book notes that Bárdossy's successive decisions gradually narrowed the country's room for manoeuvre in foreign policy, and that the country was drawn ever deeper into the maelstrom of war. Bárdossy's sense of diplomacy, was not enough to save Hungary for any length of time and to any significant degree from direct German domination and from the dangers of war. His skills may have sufficed in negotiations in which he could charm the other party, but he failed spectacularly when weighing up the most fateful issues. He was a well-trained diplomat who, nevertheless, could not measure up as prime minister of a country drifting into war. He was found wanting.

Pál Pritz, on occasion, presents the richly documented results of his scholarly research in a manner reminiscent of post-modern historiography. Beside traditional analysis of historical sources, the historian's intuition plays a role in reconstructing Bárdossy's life and career with Pritz even resorting to fictitious dialogue. The author's picture of his "hero", László Bárdossy, is therefore both authentic and exciting. ❧

Klára Hamburger

Death in Bayreuth

An Unknown Document About the Death of Franz Liszt

In 2004, Mrs István Czétényi, née Márta Maróth, presented the Hungarian Franz Liszt Society with valuable papers. The documents had originally belonged to Jolán Gerster (1889–1957), who had been Mrs. Czétényi's own beloved piano teacher and a cousin of her paternal grandmother. Between 1932 and 1944, Jolán Gerster had served as the secretary of the Liszt Society in its "last but one incarnation".

Jolán Gerster was born in 1889, the daughter of Béla Gerster (1850–1923), who had designed and built the Corinth Canal. From 1907 to 1909, she studied with Bartók at the Budapest Academy of Music, receiving her diploma as a piano teacher in 1911; the document bears Bartók's signature. Between 1910 and 1917, she lived in Berlin, where she taught and trained as a singer in the studio of her aunt, Etelka Gerster (1855–1820), an opera singer who had toured Europe and the United States with great success and had been considered Adelina Patti's rival. Jolán Gerster performed as a singer both in Berlin and in Budapest. After returning home, she was a teacher of voice and piano in private music schools in Budapest. She was one of the founders of the Hungarian Liszt Society and was one of its guiding spirits until the Society ceased to function during the siege of the city in 1944–45. After the war, she lived in straightened circumstances until her death in 1957.[1]

The president of the Hungarian Liszt Society during the Horthy era (until 1943) was Countess Margit Zichy (1874–1963), who had grown up in Liszt's circle: both her father, Count Géza Zichy (1849–1924), the one-armed concert pianist, and her maternal grandfather, Count Guidó Karátsonyi (1817–1885), were intimate friends of Liszt.

I found the report, published below, among Jolán Gerster's documents.[2] It is anonymous, yet the author's identity cannot be in doubt, as the writer must have been both professionally concerned with nursing and a clerk; furthermore, he identifies himself as one of those who had prepared Liszt's death mask. Bernhard Schnappauf (October 5, 1840–March 13, 1904) was a barber-surgeon in Bayreuth. He had served as Richard Wagner's valet since 1872 and accompanied him on his Italian journeys. Since I had been previously unaware of this

Klára Hamburger
has published widely on Liszt, including a biography in English (Corvina Books, 1987).

report and had no knowledge of its contents, I asked Professor Alan Walker, who is the best authority on the Liszt documents. He replied on January 21, 2005:

> I did not know that B. Sch. had left some recollections about the death of Liszt, but it does not surprise me. He and Cosima placed Liszt's body into the coffin and wheeled it on a handcart from Frau Fröhlich's house to Wahnfried, so I am sure that Sch. had some vivid memories.

I also made inquiries at the Richard Wagner Archives in Bayreuth. Frau Kristina Unger was kind enough to inform me that, albeit they have a few documents that originated from Schnappauf, this report is not one of them. I am indebted to Frau Unger for information on Schnappauf.

The report may have reached Budapest through the intermediary of Countess Zichy, who was in contact with Schnappauf's son, Dr Hans Schnappauf, a physician in Bayreuth. There are many handwritten letters, notes and instructions from Countess Zichy to Jolán Gerster, and from one of these—a letter written at the Countess's Nagyláng estate on August 8 1936—we learn that Dr Hans Schnappauf was planning to sell the shirt in which Liszt died to the Liszt Society. In another, undated note, the Countess notifies her secretary that Dr Schnappauf was willing to donate the shirt as well as a death mask authenticated by Cosima Wagner. The director of the Society, Gyula Novágh, must act without delay, since the Liszt Museum in Weimar was also interested in these relics. A further typewritten report, sent by Jolán Gerster to the Countess on August 29, 1936, informs her that the Liszt Society wanted the relics.

On the occasion of the 50th anniversary of Liszt's death, the Budapest Opera performed in Bayreuth on October 19 and 20, 1936, a staged version of the *Legend of St Elisabeth* as well as two ballets to Liszt's music: *Hungarian Fantasy* and *Carnival in Pesth* (that is, the Hungarian Rhapsody No.9 in Franz Doppler's orchestration). Countess Zichy travelled on their special train to Bayreuth. There she must have met Dr Hans Schnappauf and received the relics from him and with them the manuscript of the present report. There is a note, half handwritten and half typed, among Jolán Gerster's papers which states: "During the anniversary year of 1936, Dr Schnappauf donated these relics belonging to the estate of his father Bernhard [Schnappauf], Liszt's last attendant, to the Hungarian Liszt Society."

The Richard Wagner Archive in Bayreuth has no knowledge of any Dr Hans Schnappauf papers. However, Mária Eckhardt, the director of the Liszt Ferenc Museum and Research Centre in Budapest, prompted by the present article, made the fortunate discovery of the following items that obviously originate from the Schnappauf estate and which have since then been placed on exhibit:

(1) The shirt Liszt wore last as well as a handkerchief;

(2) A photograph, taken by I. Ganz in 1882, as well as a lock of Liszt's hair.

(3) Franz Liszt's death mask made of alabaster, signed by its makers, Schnappauf and Weißbrod.

However, there is no trace of the original of the present report; it must have been destroyed during the war.[3]

In the course of the last decade, we have learned a great deal about the elderly Liszt's state of health and sudden death in Bayreuth on July 31, 1886. Our main source is the third volume of Alan Walker's monumental Liszt biography.[4] A more recent publication by Professor Walker gives a detailed account of Liszt's death, based on the recollections of a reliable eyewitness.[5] Walker has much to say on the relationship between

Liszt and his daughter Cosima Wagner (1837–1930), as well as on that between Liszt and his grandchildren. The collection of letters from Liszt to Cosima and to his granddaughter Daniela, edited by the present writer, contains some further new facts.[6]

Liszt's illness and death, at the end of July 1886, could not have come at a more inopportune time for his daughter. The Bayreuth Festival, vital for the preservation of Wagner's work, was in full swing, and Cosima herself was making her debut as a director of *Tristan und Isolde.* Liszt, who was tact personified, especially where his widowed daughter was concerned, was extremely embarrassed to have become ill at this very time and place. His biographer Lina Ramann writes in her memoirs: "The master repeatedly said, 'I wish I had fallen ill somewhere else; to become an invalid here in front of the entire world is really too stupid.'"[7] At the time, before modern drugs, pneumonia was a serious illnes at any age. A 75-year-old man whose constitution had been weakened by various ailments really had little chance, even with the best care available. What the patient needed to make the suffering of his final days more bearable would have been human warmth and loving nursing around the clock. A kind gesture, a comforting word, someone to wipe his face, to help him sit up or change the cold compress to lower his temperature, someone to offer him food or drink: these were precisely the things that Cosima had neither the time nor the desire to provide. As for her daughters Isolde and Eva,[8] the thought didn't even occur to them. Her two older daughters were not present. Daniela von Bülow[9] was on her honeymoon at the time, and Blandine von Bülow[10] was living in Italy with her husband. Liszt's young pupil Lina Schmalhausen (1864–1928), who had looked after him in Rome and Budapest, would have been eager to take over the task of taking care of "the beloved master", but she was hated in Bayreuth, and Cosima forbade her to set foot in Liszt's apartment. There is something else for which Cosima has been rightfully reproached by posterity: she neglected to call a Catholic priest to her father—an abbé—to administer the last rites. (Cosima herself had converted to Protestantism to please Wagner.)

The present, hitherto unknown document shows that Cosima entrusted her father to a professional attendant at least for the last days of his life. Schnappauf may not have been able to offer love, but at least he provided the patient with adequate medical care. The report shows that he knew his job and did whatever was necessary and possible. It also relates to us what Lina Schmalhausen couldn't see from her hiding place on the balcony.[11] In particular, what injection Liszt was given.

In my opinion, Schnappauf's report and the invoice attached to it can be accepted as authentic and reliable evidence on Liszt's death and all the technical matters relating to his body. This remains true even though the document is available only in a typewritten copy produced fifty years after the event. Schnappauf knew all the people he hired: the sculptor, the undertaker, various specialists, the employees of the undertakers and the pall-bearers whom he lists by name. The invoice, which of course includes his own fee, shows that he organised and paid for everything. The significance of his report is in no way diminished by his failure to mention a number of people who attended the funeral, such as Daniela von Bülow and many of Liszt's pupils.

The English translation of Bernhard Schnappauf's unsigned report, *"Bericht über den letzten Lebenstag, Tod und Beerdigung des Abbé Dr. von Liszt",* follows.[12]

[Bernard Schnappauf:]

An Account of the Last Day, Death and Burial of the Abbé Dr von Liszt.

[Anonymous typescript, on paper (34 x 20,5 cm). 2 pages. Invoice on p.3.]

The condition of Dr von Liszt, who had arrived here on July 22, had in recent days deteriorated to the point that occasional somnolence set in. I went on duty at 9 o'clock in the morning on Saturday, July 31. His pulse was then 110, his breathing 32, his temperature 38.4. The patient still had the strength to expel the [phlegm] that had accumulated in his bronchial tubes. He was made to sit up from time to time and, all through the day, was given alternately strong consommé, red wine, very special white wine with seltzer water, and *Knickebein* (a mixture of cognac and sugar).

Around 5 o'clock in the afternoon came Dr Landgraf, Physician to the County Court,[13] and University Professor Fleischer from Erlangen.[14] The examination revealed that the pneumonia, which had previously been only partial, had spread to the entire back of the lungs. The patient's temperature when last taken by me was 39.4, his pulse 110–115.

It was agreed that both physicians would return at 8 o'clock, and that Dr Fleischer would possibly stay for the night. Around 6 o'clock, I noticed that the phlegm which until then was expelled in powerful bursts was suddenly becoming congested. I made the patient sit up more frequently in order to help him expectorate, but in so doing, I noticed that his pulse was getting weaker and slower. Dr. Fleischer, who had just arrived, immediately sent me to the pharmacy for camphor oil. I had sulphur ether myself; both substances were injected several times, and a mustard compress was applied simultaneously on the chest and calves. The feet were placed on a hot-water bottle. Yet the patient no longer responded to these drastic measures. His pulse became weaker and weaker, his breath shorter and shorter, further impaired by the rattle caused by the accumulated phlegm. Death occurred at a quarter past eleven, without any struggle or agony.

Present at the time of death were Frau Cosima Wagner, Drs Landgraf and Fleischer, the servant Michel[15] and me. Dr von Liszt's two students, Herr Göllerich[16] and Herr Stavenhagen[17] sat in the next room. Frau Cosima remained alone with the body; I was in the next room. The other gentlemen went home, Michel went to bed. At 5 in the morning Frau Wagner came; I shaved the deceased and washed the body and placed it on the couch with Michel's help. We dressed the body in a shirt and white undergarments, black stockings and buckled shoes, black trousers, a vest, a soutane and cravat. He wore a white flannel on his chest, with an amulet sewn in. We then laid the body on the bed, which had been adorned for the solemn occasion. I woke up the undertakers Eifer and Fariberger to have them decorate the room and called a Catholic priest to bless the body. Prelate Korzendorfer expressed surprise that the deceased had not received the last rites before his passing. After the room had been draped in black and decorated with flowers, a bust of Wagner was placed at the head of the deceased and, at his feet, a precious crucifix loaned by Dr Beer, Senior Medical Officer. They lit the wax candles on stands provided by the Catholic Church. The priest came around a quarter before nine and performed the blessing. Then came Dr Gumein; he examined the body and issued the certificate right away. Herr Korzendorfer and Herr Gross[18] notified the Registry Office.

The family then gathered in silent prayer. At her own request, even Miss Schmalhausen was admitted. The first donation was a bouquet of forget-me-nots.[19] The general public was now allowed to enter. Miss Isolde became indisposed because of the heat and had to leave the room. The family withdrew around 1 o'clock, and the room was closed. Weissbrod, a sculptor whom I had called in, Peter Kästner and myself prepared the death mask, which turned out excellently.[20] The photographer Brand took five pictures of the body.[21]

[p.2] Around three o'clock I went to the Festspielhaus. Michel stayed with the body. Mrs Fröhlich, the wife of the forester,[22] expressed her disapproval that the body had been laid out in her house and none had asked for her leave as the householder.

On Monday, August 2,[23] I went to the house of the deceased at six o'clock in the morning and noticed that the body was already starting to decompose, a process that manifested itself in the swelling of the head. Michel had rashly informed Herr Fröhlich about this state of affairs. In great agitation, the forester told me that the corpse must leave the house, or else he would have recourse to the help of our police, something he had a right to do for sanitary reasons.

I hurried at once to Frau Cosima, who was still in bed, told her what had happened and received orders to transfer the body to Wahnfried as soon as it was placed in a closed coffin.

I hurried to [the undertaker] Bayerlein, and hastened the making of the metal coffin, which was then lined with white satin by the upholsterer Nachtigall. Then I rode to Dr Landgraf's, informed him of Fröhlich's plans and procured chloride, sulphuric acid and some bowls for disinfection. Herr Fröhlich confirmed to Dr Landgraf as well that he insisted on the removal of the body. I charged Frau Hübner from the undertaker's and ... *(sic)* to bring a coffin. Around 9 o'clock, Dr Gumein, Frau Hübner and I laid the body in the coffin. Frau Cosima spent a few minutes in silent prayer, then the coffin was closed, screwed down and carried by Bayerlein's people (Bleil and Körner) and the gardener's apprentice. Frau Cosima supported the coffin at the foot and I at the head. It was brought into the main hall of Wahnfried through the side door, placed on a makeshift stand and covered with black material taken from the room decoration.

The burial was set for Tuesday, August 3,[24] and the time was fixed for 10 o'clock in the morning. I requested the ringing of the bells from the Protestant Deanery; my request was granted. Mayor Muncker[25] selected the burial site. Herr Wolfel, the mason, had the grave covered with stones. Eiser provided the hearse, coachman Stemmer the horses. I asked Messrs Brand, Senf, Weih, Seiler, Staudt, Stopp,

Zeisel, Schamel, Heller, Händel, Golz, Richter and Zimmermann to be pall-bearers. Herr von Loën,[26] then representing the Grand Duke of Weimar,[27] as well as Mottl,[28] Glasenapp,[29] and Mihalovich (as a Hungarian)[30] were asked to hold the four corners of the coffin cover. About half past nine the pall-bearers took their places in front of the coffin, surrounded by lights, and prelate Korzendorfer began the blessing. Liszt's friend, the Baroness Meyendorff, née Princess Gortschakoff,[31] fainted in the hall and was carried by Stopp into the dining room. I helped the lady on to her feet with ... *(sic)* and with a glass of red wine. At Frau Wagner's behest, a branch of ivy, presumably from the Master's grave, was wound around the cross on the coffin. After the coffin had been placed on the four-horse carriage, the funeral cortège started on its way. In front of the carriage walked Michel, Pauline[32] and myself, carrying the decorations. Behind the coffin followed Count Wedell,[33] the representative of the Grand Duke, Joukowsky,[34] Siegfried,[35] and Dr Thode.[36] Frau Wagner with the children rode in the first carriage, the Princess Hatzfeld[37] and the Baroness Meyendorff in the second. The banners, borrowed from the gymnastics club, were carried by Liszt's pupils Reuss,[38] Stavenhagen, Göllerich, etc. The carriage stopped at the black gate, the pall-bearers took the coffin to the grave and lowered it to its resting place. Muncker, Reuss and Court Councillor Gille[39] spoke after the blessing. The Requiem Mass took place on Wednesday at 10 o'clock in the Catholic Church. Court organist Bruckner[40] played the organ and five teachers sang the vigils.

Afterwards, I took the decorations to Wahnfried and the wreaths to the cemetery. In order to prevent the theft of the wreaths, I had them hung in the church. A requiem mass was planned by Frau Cosima for 11 o'clock at night on Thursday, August 5,[41] in the cemetery chapel, but it came to naught because the Protestant clergy did not allow the use of the cemetery church.

Invoice [p 3]

Municipal costs	99.84 Marks	Carriage with flowers (from Renner)	15
Coffin, provided by Bayerlein	311	Torches	7.80
Wax candles	10.30	Posters, announcing the Requiem	2.80
Catholic church charges	12	Servants, police	11
Sashes	63	Impregnation of the body	30
Gloves for the pall-bearers	18	Planting of the gravesite	13
Pharmacy	12.85	Miscellaneous	80
Bells at both Protestant churches	10.50	Personal expenses	120
		Transplanting flowers	4.50

NOTES

1 ■ I am grateful to Mrs István Czétényi for providing me with valuable family information, in addition to the precious documents.

2 ■ The typescript, on larger-than-usual paper, fills two pages and is single-spaced. A third page contains the list of expenses. It is likely that the typescript was prepared in 1936 by Jolán Gerster, who worked from the original German document.

This hypothesis is based on the fact that Miss Gerster had been using this paper format, which is no longer standard not only earlier but occasionally later on as well. The typewriter must have been Hungarian: it had an "ä" but no "ß". The typist must have had an excellent command of German in order to decipher the old handwriting.

3 ■ The copy contains numerous errors, due in part to the typing and in part to a faulty reading of the manuscript. Sometimes the copyist left certain signs blank if she could not read them. Schnappauf had committed some errors of his own.

4 ■ Alan Walker: *The Final Years*, 1861–1886. New York: Alfred A. Knopf, 1996.

5 ■ *The Death of Franz Liszt Based on the Unpublished Diary of His Pupil Lina Schmalhausen.* Ithaca—London: Cornell University Press, 2002. Unfortunately, like many publications from the English-speaking world, this important volume presents German-language documents only in English translation.

6 ■ *Franz Liszt. Lettres à Cosima et à Daniela.* Présentées et annotées par Klára Hamburger. Sprimont, Mardaga, 1996.

7 ■ Lina Ramann: *Lisztiana. Erinnerungen an Franz Liszt* (1873–1886/87). Hrsg. Arthur Seidl. Textrev. Friedrich Schnapp. Mainz, Schott, 1983, p. 375.

8 ■ Isolde Wagner (1865–1919), Eva Wagner (1867–1942).

9 ■ Daniela von Bülow (1860–1940) had just married the art historian Henry Thode (1857–1920).

10 ■ Blandine von Bülow (1863–1941) was married to Count Biagio Gravina.

11 ■ See Alan Walker: *The Death of Franz Liszt* (see 5 above).

12 ■ The original German text was published in the Autumn 2005 issue of *Studia musicologica.*

13 ■ Dr Karl Landgraf, Richard Wagner's family doctor.

14 ■ Dr Fleischer was called in by Cosima.

15 ■ Mihály Kreiner, Liszt's Hungarian manservant [called Mishka].

16 ■ August Göllerich (1859–1923), pianist.

17 ■ Bernhard Stavenhagen (1862–1914), pianist.

18 ■ Adolf von Gross (1845–1931), a Bayreuth banker, was Cosima's advisor.

19 ■ The typescript says "Kranz", but it is likely that a *Strauss* or bouquet was meant, which was placed in his hands by Lina Schmalhausen. She later added a rose. "I placed forget-me-nots and a red rose in his hands before the coffin was closed. I was the only one to adorn the body with flowers", as she writes in her diary. See Ernst Burger: *Franz Liszt. Eine Lebenschronik in Bildern und Dokumenten.* Munich: Paul List, 1986, p. 322.

20 ■ The painter Paul von Joukowsky (1845–1912), who lived in the same building, was also present when the death mask was made.

21 ■ Lina Schmalhausen wrote: "Hans Brand took some photographs at my request." See Burger, *Franz Liszt,* p. 322.

22 ■ Liszt used to stay not at Wahnfried, but with the Fröhlichs across the street in the Siegfried-straße. The street is now named after Liszt, and the apartment where he died is now the Liszt Museum of the City of Bayreuth.

23 ■ From here on, Schnappauf is consistently off by one day.

24 ■ Schnappauf, erroneously, has August 2.

25 ■ Theodor Muncker (1823–1900), mayor of Bayreuth since 1863.

26 ■ Baron August von Loën (1827–1887), the director of the Weimar theatre.

27 ■ Grand Duke Carl Alexander (1818–1901).

28 ■ Conductor Felix Mottl (1856–1911).

29 ■ Carl Friedrich Glasenapp (1847–1915), Wagner's biographer.

30 ■ Composer Ödön Mihalovich (1842–1929), Liszt's friend.

31 ■ Baroness Olga von Meyendorff, née Gortschakoff (1838-1926).

32 ■ Pauline Apel, Liszt's housekeeper from Weimar.

33 ■ Count Oskar von Wedell (1835–1908), Weimar court chamberlain.

34 ■ See n.20 above.

35 ■ Siegfried Wagner (1869–1930), the son of Richard and Cosima Wagner.

36 ■ See n.9 above.

37 ■ Princess Marie von Hatzfeld (1820–1911), a close friend of Liszt.

38 ■ Eduard Reuss (1851–1911), conductor in Karlsruhe.

39 ■ Dr. Carl Gille (1813–1899) from Jena, a friend of Liszt.

40 ■ Anton Bruckner (1824–1896), the composer.

41 ■ Schnappauf here, as always, mistakes by one day.

Paul Griffiths

Austerity and Exuberance

Contemporary Music at the 2005 Budapest Autumn Festival

Where music is concerned, the Budapest Autumn Festival, founded in 1992, is the direct successor to the Contemporary Music Weeks that similarly took place in late October, with the same function of offering a two-way window. New Hungarian music is shown to the world, or at least to a decent number of professional and non-professional visitors, while Budapest audiences—and composers—are exposed to new work from abroad.

This time the big Hungarian event was the première, on October 22, of Zoltán Jeney's *Funeral Rite,* a composition a quarter century in the making, scored for full choral and orchestral forces with vocal soloists plus a concertino percussion quartet (Amadinda), and lasting over three hours. These hours pass slowly, no doubt by design; they hang heavy. The work is a sequence of immense slabs, each uniform in texture and colour, each starting, continuing and stopping. Harmony, as one might expect from this composer, is not a progressive force but static. Perhaps more surprising is the dependence in the vocal writing on plainsong and folk melodies, or on modes and motifs typical of these—not least in the opening 'Motto', which sets a striking allegory by Pilinszky, this being one of many modern or folk poems alternating with the liturgical Latin that provides the bulk of the text.

The scale changes all the time. Latin texts generally call on the full orchestra to accompany the chorus or soloists, whereas some of the other sections are composed for a solo singer with just one instrumentalist (baritone and pizzicato cello in the 'Motto') or a small group (the mezzo-soprano Katalin Károlyi and Amadinda in an adagissimo setting of a poem in Italian by Laura Romani). The pace, too, is not unvaried, even if much of the music is slow. Yet Jeney avoids drama. In what may be the longest Requiem ever written, there is no *Dies irae.* Many of the texts, both ancient and modern, are given as prayers or readings, evenly delivered.

As a consequence, some few excited moments stand out. In three widely separated passages, verses from the psalm *De profundis clamavi* each time instigate, to those opening words, an image of clam-

---

Paul Griffiths
is the author of books on Stravinsky, Bartók, the string quartet and, most recenty, of The Penguin Companion to Classical Music *(2004).*

our in which the whole range of the chorus is scanned at lightning speed, from the basses' low D sharp to the sopranos' high C. Not so thrilling but certainly effective is the setting of the Lord's Prayer for men's choir and orchestra in staggered rhythms, producing a stretch of dark haze. There are also touching arrangements of folk laments for solo women's voices with ensembles including *cimbalom* and percussionists stationed in a balcony.

Through most of its course, however, the work makes little effort at musical interest. Such is its austerity—despite the large forces involved. It proceeds. And that is supposed to be enough. Jeney does not, as Stravinsky did, reinvent rituals and reinvoke faith for an age lacking both. His position, with regard to the material he assembles, is that of an anthologist, not a forger of some vital unity. He stands curiously apart and leaves us, his audience, with no option but to do likewise. Attending the performance was rather like being present at a ceremony in a distant culture. One could admire the dedication on stage—especially from the soprano Klára Kolonits, from Károlyi, from the baritone Róbert Rezsnyák and from Zoltán Kocsis conducting the National Philharmonic Orchestra and Chorus—but not share in it.

One could certainly appreciate, though, the clarity of sound and sense of space in the National Concert Hall, which is the large auditorium in the new Palace of Arts. The building—near but thankfully apart from the bizarre National Theatre—has an inviting frontage of glass and soft, twinkling neon bands, while the interior is spruce, not grand.

The next night, in the small-scale theatre within the same building, was music as different from Jeney's as may be imagined—and by no means only in coming from outside Hungary. Where Jeney's music used normal instruments in normal ways, this did not. Where Jeney's summoned auras of antiquity, this was breathtakingly new. Where Jeney's was content to present, this acted, driving onward. Excellent performances helped, from the Ensemble Modern expertly conducted by Bradley Lubman. But propelling those performances were the scores and the imagination of Helmut Lachenmann, who was being celebrated in the year of his seventieth birthday.

Lachenmann's course, over the last three decades and more, through a period of decaying musical values, has been hearteningly sure. In the late sixties he made the discovery that non-standard ways of playing instruments—scrapes, rustles, breath tones and a myriad other noises—could support musical forms as persuasive as those produced in the past by tonal harmony. *Mouvement (—vor der Erstarrung),* or *Mouvement (—before Paralysis),* the Lachenmann classic in the first half of this programme, showed the strength of this approach applied to an ensemble of fifteen players. Lachenmann's music is about the discovery of new beauty, but its purpose is fundamentally moral. In expanding the limits of musical sound, he questions received opinion. What he wants, he has said, is "Art as a foretaste of freedom in an age without freedom."

Of course, freedom, once found, easily becomes limitation, and the search has to proceed. Once Lachenmann had shown that music could be made in the absence of defined pitches, and therefore in the absence of anything like conventional harmony and melody, the abnegation might itself have turned into a set of rules, a standard practice. He had to go further by allowing regular sounds back into his music, in a process that he had begun by the time he wrote *Mouvement* in 1983–4, which has now resulted in a work as exuberant as *Concertini.* Completed in the early summer of 2005, and playing for about three-quarters of an hour without interruption, *Concertini* is scored for an ensemble almost twice as big as that of *Mouvement,* but an important principle remains: the sense of instruments—and instrumentalists—listening to one another. Lachenmann's music brings to larger groupings the responsibilities and the rewards of chamber music, how sounds and rhythms have to be matched.

Concertini makes a special point of that matching by splitting the ensemble between front and back stages. The tuba at the back may discourse with a trombone at the front, the guitar at the back with the harp at the front. As the composer has pointed out, the piece warrants its title by virtue of the small groupings that are constantly being brought forward. But rarely are these maintained for long. The piece moves with unflagging energy, all the way from the wooden knock on the piano at the front with which it begins to the metal resonance from the rear in which it vanishes. ❧

THEATRE & FILM

Tamás Koltai

Cloth Supplied

István Tasnádi: *Phaedra* • *D.J. avagy az istentagadó büntetése* (D. J., or the Punishment of the Atheist) • *Passion*

When I was a boy, some tailors' shop signs (if a tailor had a sign at all, as most worked at home in straightened circumstances, with only a few customers knowing about them) would state that they undertook to cut suits from cloth supplied by the customer. Cloth supplied did not always mean something bought in a shop: often new clothes would be made up from old. More than once I was given an old suit of my father's. On these occasions the tailor would ask, "Adjustment to fit?" Then he made a new suit out of the old.

The theatre, too, often works with cloth supplied. There were the great myths of the Ancient Greeks, and it is from these that the tragedies were tailored. Later ages would often look on the Greek tragedies as finish-ed suits, merely refitting the subject to their own size. But later on, still, a significant proportion of playwrights did not hesitate to borrow written and unwritten stories, tales and legends no matter where they found them, or to rewrite works that had already been published in print. This did not constitute plagiarism: Shakespeare, Molière and Brecht worked in this way, not to mention many other important theatrical tailors.

Refitting is not uncommon today. István Tasnádi's adjustment of *Phaedra* was born out of the wish to replace the sacrality of antique myths with the contemporary and the profane. If we draw an imaginary straight line from the Ur-myths to the variants of our own age, his play lies at the end of the end—not just for chronological reasons, but because of the matter-of-fact, rather dispassionate perspective and because of an irony that is intellectually detached.

Recent Hungarian productions of *Medea* come in handy if one wishes to clarify the degrees of detachment from, and disenchantment with, mythology. Director Sándor Zsótér's version of *Medea* by the German Expressionist Hans Henny Jahnn keeps to the original myth of visceral passion, in which the surface is soaked in concealed instincts, identity crises and sexual and power orientations as linen is soaked in blood, and the story inevitably leads to the collapse of the "bourgeois" family. To some extent, Gábor Zsámbéky's interpretation of Euripides' *Medea* (Katona József Theatre,

---

Tamás Koltai

editor of Színház, *a theatre monthly, is* The Hungarian Quarterly*'s regular theatre critic.*

2004) demytholigises it, as the setting is a neutral everyday environment, with echoes of familiar problems (adultery, divorce, custody of children). Still, Zsámbéki's production conveys an absolute faith in a moral order as a transcendent divine system of justice. The validity of tragedy is ensured here in the confrontation of the mythic and the profane. Mihai Măniuţiu, a Romanian director, no longer believes in a supreme moral order, so while re-establishing the rite, he annuls the tragedy. In the production by the Tamási Áron Theatre from Sfîntu Gheorge, Transylvania (which recently came to Pécs) Medea does not kill her children: she just pretends to do so for the benefit of the outside world. Through this she hopes to move away ("emigrate") from a ritual in which the general loss of values is manifest in a grotesque mass hooliganism, a ritual acting as a symbol of a way of life, a ritual that takes the form of a folkloristic choral dance.

Tasnádi's *Phaedra* goes even further than this, embedding the figures of the myth in inadequate, degraded living conditions. Here, Theseus—his mythical counterpart was fighting somewhere far away—is lying on a hospital bed, a living corpse who has been in a coma for three years. What in the myth was a power vacuum generates here a feeling of awkward insecurity from the outset. For Tasnádi, the father idol becomes an even greater obstacle to Hippolytus' retarded development: the young man, though both intellectually and biologically mature, appears infantile. Neither is Phaedra's situation enviable, as partner in power to a vegetable, a pseudo-widow, a wife left to waste away and a stepmother—ultimately, a woman on the brink of her change of life, whose last significant sexual experience was when her four-year-old stepson slid a teaspoon under her panties at the dinner table. Thus the representatives of both generations are impotent, both as men and as rulers. Neither does the situation change when Theseus unexpectedly comes out of his coma. Unable to decide whether to believe his son or his beloved (Phaedra claims that Hippolytus raped her, while Hippolytus claims that she seduced the macho Sauros), out of revenge he tries, unsuccessfully, to cover his wife. We know the truth: Phaedra has declared her passion to her stepson, who has rejected her as too old and forced his thug of a friend on her. The boy and the friend will both be liquidated, the status quo is restored, and they can go to dinner. Phaedra's real son, the retarded Minitaurus (sic!), who has thus far been fiddling with his mobile in silence, now recounts his poetic vision of the end of the world, which is eerily similar to a description of a tsunami.

The text surfs between the ancient metric form and contemporary vulgarism; hexameter alternates with stark prose, and mythological images clash with psychoanalytical, economic, political and computer jargon. Right through the verse, the chorus takes on a fully alienating role. Tasnádi deliberately makes a montage of contrasting historic periods, ways of speech and behaviour and layers of style in order to capture the clichéd emptiness of a world ridden of its myths by rubbishy ersatz. The laconic severity, coldness and sardonic irony of the text mostly works well. The problem is that it has no focus, direction or structure; in short, it has no dramaturgy (to the extent that it could be cut or extended at any point; there is no structural connection between its parts). The conflict is between the statements delivered, rather than between dramatic characters, layers of style or people. Ultimately, even if we are aware that this is a deliberate, cold, Germanic act of "word-processing", this leads to a loss of all that is personal. It is a glaring example of dramatic carelessness that not even the multifunctional role of narrator (priest, doctor, psychiatrist, anyone), displayed emphatically at the beginning, is carried through; the production lets one of the outstanding actors, Tilo Werner, gradually vanish from the scene. Its function clashes with that of the chorus, and by the end, more or less non-existent, it vanishes too. The whole play has been sacrificed on the altar of cool, cerebral writing à la German theatre.

This was an international project, premiered at the Salzburg Festival. The companies involved were the Busche und Mans und Sophiensäle from Berlin, the Schauspiel/Staatstheater from Stuttgart and the Trafó and Krétakör Theatre from Budapest, the latter currently the Hungarian company best known internationally. Its manager, Árpád Schilling, staged the production. Schilling is known for not having a characteristic "style", preferring to try new ventures, treating each one as a test for himself. One such test is bilinguality. The blend of text well-nursed in both Hungarian and German causes no problems, and the production finds an ingenious framework for it by projecting a translation as a backdrop for the benefit of audiences. With the exception of the tirade in which Hippolytus is impeached, the only words spoken in Hungarian are those of Dorottya Udvaros in the title role, and those of Gergely Bánki, who delivers the final tsunami soliloquy; they are answered by the bilingual Tilo Werner, currently a member of the Krétakör company. Schilling does not provoke his audience; the actors intone in the matter-of-fact everyday style that German productions have a reputation for. The professional standard and coordination of the actors cannot be faulted; hard work in rehearsal makes those not in the know believe that this *ad hoc* team has been working with the director for years. The three-person female chorus negotiates with superior ease an ironical song style as well as those glissandos rising to piercing screams. The composer Albert Márkos himself provides the cello accompaniment. As the stranger within the group—in part, the production is about this strangeness—Dorottya Udvaros brings Phaedra's inner changes, emotional range and menopausal problems to life through her diction alone. At the end, what remains of the family, complemented by the conforming chorus, groups together into a photograph, and sucks her in, too.

A more delicate experiment with cloth supplied is a production by an *ad hoc* team. The cloth was Mozart's *Don Giovanni* and it was recut in Zsámbék, in an amphitheatre constructed in a natural environment (a hillside), under the title of *D. J., or the Punishment of the Atheist.* The premiere was a so-called public rehearsal, a half-ready production, and director Balázs Simon warned the audience in advance that it was being shown a phase in their work on the play: they wanted to test the effect of what they have done, and discover how to go on with it. The D. J. of the title refers to Don Juan (as well as to disc jockey, of course), and the opus that is staged is a paraphrase, as the subtitle reveals—*"Light drama" in two acts, based on, and perhaps in the spirit of, the operas of Mozart and Da Ponte.* The "light drama" is a rough translation of *dramma giocoso,* so all intentions refer to the original, even though Miklós Paizs has written new text for both the arioso parts and for the prose scenes used in place of the recitatives. Attila Pacsay has re-orchestrated the music for a small ensemble using electronic and acoustic instruments. As to the question whether this is permissible, the answer is that everything is—provided it works. The goal is clear: to bring the play closer to the present. This is the objective of all interpretations worth their salt, even those that don't change a thing in the score, or in the text (the latter assumes that the performance is in the original language). Nowadays the attic is full of performances that transpose the events of *Don Giovanni* to a modern-day environment, with the wildest of directorial associations, from Patrice Chéreau to Martin Kuseji and Luca Ronconi, to mention just a few productions of recent years. All of these parade their profane everyday nature, ignoring the universal dimensions of the work, dimensions which were brilliantly explored in a 1982 Budapest production by the Russian director Yuri Lyubimov. In order to emphasise a direct contemporary attitude, one need not rewrite the play. There are two well-known examples of this: one is Peter Sellars' famous (1987) staging, which transports the events to blackest Harlem with Don Giovanni as a drug baron and the other by Peter Brook (1998, Aix-en-Provence), which places them in an abstract geometrical space.

In terms of its attitude, the present experiment is closest to Brook's famous 1983 *Carmen,* which was a version rewritten for four singers and three actors, and orchestrated for an orchestra of fourteen, with no chorus or ballet (that is, with a completely new musical context). There was vehement criticism and keen support from the best circles; the opinion of the latter, which I agree with, is that it was good for Brook, not Bizet. That is the point. It is a fruitless task debating fidelity or the lack of it—if something of quality is created, it matters not what its parentage is. The procedure is patented; it is not a new discovery. *Don Giovanni* was performed "fitted to size" (though not rewritten) twenty-odd years ago by a provincial touring company in Hungary. The principal director of the Budapest Opera House at the time wrote of it: "It was a dilettante production in the best sense, performed as it was in a courtyard. Without bias I can say that it was fantastic. The environment suited the play, the music was good, and the whole thing felt like a Mozart musical without the customary rapture. This despite the fact that many of the cast were not competent singers. Strangely enough, this did not detract from the final experience. It was much more exciting than any performance that is perfectly professional but empty."

A comment like this makes it clear that it is reflexivity that gives meaning to this operation. It is not that one must act in the spirit of Mozart or Da Ponte, but that one must relate to it. The handling of the Masetto–Zerlina relationship is a good example from the staging of Balázs Simon and his team. In the wedding scene, a "bigshot" mocks them and, by the end, they become completely confused. How can they cope if they cannot trust each other enough to leave the other for a single moment? The slang, the psychology and the behaviour are all spot-on. Zerlina, of whom the directorial genius Ponnelle once said that she spends her days waiting for the call from Hollywood, is fed by D. J. with the perfect phrase—that she is talented. In a later scene, however, Zerlina's rather down-to-earth emotion is so forcefully expressed that it ill matches what follows in the mellow melody line of her aria. The coordination of text, situation and music is sometimes successful, sometimes not. The text is sometimes distinctly witty (in a few arias the Hungarian rhymes with the same sounds as the original Italian), sometimes inane, or clichéd and vulgar; the music is sometimes humorously orchestrated (with the hearty sound of brass), sometimes not orchestrated at all (the second part closes with a duo for a piano and viola).

The Champagne aria, the only item to be turned into rock music, could be a cornerstone. Péter Novák grabs the microphone and sings the bravura piece as if it were a rock number, his trademark that is—the new orchestration offered many like opportunities where such and other devices could have been employed. Novák does not have an operatic voice, but then he does not need one: his singing is just as "below" Mozart's music as the role he plays. The deviant is replaced by an unscrupulous nobody; the libertine aristocrat, brutal and sophisticated, is replaced by a hero of our times, the flamboyant media star. This is a good aperçu, and it also shows how the world has changed. Other motifs are not dealt with at all. If those behind the production are taking their work seriously, there is much work left for them to do.

Also in Zsámbék—where performances are staged in the concrete silos of a Soviet rocket base built into the side of the hill (hence its name: Zsámbék Theatre Base)—the cloth supplied was what is perhaps humanity's best-known "story", a production of the *The Passion.* The concrete bunkers, paths, balconies and roofs in the forests and clearings provide a wild, "uncivilised" environment for theatre-makers keen to escape from their usual surroundings. Resourceful directors find a number of new locations each year. The creators of *Passion,* director Árpád Sopsits and choreographer Csaba Horváth, moved into an unused reinforced concrete building, whose sombre beauty would be the envy of the world's theatrical nonconformists, from Brook to Warlikowski. Pure concrete, the glow of the trees in the spotlights can be seen through the high windows. The walls are concrete grey, almost white, and on the floor is a thick layer of flour. As the actors move, a white cloud of dust rises as if the cracks in the floor were breathing as the feet squeeze the air from under them, keeping that white mist suspended above them. The text is just an extract, details from the Gospels and the Apocrypha; it is the music and the movement that count. The passion of Christ emerges from the continuous drift, flow and unstoppable dynamic of the group, of the "masses". In places it sets off to or from known iconographic signs, depictions of churches, the *topoi* of icons and paintings —all the while using an unusual melange of the raw, the sacred, the tragic and the grotesque to narrate the stations of the Cross. The parallel music—not just accompaniment, as it has an inspirational function on par with that of the movement—uses sacred music and details of oratorios, just as it involves motifs from jazz and contemporary music, or the tense acoustic of the one sustained note.

The story of *Passion* can be followed, as text and movement are subtly interwoven. More important than the narrative, however, is its emotional and intellectual content, enriched as it is by a wide array of associations. And the *image.* The body language is a sight in itself; neither backdrops nor particular lighting effects overtake its theatricality: every dancer is an actor, and every actor is a dancer. Tibor Pálffy as Christ is an emblem just being himself, with his charismatic presence, to which he adds the exceptional concentration of his movement (such as the leaden slowness with which he takes up the iconographic poses of the Crucifixion or the Resurrection). His being radiates corporality and unworldliness—anything more would be out of place. The choreography creates many beautiful moments, the most beautiful perhaps being the Calvary scene and the scenes following the Crucifixion, in which a "living" cross (a human body clinging tightly to the suffering Christ) shares in His agony and metamorphosis—in shocking counterpoint to a hostile, inimical, uncaring world. Cloth was supplied for this production, too, but fortunately those who created it felt no need to add ideological frills to it. Christ's Passion in this staging can be experienced as art, in its immediacy, without any explanation. ❧

Erzsébet Bori

And Yet It Moves...

Áron Gauder & Erik Novák's *Nyócker* and the Revival of Hungarian Animation

After long lean years, Hungarian animation has once again reached the world's big screens. A young production team headed by Áron Gauder and Erik Novák has seen their animation feature *Nyócker* (The District) haul in one international prize after another in 2005: best feature-length European animation, Annency (France); grand prize of the International Animation Film Festival of Kecskemét; grand prize of the Ottawa Animation Festival; Seoul International Animation Festival grand prize. Perhaps even more important than critical success has been the public's enthusiastic response worldwide to *The District.**

This has happened at a time when we thought we were counting down the last hours of Hungarian animation. In the summer of 2005, a convention was held of film-makers, producers, curators, state and foundation fund executives and decision-makers and directors of TV channels; it was suffused with a sense of bleak prospects and a profound despair. Of the paltry funds allocated by the state to film-making, only a disproportionately small amount is earmarked for animation, so small that even contemplating an animated feature or a cartoon series has been out of the question for many years. Foreign commissions have dried up; workshops can only count on mundane sub-contract work, if any at all, to keep themselves going. The final blow to animation in Hungary was delivered by television, formerly its main customer. After 1989 there was a dramatic increase in the number of channels, but none of these has been prepared to finance new animation work. It's not as if there's no demand for it, for there certainly is; what is happening,

*Some of the reactions of foreign viewers: "Oh, sweet lord. Hungary's gone and done it again. We got all worked up over Nimród Antal's stylish *Kontroll* last year, and now animator Áron Gauder has put out *Nyócker* (The District), an absolutely stunning—in a very seedy sort of way—animated feature revolving around aimless youth in Budapest"; "If this is as good as *Kontroll* (a movie that gets better and better with each viewing!)... I'll be a happy customer."; "My God... downloads for the second and third trailers just finished... this is the best thing I've seen in ages..." "Cracking, stunning animation and style, very individual and unusual."

Erzsébet Bori
is the regular film critic of this journal.

however, is that the favourites of the 60s and 70s are being rerun again and again.

Given the crisis of today, it hardly seems credible that, not that long ago, Hungary was a superpower in the animation world and Pannónia Studios one of the world's five most significant animation workshops.** That development was organic and gradual. The painter Sándor Bortnyik established the first important workshop in 1928, where graphic artists like Gyula Macskássy—regarded as the founding father of Hungarian animation—and the internationally celebrated cartoonist, Félix Kassowitz, worked. They were primarily making animated cinema commercials. As film-production slowly revived after the Second World War, and until television began to flourish at the beginning of the 60s, animation still didn't play a major role. Cartoons were almost exclusively short (and moralising) folk and fairy tales. Naturally, television as well mainly required children's films. This huge increase in product, however, enabled a great number of the young and talented (like József Nepp, Attila Dargay, József Gémes, Marcell Jankovics, Sándor Reisenbüchler) to learn their craft and find their own style. Hungarian animation then came of age: alongside films for children, more and more humorous, satirical and even philosophical short animated films for adults were being made. Hungarian cartoons of the 70s had a variety of themes, were of high aesthetic standards and were experimental in both technique and form. Indeed, they could no longer simply be called cartoons, as sand, plasticine, cut-out and object animation also appeared. In other words, anything that moves. It was in the 70s, too, that several of the succesful cartoon series of the 60s started to enter their prime and provided an indelible experience for generations of children and the young. Among these we can cite: Macskássy–Várnai, *Peti and the Robot;* József Nepp, *Gustavus;* Marcell Jankovics, *Hungarian Folktales;* Nepp, *Next, Please;* Nepp, *The Mézga Family;* Attila Dargay, *Vuk.* One by one, their creators were awarded prestigious international prizes of which Ferenc Rufus' animation Oscar (for *The Fly,* 1981) and Ferenc Czakó's Grand Prix in Cannes (*Ab ovo,* 1987) stand out.

The next stage had to be a feature-length film, and it came in 1973, based on a classic of Hungarian literature, Sándor Petőfi's *Johnny Corncob (János vitéz).* Marcell Jankovics made it and it itself has become a classic. Hungary was not that late on the scene; surprising though it may sound, in 1972 the world's entire output of feature-length cartoons hadn't even come up to fifty in number (one of the most famous, *Animal Farm,* was made by Hungarian-born John Halas in 1954). From then on, every year or so, a feature-length animated film would reach Hungarian cinemas—mainly children's stories, including extraordinary satirical musicals like György Kovásznai's *Bubble Bath.* A co-production, *Cat City,* achieved great success here and abroad (Béla Ternovszky, 1986). In 1991, the twenty-fifth Hungarian animated feature appeared (József Gémes, *The Princess and the Goblin*)—and then everything fell silent. The protracted crisis had begun. In these past fifteen years only three feature-length animation films were made, two of them on foreign commission.

Entering the 90s, it appeared that in Hungary and in the entire region the once radiant sun of East European animation—nurturing geniuses like Jurij Norstejn or Jan Svankmajer—had forever set. The shadow of Walt Disney had descended over the scene. Sadly, no more was heard of Norstejn, who probably never finished

**On Hungarian animation in English: http//en.wikipedia.org/wiki/PannóniaFilm

The Cloak, intended as his chef d'oeuvre; Svankmajer, the last of the all-round film-makers, is fortunately still working, but he has transferred his imagination and creative power from animation to dramatic feature films. A faint ray of light was cast by the emergence of Anime *(Princess Mononoke, Spirited Away)* and Pixar *(Toy Story, Monsters' Inc.)* with ever rising production costs, however. This did not hold out much hope of the post-socialist countries returning to a field where the costs of a feature-length cartoon easily match those of a straight feature. Today, instead of the lone wolves, it is large and specialist teams that work on animation productions, while high-capacity computers do the work that had once consisted of minute and time-consuming manual labour. It was a mistake to believe that spirits couldn't be locked into machines.

Then came the *Simpsons* with *Beavis and Butthead* in their wake, followed by the technological and thematic explosion of *South Park.* However much they deny it, the creators of *The District* owe a lot to these American forerunners. Not of course for the story or the graphics, but for their courage and the example they set. They provided convincing proof that there is a life outside giant companies and that the small and independent can compete, even against the technical perfection that state-of-the art computer-aided design can achieve. They also proved that there is demand not just for visually cute and moralizing stories but also for the crude, the oafish and the outspoken. *The District* certainly doesn't suffer from any shortage of outspokenness and cheek, though its graphics are not the least crude or basic. The photographic precision and likeness to life of the faces and voicing of the characters, along with the exteriors and interiors of their homes were created at home on personal computers—something anyone can have a go at. The project cost no more than the equivalent of some $500,000; what is best and most original in it, the concept and the thinking, didn't cost a penny.

Áron Gauder had the idea of taking a series of digital photographs of the cast, the props and the locations and, having transferred them to drawings, animating them. The story is set in Józsefváros, the eighth district of Budapest (hence the Hungarian title *Nyócker,* from ***nyolc**adik* ***ker**ület*). This central city quarter emerged in the 19th century when new immigrants came to the rapidly developing city, and was inhabited by workers, by the poor and by the dubious. Its bad reputation goes back many years and, until only recently, it was the centre for cheap streetwalkers.

The image of Józsefváros (Josephstadt—Joseph's City)—a construct of facts, actual conditions, prejudices and city legends—still has a hold on the popular imagination, best expressed by the laconic wording in Apartments Wanted small-ads: "8th district out of the question!" This is the ghetto, the jungle, Budapest's Gypsy row, the hotbed of crime, where you'd do best not to go out in broad daylight, let alone after dark. Where anything can happen, from mafia

showdowns to shoot-outs, to bombs, to knives flying through the air. Of course, this image, which the popular press, movies and rap lyrics constantly reinforce, doesn't live up to the reality; all that is true in the image is that here flats are relatively cheap and the environment is traditionally more accommodating to newcomers. For that reason many Roma, especially musicians, live here, and, more recently, an increasing number of Chinese and Middle Eastern immigrants have arrived. Józsefváros may be a bit dirtier, noisier and more run-down than other Budapest districts, but public security is no worse here than anywhere else.

But who cares about prosaic reality once you've got living full-blooded urban folk-poetry, a modern mythology deeply rooted in the collective consciousness (and subconscious), and a cavalcade of colourful figures, a modern mythology that offers itself to a foul-mouthed, true-to-life and politically very incorrect film made for the uncorrupted young?

In this ghettoized Romeo and Juliet story, Ricsi the Gypsy and the Hungarian Julika fall in love and, together with a gang of local kids, devise a plan to disarm their hate-filled parents. The kids—Roma, Jews, Chinese and 'Arabs'—put together their heads and hearts, craftiness and imagination; they travel back to the Stone Age in a time machine and create extensive oil fields beneath the "district" as a means to pacify the greedy adults of the future with worldly goods.

For a while everything works like clockwork, the fabulous wealth smoothes out the ethnic differences in no time, the children live the good life, Józsefváros becomes a factor in world politics. But where there's business and oil, sooner or later the big shots come on the scene and the struggle for control gets under way. The CIA and the KGB are involved, as are the Pope, Tony Blair and George W. Bush. So once again we can start worrying about the lovers' fate.

The refreshing novelty—an almost Copernican turn—about *The District* is that it never thinks about going up against the gross prejudices and stereotypes; on the contrary, it plays up to them. The Roma here are criminals (musicians at best), the police are corrupt and the priest is a paedophile. One of the prostitutes is a country Roma, the other is Ukrainian (with KGB connections). The local sex shop is run by gay East German Stasi agents, the Jew is a shrewd profiteer, the Arab disguises himself as a kebab-vendor but makes bombs in his basement, and in the end we discover why Osama bin Laden hasn't been found yet. On top of all this the politicians get their deserts, whether the local politicos or Tony Blair in his Darth Vader helmet or George W. Bush who, enthusiastically applauded by Arnold Schwarzenegger in Tyrolean lederhosen, once again mixes up Budapest with Bucharest.

The ghetto, the poor district, is known in every big city in the world, but in this film there are, of course, some cultural references which you have to be Hungarian to understand, better still from Budapest, and even better still from Józsefváros. Besides the actors, some of the creative team and some well-known musicians have lent their faces and/or voices to the characters. A fair number of them are Roma. People who know the district well will also enjoy the locations with which the film works miracles. It shows the district with the accuracy of a map (part aerial photo, part photo album) with its identifiable houses, squares, streets, turning it once and for all into a place of beauty, colour and adventure—a fairytale city, where even dog dirt is picturesque. The richness and variety of the rap soundtrack may come as a surprise to anyone, Hungarian or foreign. ❧